UNDER CONSTRUCTION

UNDER CONSTRUCTION

Making Homeland Security at the Local Level

KERRY B. FOSHER

THE UNIVERSITY OF CHICAGO PRESS // CHICAGO & LONDON

KERRY B. FOSHER is an anthropologist of security and intelligence who is currently working at the Marine Corps Base at Quantico, Virginia, as the Marine Corps' first Command Social Scientist. She also serves as a research and practice associate at the Institute for National Security and Counterterrorism at the Maxwell School of Citizenship and Public Affairs and the College of Law at Syracuse University.

The University of Chicago Press, Chicago 60637
The University of Chicago Press, Ltd., London
© 2009 by The University of Chicago
All rights reserved. Published 2009
Printed in the United States of America

18 17 16 15 14 13 12 11 10 09   1 2 3 4 5

ISBN-13: 978-0-226-25743-3 (cloth)
ISBN-10: 0-226-25743-6 (cloth)
ISBN-13: 978-0-226-25744-0 (paper)
ISBN-10: 0-226-25744-4 (paper)

Library of Congress
Cataloging-in-Publication Data

Fosher, Kerry B.
   Under construction: making homeland security at the local level / Kerry B. Fosher.
      p.   cm.
   Includes bibliographical references and index.
      ISBN-13: 978-0-226-25743-3 (cloth: alk. paper)
      ISBN-10: 0-226-25743-6 (cloth: alk. paper)
      ISBN-13: 978-0-226-25744-0 (pbk.: alk. paper)
      ISBN-10: 0-226-25744-4 (pbk.: alk. paper)
   1. Civil defense—Government policy—Massachusetts—Boston Metropolitan Area.
   2. Local government—Massachusetts—Boston Metropolitan Area. 3. Civil defense—Government policy—United States.
   4. Terrorism—Social aspects—United States.
   5. Terrorism—Prevention—United States.
   6. National security—United States. I. Title.
   UA928.5.B67F67   2009
   363.34'70973091732—dc22

                                          2008018266

♾ The paper used in this publication meets the minimum requirements of the American National Standard for Information Sciences—Permanence of Paper for Printed Library Materials, ANSI Z39.48-1992.

For my family, the clan, and Surry

CONTENTS

ACKNOWLEDGMENTS

As is the case with all anthropological work, this project has been supported, encouraged, kept on track, and nudged in the right direction by so many people that any attempt to acknowledge them all is doomed to fail. And yet we try.

INSTITUTIONAL: Various stages of this project were generously supported with funds and other resources by the following organizations: at Syracuse University, the Department of Anthropology, the Claudia DeLys Grant Program, the Program on the Analysis and Resolution of Conflicts, the Maxwell School's Roscoe Martin Fund, and the Graduate School; the National Science Foundation; at Harvard University, the John F. Kennedy School of Government's Belfer Center for Science and International Affairs, and the Taubman Center for State and Local Government.[1] The people of the National Security Studies Program, then at the Maxwell School at Syracuse, provided unofficial mentoring and encouragement and allowed me to participate in several of their programs. They helped me build an understanding of the military and intelligence communities that proved vital as I tracked the changes after 9/11/2001. I also wish to acknowledge the critical assistance of the Monterey Institute of Interna-

1. National Science Foundation guidelines require the following acknowledgment: This material is based *[in part]* on work supported by the National Science Foundation under Grant No. 0129762. Any opinions, findings, and conclusions or recommendations expressed in this material are those of the author and do not necessarily reflect the views of the National Science Foundation.

tional Studies' Center for Non-Proliferation Studies for providing me with access to their terrorism database without charge during the last phases of my fieldwork.

PROFESSIONAL: This book had its beginnings in my dissertation and, hence, with my graduate school faculty and cohort. Robert Rubinstein, Deborah Pellow, Mark Fleischman, and William Banks, along with Michael Freedman, were true mentors. They supported my strange topic in its infancy and nurtured it along the way. They helped me hone my ideas into something resilient enough to be accepted before 9/11/2001 and still relevant after it. Elaine Sudanowicz of the Boston Emergency Management Agency began helping me while I was in the field. She performed the dual role of key community informant and academic mentor, a balancing act she managed to my great benefit.

Outside of Syracuse, Monica Schoch-Spana of the University of Pittsburgh Medical Center's Center for Biosecurity set the perfect example of an anthropologist navigating the difficult waters of this topical area and encouraged me throughout my writing. My colleagues at the New England Center for Emergency Preparedness at Dartmouth Medical School and, later, at Air University and Marine Corps Intelligence Activity all have been generous with time and encouragement.

Last in this category, I need to acknowledge the efforts and patience of T. David Brent at the University of Chicago Press, who shepherded a naive author and difficult manuscript with great grace and diplomacy.

PERSONAL: My family and friends are patient with me about many things. I have neglected them, ranted at them, and done everything that academics do, on truly horrible topics like smallpox and explosive devices and intelligence failures. They are still with me and I am amazed. To my parents, my brother and sister-in-law, Jackie, Stanzi, and Aedan Scribner and their Jim, Penny Sharpe, Wendy Ayotte, Lana Cohen, my village neighbors who are family in behavior if not in biology, and those of you who did not want to be named, even if I promised not to do anything like this again, you would know better. Thanks for believing in me and for standing by me. I owe a special debt to Alicia Ory DeNicola, Brian Selmeski, and Paul Harrington. They have been my academic barometers, my walls off of which to bounce ideas, my cheerleaders, and my prodders. This book would not have happened without them.

SECRET SQUIRRELS: Confidentiality issues as well as practicality make it difficult to identify all the organizations and people who helped me during my field research. Where possible, I will acknowledge them privately. However, special thanks are necessary to a few who provided key insights or critical access. I cannot name them, but I can list their organizations (in order of contact): the Massachusetts National Guard First Civil Support Team—Weapons of Mass Destruction, the National Security Agency, Boston Emergency Management in Boston Fire, Massport Fire Rescue, the Massachusetts Office of Commonwealth Security (now part of the Executive Office of Public Safety), Boston Police Harbor Patrol, and the U.S. Coast Guard. In a period of chaos, they included me and helped me understand. Any errors in the following are in spite of their efforts.

Beyond the immediate sphere of my project there are a number of people in the national security community I feel compelled to acknowledge: the true gentleman from the National Aeronautics and Space Administration whose chivalry kept me sane during a nasty grant-writing phase, the thoughtful workaholic from the National Ground Intelligence Center for an early organizing image, the fabulous international intelligence agent masquerading as a short soccer dad, the Buddhist-colonel for a much-needed kick in the pants he may not even know he delivered, and not least of all to the emergency exercise designer from Connecticut and certain members of the New York City Fire Department for making me laugh so hard that my heart unclenched and I was able to write again.

INTRODUCTION

I sat looking across the table at the fire captain. Around the table sat representatives from twelve other agencies, all trying to figure out how to plan for the possibility that a very hazardous substance might have to be moved through a crowded neighborhood of homes, past a hospital and a school. They had to consider the likelihood and possible consequences of an accident or an attack on the truck. They had to think about whether or not the public should be informed, whether the school should be closed. Is there any guidance on this from the feds? Yeah, right. They only said it had to be escorted and kept safe from attack, whatever that means. Maybe the truck could come through at night? No, too hard to see possible attackers. Maybe there was some way to move it through another location? No, they had already been through all that. And by the way, who was going to pay for the overtime for all the police escorts? Could they close down the side roads? At that time of day?! Please! Get real. What would they do about pedestrians? How hazardous is this stuff, really? Isn't this a decision the mayor should be making? Do you see him here? Everyone turned to the fire captain as the person most knowledgeable about hazardous materials. His face sank a little as he realized that he would have to lead the way to a solution, despite the fact that he knew little about the legal aspects of the situation, the likelihood of attack, the neighborhood in question, how much of an escort made sense, or many of the other factors that had to go into a decision about what it meant to make this shipment "secure." He took a breath, pushed back from the table, and began with, "OK, I'm just thinking out loud here . . ."

Homeland security consists not only in policies and grand sociocultural shifts but also in the daily lives of responders and planners. At every level of government, people's activities, assumptions, confusions, worries, relationships, frustrations, and decisions influence the shape of this aspect of American life. At the local level, people's practice *creates* the shape of security with which most of the public interacts. While I was in the field, people were very much making it up as they went along. I heard the phrase "I'm just thinking out loud" or its equivalent so many times that it became fundamental to my interpretation of what I observed. Far from being dictated by national-level policies, homeland security was under construction. It involved all the confusion, delays, detours, and potholes that phrase usually implies, made all the more complex by the lack of a common conception of what things should look like at the end of all the work.

The ideas and institutions of security in the United States have tremendous power in the world. People's practices at the local level of homeland security provide an opportunity to examine one aspect of that security, how it is constructed, maintained, and potentially transformed. In the case of homeland security, practice is accessible at an unusual level. No longer the exclusive province of elite policymakers, military planners, and bureaucrats, this area of security involves firefighters, emergency room doctors, cops, city planners, public works truck drivers, and local emergency managers, among others. This area of practice began to emerge from the ashes of civil defense programs and ongoing emergency management initiatives in the late 1990s. After the attacks in the fall of 2001, the pace of development and elaboration increased. While the country tried to sort out its ideas about defense and security within its national borders and while the federal government debated how involved it should be and what guidance to give, local people had to make it up as they went along. As they muddled through, talking, trying things out, arguing, making mistakes, getting confused, laughing, their practice was ethnographically accessible.

My aims in writing this book have been relatively simple. First, I wanted to show U.S. homeland security as practice, as something that is not monolithic but constructed, not impenetrable but accessible to field research and analysis. Second, I wanted to describe the methodological and ethnographic challenges faced by those studying (and/or engaging with) security-related topics at a time when the discipline is struggling with how to position itself with respect to U.S. national security. Finally, I wanted to provide some insights on U.S. homeland security from the perspective of an insider/outsider, an anthropologist who set out to study, but has ended up working with, one of the communities involved in creating security and emergency preparedness. In particular, I argue that some of the circumstances and actions described in the ethnographic chapters have led to a situation in which much of what constitutes local homeland security in the United States exists at least partially outside of official policy and, thus, outside normal processes of monitoring and accountability.

The following chapters are based on interpretation of data gathered during more than two years of fieldwork, largely participant observation, among the planners and responders involved in developing homeland security for the Boston area. I had a level of access that was both wonderful and methodologically challenging. Starting with three key informants, an expanding circle of planners and responders opened their doors to me, accepted me in their meetings, found ways to give me glimpses of operations, and put me to work alongside everyone else who was trying to figure out what homeland security was going to mean for the Boston area.[2] My commentary and critique are further informed by three years spent as an academic researcher/practitioner in the field of homeland security and emergency preparedness in New England at the New England Center for Emergency Preparedness at Dartmouth Medical School.

Although the research and much of the writing for this book were done before the devastating effects of the 2004 and 2005 hurricane seasons in the United States, much of the analysis presented here applies to the preparedness for and response to those disasters. Despite, or perhaps because of, several years of intensive planning and policy work at all levels of government, expectations of what could be accomplished in a natural disaster did not match up to the constraints on local capabilities. As the following chapters will show, the homeland security and emergency preparedness with which the disaster and the public interacted was created at the local level and can only be analyzed and understood if local practice is addressed.

ORGANIZATION

The remainder of the book is divided into three sections. The first section, chapters 1– 4, sets up the background and context of the study. The second

2. Throughout the book, I use the following terms interchangeably: "planners and responders," "homeland security community," "homeland security policy community," "people involved in homeland security."

section, chapters 5–8, provides the account of homeland security practice. The third section, consisting of only the final chapter, provides commentary and conclusions. This arrangement, along with the segmenting of the chapters, is intended to help different audiences navigate the book more easily, focusing on aspects that are of more interest to them. For example, some practitioners may be less interested in the chapter on methods or the theoretical segments within other chapters than they are in the analysis of homeland security practice. Anthropologists may be less interested in the intricacies of how practitioners coped with the incident command system than they are in the discussion of authorial identity or with some of the theoretical and ethical discussions. Students may be most interested in the exploration of the rocky relationship among field methods, secrecy, and ethnography.

In the balance of this introductory chapter, I set out the organization of the book, address some of the more problematic terms used throughout, and close with a brief account of how 9/11/2001 influenced my working relationships in the field and academia.[3] Chapter 1 briefly situates the study in several contexts. In it, I discuss disciplinary politics related to the study of national security and the implications of engagement for the discipline and authorial identity. I describe the approaches that guided the study with respect to critique, theory, and interpretation. Finally, I describe the advantages and disadvantages of my vantage point in the research community. Chapter 2 presents the policy context of homeland security in the immediate aftermath of the 9/11 attacks. In it, I provide an overview of the federal policies that influenced local action from civil defense to the present. I also describe some of the features of the Boston area that created a special context for homeland security operations, particularly the inconsistent patterns of regionalization and the impact of the Big Dig, the largest highway construction project ever started (and possibly never finished).

In chapter 3, "Muddling Through," I canvass some of the methodological, ethical, and practical challenges I faced during this project and explain the solutions I chose. I briefly describe the research site and community, then cover the practical realities of sampling and studying in such a community. The chapter addresses several methodological and ethical concerns that affected writing, specifically, how the choice of participant observation affected writing and the interplay among ethnographic writ-

3. Henceforth, "9/11" will stand for "9/11/2001" unless there is possible confusion about the year.

ing and informant confidentiality, continued access to the community, and security concerns.

Chapters 4–8 provide ethnographic material on homeland security based on field research. The story of homeland security during my time in the field is the story of people developing a process, figuring out a new area of practice amid some substantial pressures and cultural changes, rather than a defined account with accomplishments and an endpoint. The organization of these chapters reflects that process, focusing on the framework necessary for understanding practice rather than on narratives or chronologies.

Chapter 4 is about finding the community. In the first part of that chapter, I describe the difficulties of access and, quite literally, finding the community amid the forest of organizations. The next two sections support an argument that homeland security in the greater Boston area was being practiced through a policy community, a community formed by the direct or indirect influences of policy. The chapter closes with an exploration of the generative properties of practice within the policy community, drawing on themes from globalization theory.

Chapters 5–8 examine homeland security as practice. Chapter 5, more of a coda than a chapter, is a brief introduction. It frames the two subsequent chapters, provides examples of some of the questions facing practitioners, and introduces two important themes that run through them, coordination and information sharing/secrecy. Chapter 6 addresses the more workaday aspects of practice, the daily tasks that took a large part of the time of frontline staff. It covers intelligence gathering and processing, watching, guarding, and incident response. Chapter 7 engages with the more conceptual work of those involved with homeland security. It covers defining hazards, identifying targets and vulnerabilities, figuring out what "secure" means in various contexts, negotiating roles and responsibilities, meshing homeland security with existing concepts of emergency management and security, and creating a shared sense of community among the involved organizations.

Chapter 8 addresses how the work of homeland security gets done. It explores the tension between the desire for local autonomy and flexibility and the pressures to codify practice and institutionalize relationships. It then explores the ways that people in the policy community were able to get things done while resisting these pressures. In particular it focuses on four processes. First, it identifies the key roles and categories of individual innovators who were able to stretch or step outside normal boundaries to suggest and teach and learn. Second, it examines the roles of affiliations, relationships, and community channels in practice. Third, it looks at the role of temporary, task-based organization as a means of resisting institutionalization of community relationships. Fourth, it describes the critical role of tacit knowledge in the community and the problems with attempts to codify that knowledge.

In the concluding chapter, I identify areas I see as possible opportunities for anthropology to contribute to policy. I then comment on five "ugly secrets" of preparedness, some of which are directly related to the importance of practice as a shaping force in homeland security. I close with a few thoughts summarizing the impact of practice and considering the need for disciplinary discussions on the realities of contemporary fieldwork and on the importance of practice research for understanding complex, powerful institutions.

PROBLEMATIC TERMS

This book is not a critique of national attitudes toward security, war, terrorism, and resistance. However, the people with whom I worked operated in a context that was politically charged. On a day-to-day basis, they used terms that begged to be unpacked and picked over for their assumptions and connotations. While I cannot address each of these in the context of this work, there are three—terrorism, weapons of mass destruction, and homeland defense/security—that require at least some mention.

At a makeshift memorial arranged on a seawall in Quincy, Massachusetts, on September 14, 2001, people's minds were on revenge, recovery, and future protection. As I walked along the beach that night, the conversations I heard were about who was responsible, how to pick up the pieces, and how to make sure it didn't happen again. Nobody was engaged in debate about whether the attacks on the World Trade Center and the Pentagon had been crimes or acts of terrorism or of war. Similarly, this project addresses the construction of homeland security in the United States rather than any particular type of perceived threat or enemy—terrorist, criminal, or otherwise.

Most initial homeland security programs were geared toward "terrorist" threats and, more specifically, "terrorism" involving weapons that have the potential to cause damage or disruption on a large scale. However, these were largely catchall categories for unexpected attacks, regardless of how they were politically categorized. Many definitions of "terrorism" focus, with reason, on the intentions and methods of people doing whatever it is that others are calling war or terrorism or crime (Tucker 1997). Any definition of "terrorism" is culturally constructed and highly problematic. However, the primary distinction usually made between terrorism and war has been that terrorism involves deliberate attacks on noncombatants (Tucker 1997). Throughout this work, I use the words "terrorist" and "terrorism" to refer to actors and acts that are covert and/or unexpected without regard to target, as there is no way to make a clean distinction between combatant and noncombatant in current geopolitics. It is not my purpose in this research to question how and why certain groups or actions are defined as terrorist. As much as possible, I work with the emic usage of the security planners and legislators who control the shape of U.S. policy as it affects my research context.[4]

For the majority of the people involved in homeland security at the local level, what matters is how to stop attacks, catch attackers, minimize the harm attacks can do, respond adequately to them if they occur, and help the community pick up the physical, sociocultural, and economic pieces after an attack takes place. The intentions and methods of the warriors or criminals or terrorists or freedom fighters matter very little, except as they bear on the practical aspects of saving lives and property.

"Weapons of mass destruction" was another term closely associated with early homeland security work. It is no longer used to any great degree among local-level responders and planners. However, it was a major part of the initial discussions of homeland security even before 2001. In the buildup to the war in Iraq in 2002 and 2003, the term gained even more currency. In common use, the phrase was supposed to refer to nuclear, biological, and chemical weapons. It did not include radiological devices or conventional explosives. It certainly did not include using fuel-laden airliners to destroy buildings. It did not account for the wide range of damage that could be caused by different agents within the subcategories. For example, in the biological category, different diseases have different potential for causing widespread harm. While anthrax is a dangerous disease, it is not communicable. Creating mass destruction would be much easier with something like pneumonic plague or smallpox, which spread with some ease.

The term also did not account for what was perceived to be the major goal of terrorism, disruption. Disruption and fear, not mass illness and

4. Here I use "emic" in the standard anthropological sense of trying to rely on categories and definitions as they are meaningful to the study community. I do not mean to suggest that the community was uniform in its application of the terms, only that they do not problematize them to the same degree that is found in anthropological discourse.

death, were what made the anthrax attacks in 2001 successful. With only a few whiffs of powder, the attacker disrupted a major national social service, created public fear of handling mail, and nearly exhausted the public health and safety resources needed to respond to "white powder calls" even in places where no anthrax was ever found.

Finally, we come to the term "homeland security" itself. When I first began research in this area, the terms I tracked included "domestic terrorism," "terrorism preparedness," "domestic preparedness," "weapons of mass destruction preparedness," "wmd terrorism," "homeland defense," and, as time passed, "homeland security."[5] The formation of the Office of Homeland Security and later the Department of Homeland Security cemented "homeland security" as the term that would be used to aggregate the messy accumulation of new and existing ideas, practices, structures, and resources. The choice of the word "homeland" with its exclusionary connotations has been picked over enough that I need not repeat the process here (Bartlett 2001; Greenspan 2001; Kaplan 2003; Mullian 2001; Safire 2002). Suffice to say that its association with other political causes and its lingering hints of the German *heimat* made it a much more controversial term than "domestic security" or "domestic preparedness" would have been. In some ways, I think this is a positive thing. Questions about the term drew more press and academic attention to the development of the field than an ordinary bureaucratic reshuffling might have attracted.

The conceptual distinction between "homeland security" and "homeland defense" has been less thoroughly explored. Safire suggested that the choice was predominantly made to distance the military from responsibility for missions inside the United States, many of which could be seen as simple expansions of traditional public safety and health activities (Safire 2002). This assessment was born out in my field experience. Most members of the military to whom I spoke were wary of involvement in what they perceived as a civilian area of responsibility. In fact, the U.S. Northern Command's website tried to make exactly this distinction, although not especially successfully, to a lay audience. According to their definitions:

Homeland security is the prevention, preemption, and deterrence of, and defense against, aggression targeted at U.S. territory, sovereignty, domestic population, and infrastructure as well as the management of the consequences of such aggression and other domestic emergencies. . . . Homeland

---

5. Although capitalization of the terms "weapons of mass destruction" and "wmd" is common, I have chosen not to accord them that weight except in citations or emic use.

defense is the protection of U.S. territory, domestic population and critical infrastructure against military attacks emanating from outside the United States. (U.S. Northern Command 2004)

Regardless of the reasons for the decision to use the word "security" over "defense," it had implications for both policy and practice. The idea of defense implies a known something or someone who is presenting a threat or is attacking and can be repelled. It is directed externally in ideas about deterrence, prevention, thwarting, and resisting. In contrast, security connotes a state of being constructed with reference to possible dangers, rather than known ones. It includes the ideas associated with defense, but also other internally directed concepts that presume damage will occur, such as personal preparedness, mitigation, response, consequence management, and recovery.

These are concepts from general emergency management and they are the language of the inevitable. Floods, fires, earthquakes, tornados, and accidents will happen no matter what we do. The best we can hope for is to mitigate against their consequences, to respond swiftly and well when they occur, and to recover quickly. Regardless of intention, one effect of the use of the word "security" has been to pull war, terrorism, and crime into the realm of the inevitable, with all that implies for U.S. culture and foreign policy.

Another effect was to create a field of practice with parameters so broad as to be meaningless. As described in detail in the following chapters, a great deal of the work of homeland security at the local level was simply figuring out what they were supposed to be doing. Preparing to counter every possible threat? Assessing risks and choosing those that were most likely? Those that would cause the most damage? Worrying about terrorism? About natural hazards and terrorism? About hazardous events regardless of cause? This was the conceptual morass into which the homeland security policy community in Boston was plunged.

9/11

It was tempting not to write about 9/11. It feels like writing about the pinprick through which light flows rather than about analyzing what one can see in that light. However, my experience of that day and the months that follow formed an important basis for how I interacted with my informants, my department, and my academic colleagues.

I moved to my field site in early June 2001. I had a small grant to conduct preliminary research and anticipated starting in-depth fieldwork in January 2002. I spent the summer working on grants, position papers, learning something about the organization of preparedness in Massachusetts, and dealing with a difficult and unanticipated living situation (what anthropologist has not started out that way?). At the end of August, I took a week off to visit friends, correctly expecting that it would be difficult to get away once preliminary research began. From that little vacation, I headed out to Syracuse University to spend two weeks sitting in on a National Security Studies leadership course for Department of Defense officials at Syracuse University. One of the last exercises in the course dealt with response to conventional and biological terrorism in the United States. I gleefully handed out the latest simulated "news bulletins" to the work groups who were supposed to be acting as decision makers in the response.

Leaving the Security Studies group at the end of the two weeks, I felt refreshed by the practical tone of the course and by a few weeks off from my own work. I stopped at my family's home for a few days, arriving back in eastern Massachusetts just after Labor Day. I had about a week to get all my plans and contacts in order before kicking off my preliminary fieldwork by attending a multiagency exercise at a nearby National Guard armory on September 13.

I was preoccupied on the morning of September 11. I knew I was going to have to tell my current housemate I had to move out, a delicate situation. I went for my usual walk to the local beach, where I sat on a bench reading an article and watching the early morning planes take off from Logan Airport. In retrospect, there can be little doubt I saw Flights 11 and 175 take off, less than an hour before they were flown into the World Trade Center, but at the time, oblivious to what was happening 188 miles away, I went home to explain the move to my housemate. Just then, a friend called and said somebody had crashed a plane into the World Trade Center.

I went to the office area of my room, turned on my radio, and launched a web browser. National Public Radio was still trying to make sense of what was happening. I tried to load CNN, but the web was clogged and all I could see was one picture of a smoking tower on a white background. My housemate came in, looked over my shoulder at the picture, and asked whether what we were seeing was a second plane. I said, "yes," and started collecting information, something I did compulsively for the next three years.

The rest of that day is a little blurry around the edges. It seems melodramatic in retrospect, but the experience of it was not. I tried to create archives of news stories and websites for future analysis while listening to the radio and occasionally wandering out into the living room to see television coverage. I joined the masses of people trying to contact friends in New York City, as the Boston phone systems overloaded. I fielded telephone calls from friends and family suffering various degrees of anxiety, depending on how long it had taken them to get a phone line into my area—that is, how long they had been wondering whether something had happened in Boston. I watched the escape routes from eastern Massachusetts clog with frantic commuters and self-evacuees, although I would later learn that this process had actually gone quite smoothly as a result of the police department having had prior experience with commuters leaving work early during bad snowstorms. My family urged me to leave as well. While Boston locked down and officials began searching for the supporting area terror cell, academic colleagues called to make jokes about my no longer having to worry about getting funding.

Outside, the constant hum of air traffic and the usual crosshatch of contrails in the sky disappeared. The sound of approaching military jets made people cringe against storefronts. Was it over? Was Boston next? Would there be secondary devices? A suitcase nuke? Were there other terrorists in the city? People on the beach stared across the bay at the painfully intact Boston skyline, thinking about what it would look like after an attack such as New York City had suffered. The first night felt interminable. No one knew yet that people in the ruins were mostly already dead. Even though I knew there was plenty of other suffering to go around in the world that night, I could not keep the image of trapped, terrified people out of my mind. My constant focus on collecting information preoccupied me enough to keep me from entering the walking stupor that affected many Boston-area residents for the next few weeks.

It was hard to know where to be after that. I shared the sentiments of many of my academic colleagues that this was something the United States should have expected even sooner, given the impact of its policies and businesses. I was horrified by the loss of life, as I have been when exposed to images of death and suffering anywhere. I feared how we would react. But as my time in Boston progressed, I also came to sympathize with the people in my research community. Few of them engaged in the kind of bloodthirsty xenophobia that gripped some Boston residents, but when they saw images of the 9/11 attacks, they saw their professional brothers and sisters being killed. They felt fear and anger and sadness. Many described long periods of depression. When I looked at them, I felt a sick confusion.

There was no good way to feel. No position to take that did not somehow minimize the concerns of colleagues or informants.

On a workaday level, I came to terms with it fairly easily. I simply did not discuss the events of that particular day with my department and my academic colleagues. With informants, I listened when they talked about their feelings or about their experiences of participating in digging through the rubble of the Trade Center, but I only engaged in discussions of the response to the attacks and subsequent impact on their fields. I was honest with them about my political leanings but made an effort not to insert them into what were essentially narratives of grief. This worked pretty well until I found myself sitting at a bar with an informant, a New York firefighter who had lost eleven people from his house. When somebody else brought up 9/11, neither of us entered the discussion, but he looked at me like a drowning man looks at a drifting rowboat. Would I come close enough to help him get to a safer place? I found a way to change the topic, but episodes like that kept the tension fresh in my mind. I have not resolved it.

PART 1 Background and Context

CHAPTER 1 // POSITIONS

In this chapter, I situate the study briefly in several contexts. I address my position, in what follows, with respect to the changing disciplinary ideas about national security and the researcher-subject relationship, the approaches to cultural critique, theory, and interpretation that guided my research and writing, and the particular vantage point I had in the community.

DISCIPLINARY POLITICS AND AUTHORIAL IDENTITY

It is not unusual for an ethnography to begin with the story of how the researcher came to be interested in the topic. In this case, that account is necessary to position the work within the context of the current disciplinary debate about how anthropologists are engaging with the military, intelligence agencies, and other organizations involved in national security.

Usually when I discuss the history of my interest in security, I trace it back to the summer of 1999 when I was in San Lucas Tolimán, Guatemala. I was supposed to be doing preliminary research to see if the area might be an appropriate field site for a medical anthropology project. Instead, I found myself looking at the way the physical and social artifacts of the country's national security checkpoint gates and patrols that appeared to have both police and military officers involved. In fact, that experience was only the final straw. The project's beginning actually goes back as far as 1998, to an offhand comment I made to a faculty member.

I was at Syracuse University's Maxwell School, which housed not only my anthropology program but also the Department of Defense's National Security Studies program a few doors down the hall. The program brings in military and civilian employees of military and intelligence agencies, generally at the equivalent of the colonel or brigadier general rank, for two- or six-week educational programs. One day I paused in front of a display case with photos of the current class. I knew students and faculty in my department had been involved in protesting the program but had not thought much more about it. When Michael Freedman, on the faculty in our department, came up to me at the display case, I made a joke about whether their presence meant we were contaminated, à la anthropologist Mary Douglas. I no longer remember the specifics of his rebuke, but it was sufficient to send me to the departmental couch, where I sat staring into space and thinking. Why had I felt like it was okay to make that joke when I would never have done so about any other visiting group? If we wanted people in military and intelligence organizations to listen to us, why were people protesting the program without talking to the men and women it brought into our hallways and lounges? And then, why didn't I recall seeing anything in any of my books about contemporary national defense/security as an area of human activity?

It didn't take long for idle curiosity to blossom into serious interest and intent. Over the next several years, I spent as much time as possible talking with the people who came to the National Security Studies program. I tried to both learn and inform, and it is in these interactions that the seeds of my later engagement can be found. I talked with men and women who were about to send troops abroad into situations where the possibilities for misunderstanding and needless violence seemed great. I talked with people who were contributing to the doctrine that would guide operations. In those conversations, I found it impossible not to try to engage, to inform, to help.

I began research on what would come to be called homeland security in 1999 and 2000 when the discipline as a whole was not particularly concerned about the politics or practice of national security. In fact, the project itself was something of a hard sell. Why would I try to understand national security by talking to firemen and FBI agents? What made me think they would talk to me? Sometimes the questions betrayed a lack of understanding that "national security" was not an entity unto itself but, rather, an arena of socially and culturally constructed actions undertaken by real people. More often, I think people simply did not really think about national security as a topic of ethnographic study so much as a topic of cultural critique. Certainly few anthropologists were interested in what was then referred to as domestic preparedness, homeland defense, and occasionally homeland security. I had a hard time making the case that this was a trend that needed anthropological attention, even as national security analysts began to examine security in the context of things normally of interest to anthropologists, such as the impact of globalization. Even now at conferences and in informal conversations in the discipline, I sometimes am not believed when I talk about what practitioners were doing before 9/11. There still is a pervasive sense (perhaps hope?) that the focus on domestic national security sprang full-blown, like Athena from Zeus, from the head of the George W. Bush administration.

In early 2001 I was turned down for a Wenner-Gren grant in part because they said I had shown no proof that I was able to talk with people in these communities. I had wrestled with that concern before submitting the proposal. How could I demonstrate access without breaching informant confidentiality? A few people on my dissertation committee were concerned that I did not provide a complete list of the organizations involved in the activities I planned to study. My protests of "nobody knows" were not well received until I presented an e-mail, a section of which appears at the beginning of chapter 4, from the agency supposed to be in charge of state and local domestic preparedness. The agency hoped that, if I was able to figure out who was involved at the local level, I would share that information with them.

Nevertheless, with small grants from my department and university, I headed off for the field. I spent several weeks in June writing a National Science Foundation proposal, which I submitted for their autumn review. That proposal was being assessed as the events of 9/11 and the subsequent anthrax incidents unfolded. Although one reviewer said that the time for research on homeland defense had "clearly passed," I did receive the grant. Between that, a fellowship from Harvard, and copious student loans, I was able to stay in the field for over two years.

I have been approved for virtually anything I requested ever since. Like my informants, I was suddenly in the spotlight. Some of my internal conflicts over 9/11 are described in the introduction. Nevertheless, the disciplinary experience is worth relating in brief, although I must rely largely on informal conversations and correspondence, bits of discussions at conferences, and the other discursive precursors to more formal reactions and publications. I realized the shift rather abruptly at the 2001 American Anthropological Association (AAA) meetings. When I was late arriving to meet colleagues, because I had been conducting fieldwork at the National Security Agency at Fort Meade, well, that was no longer bizarre. Instead, it was quite chic. Some anthropologists were happy to know that there would be ethnographic data to underpin what they correctly perceived would be a storm of political and cultural critique. However, others seemed far less concerned with what I was actually doing than they were with being able to say that an anthropologist was working on the topic. In the political imaginary of parts of the discipline, I was cast as an infiltrator, as somebody who was going to expose the dark underbelly of security or the militarization of society. Other colleagues, despite my protestations, seemed to think that I was talking to politicians rather than planners and responders. They asked for my assessment of the latest Beltway debacles, something of only marginal interest to my research. When I pointed out that I really just wanted to do a descriptive ethnography and that it would be on people at the local level, many were skeptical. Even after the post-9/11 national love affair with first responders, there still was hesitancy to humanize the construction of national security, an atmosphere that encouraged confining our engagement to political critique.

By the 2002 AAA meeting, things had started to solidify. When I presented a paper on the ethical challenges of providing help to those in my research community, something that has long been part of normal anthropological practice, one audience member compared my work on firefighters and police officers to writing a sympathetic portrayal of concentration camp guards. At the 2005 conference, a fellow attendee with whom I had been having a pleasant conversation asked what I did. When I told him I did ethnographic research on national security, he physically backed away from me as though I might be contagious. By 2006, the discipline felt comfortable holding two presidential sessions on anthropological practice and national security without including as a panelist or discussant even one anthropologist who engages with the community in anything other than a research-subject relationship. A segregated, short panel of anthropologists practicing in the security sector was provided during the lunch hour.

Negotiating the tension between my positioning of my research and the way the discipline wanted to engage with the topic of security became more complex as I further blurred the line between researcher and practitioner in my own professional life. I took a job at a new center for emergency preparedness at Dartmouth Medical School. I worked directly with security and emergency planners from several states as they struggled to create sustainable programs. I dealt with sensitive information and helped craft policy. On the side, I continued to talk with informants and acquaintances from military and intelligence organizations who were trying to think about counterterrorism, culture, social networks, and human behavior in new ways.

In several recent publications, George Marcus writes persuasively of the need for anthropology to reexamine the complex relationships that exist between anthropologists and their research communities or subjects (Marcus 1998, 1999). In particular, he identifies the need to examine how new types of projects (or perhaps newly acknowledged aspects of projects) challenge disciplinary norms of fieldwork and what it means to be an ethnographer enmeshed in these relationships. My growing identification, in some parts of my professional identity, with the people in my research community was problematic in the usual ways. Most anthropologists have had the difficulty of not wanting to oversimplify, misrepresent, or expose their informants. However, Marcus is correct that there is something stranger going on in these new or newly acknowledged relationships in the production and constraint of anthropological knowledge. We lose our illusions of autonomy and independence. We lose our feeling that we can, at any time, extract ourselves from the field and distance ourselves from our subjects.

I engaged in flawed systems, believing that the consequences of inaction were greater than the consequences of action. I began to communicate with other anthropologists engaged with national security organizations in a wide range of roles and with varied goals and perspectives. We discussed the problematic nature of engagement. Was our role as anthropologists compromised? By what specific types of engagements? Were we "weaponizing" anthropology by helping national security organizations understand themselves and others in the world, or were we contributing to a flawed and gradual, but ultimately positive, transformation of how the United States interacts with the world through these organizations? These historically rooted concerns are, of course, related to a more contemporary tension, that between applied anthropology, with its subtle quiet, internal critiques, and the more overt and direct critical analysis opportunities in academic research. There has been a tendency for mainstream anthropology to treat applied/contract research as somehow contaminated by the research-client relationship (Fluehr-Lobban 1998). This can be the case even when there is no contract, only a desire to make one's research accessible and useful to one's research participants or the sort of coordinate goals that characterize action anthropology (Bennett 1996; Rubinstein 1986). For example, one senior anthropologist warned me that

I should be careful with my inclination toward practicality, saying that "if you lay [*sic*] down with dogs, you'll get up with fleas."[1]

Engaging with those flawed systems is the issue at the heart of the current disciplinary debate, the disciplinary context in which this book is located. This context has been characterized by a nearly exclusive focus on covert fieldwork or applied research for military and intelligence agencies or on the use of information generated by anthropologists in ways that increase harm to the subjects of that research (Collins 2006; Fluehr-Lobban 2006; Gusterson 2005; McNamara 2006; Moos 2005; Price 2006). Although these activities comprise a very small percentage of the possible types of engagement, the sometimes virulent informal discourse tends to elide nuance into a sort of "you're either with us or against us" dichotomy in which people who have crafted carefully monitored engagements are placed in the same camp with anthropologists alleged to be "rogues" or to "stand with the torturers" (Jaschik 2006; Price 2006). Anthropology has come to terms with studying practices that are unsettling, as evidenced by works on headhunting and infanticide, to mention only two of the more canonically prominent (Rosaldo 1993; Scheper-Hughes 1992). It may take a little more time before the discipline can come to terms with national security practices in the same way, grappling with the internal logics and then teasing apart the practices we want to critique from those that are simply suffering by association. Understanding engaged anthropology in this topic is likely to be even more challenging.

Anthropological involvement in any policy debate will always need discussion and oversight. Anthropological engagement can contribute to solutions that are insufficiently critical and that serve to maintain solutions based in flawed, unexamined logics. However, disengagement also serves to maintain those structures by not contributing anything to the decision-making process. Maintaining scholarly disinterest and detachment is, itself, a statement. Few policymakers read anthropological journals. To engage in the conversation, anthropologists must act in extra-disciplinary, often extra-academic contexts. Those contexts can require uncomfortable compromises in presentation style and conversations with people whose comfort zones start so far from our own that the middle ground seems off in the hazy distance. However, we cannot expect people outside the discipline to listen to us if we pick and choose the problems with which we engage largely on the basis of our comfort level with pos-

---

1. The anthropologist in question will remain anonymous for obvious reasons.

sible partners and their politics. It is one thing to pick one's path with care; it is another to refuse to leave the yard and then complain about what one sees over the fence.

A careful and detailed account of the current debate—its history, key arguments, and possible outcomes—is provided by Brian Selmeski in his recent piece on the "slippery slope" of engagement (Selmeski 2006). I will not duplicate his exposition here, but I will comment on the title as it comes from some of the conversations back and forth among colleagues with different positions in the debate. In mid-2006, I wrote to one colleague,

I guess if I am going to rappel down that slippery slope and try to bring information back up, then I want two things. Firstly, I want good critical thinkers, like Hugh Gusterson, David Price, and Laura McNamara, leaning hard on the rope so that I don't go too far, too fast. Secondly, I would prefer it if the discipline had a little care for the fact that I am in a precarious position with regard to my academic and practitioner positions. I'd like it if I wasn't always having to be worried that they were going to let go of the rope all of sudden. And, most particularly, when I try to hand up information, I'd like it if people spent at least half as much time looking at the value of the information I am able to give as they spend complaining about the fact that I am using some of my energy to cling to the slope.

Those of us who deliberately bridge the insider/outsider divide also occupy a strange place in the debate. We exist partway down (or up) the slope and, as Selmeski rightly notes, it is a position that requires a lot of energy to maintain.

Rather than couching my own insider/outsider status in terms of applied versus academic research, I prefer to understand it through the lens and problematic articulated by Lila Abu-Lughod. What is the anthropological relationship to our subjects? What are the underlying tensions when the anthropologist confronts his or her inevitable involvement with the subject? She wrote:

The problem with studying one's own society is alleged to be the problem of gaining enough distance. Since for halfies, the Other is in certain ways the self, there is said to be the danger shared with indigenous anthropologists of identification and the easy slide into subjectivity. These worries suggest that the anthropologist is still defined as a being who must stand apart from the

Other, even when he or she seeks explicitly to bridge the gap. . . . The obvious point he [Bourdieu] misses is that the outsider self never simply stands outside. He or she stands in a definite relation with the Other of the study. (Abu-Lughod 1991, 141)

Even before I began trying to help the people in the Boston homeland security community, even before I took a job that involved direct assistance under contract, I was a U.S. citizen, a northeasterner, and, perhaps most critically, a person from the lower middle class, like many of my informants. However, these intersections are not so complex as my work with the community.

People who engage with their research communities beyond data gathering—through advocacy, applied work, or simply helping—highlight this problematic in ways that the discipline has not quite worked out yet. Are we allowed to study the powerful only if our primary research result is critique rather than traditional ethnography or an applied research product? What are the implications of such unwritten rules? Being a medical anthropologist and a doctor or a political anthropologist and a human rights advocate does not resonate in quite the same way that being in a client relationship to your research community does. Nor do these kinds of engagements cause the same dissonance that arises when researchers—through traditional anthropological assistance to a community, advocacy, or applied work—engage with people whose activities are unsettling. In the case of security, the discipline's lingering questions about standpoint collide with a topic often addressed through distanced cultural critique rather than fieldwork and traditional ethnography. Even when anthropologists conduct research in security contexts, they seem to try to maintain an ironic distance from people in security institutions, as though they feel the need to prove that they emerged from the field experience still capable of objectivity and critique, a position that understandably privileges the traditional anthropological standpoint. Those of us who acknowledge our entanglement in the usual complex of researcher/Other relationships and power dynamics with respect to the security sector are, in a sense, problematizing one of anthropology's last objectified Others.

I do not wish to equate Abu-Lughod's "halfie" concept perfectly with the kinds of power dynamics inherent in applied work, advocacy, and other types of engagement. However, I do wish to make the point that these categories are not as distinct as they first appear and that anthropologists, thus categorized, experience many of the same dilemmas of personal and disciplinary identity. Bakalaki wrote of the temptation indigenous anthropologists may feel to simplify: "It is perhaps expedient for native anthropologists to negate or conceal their native identity and try to be as 'real' as any other anthropologist, or conversely, to legitimate and valorize their native identity in the name of avant-garde disavowals of anthropological authority in general. . . . Native anthropologists may be seem as impersonating conflicts and impasses generally inherent in anthropological praxis" (Bakalaki 1997, 503). I agree with her assessment that these temptations set up an unnecessary and perhaps impossible all-or-nothing identity stance. However, the temptation is there because the liminal state of anthropologists, who are substantively engaged with their communities, or perhaps even part of them, leads to a fragility of relationship and authoritative status in both worlds. This can be professionally and personally exhausting. It seems easier to choose than to insist that other researchers recognize their own, less marked, engagements with certain political agendas and power dynamics.

There are, of course, solid reasons to be concerned about how engagement can affect researcher bias. The American Anthropological Association (AAA) Code of Ethics applies equally to all forms of research but does not specifically address the kinds of dilemmas engaged researchers may face (Fluehr-Lobban 1998). Anthropological engagement with the security sector, and even more distanced academic attempts to understand security practitioners from an emic standpoint, highlights a number of older problems, as well as posing new ones. The discipline has started to address these issues in several ways: by encouraging discussion in meetings and publications and through the formation of the AAA Ad Hoc Commission on the Engagement of Anthropology with the U.S. Security and Intelligence Communities in 2006. I currently serve on the commission, which was designed to investigate the relationships between anthropology and the security sector. Our goals are to inform the AAA Executive Board and perhaps make suggestions for new guidelines. The professional and open environment of the commission thus far has been heartening. I do not think any one of us, with any one particular standpoint, is likely to be completely happy with the results. It is an opportunity to lay the problems out in a systematic, public way, set apart from the polemics this sort of debate inevitably generates. It is an opportunity to see whether there is room in the discipline for a range of researcher-subject relationships within this topic. This book is one offering in what I hope will be a peaceful, if noisy, coexistence.

CRITIQUE AND CONFLICT—PRIVILEGING THE LOCAL

This work is not a critique of national-level U.S. security policy, before or after September 11, 2001. It is not a political analysis of the Clinton or Bush administrations. It is not an exposé designed to show the gaps and idiosyncrasies of specific responses or plans.[2] I am not dismissing the need for those kinds of critiques. The United States reacted to 9/11 in ways that have significant consequences within and outside U.S. borders. My purpose here is to contribute ethnographically to the discipline's understanding of security institutions from a standpoint that blurs the line between researcher and practitioner.[3] Consequently, most of the critique in this work is either midrange problematizing of some aspect of practice done within the context of the ethnography or framed as commentary in the final chapter.

The people in my research community are neither more nor less obsessed with the context of their work than any other group of people. They alternate between considering it and getting on with daily life in the same way a university faculty member might feel strong support for or antipathy toward the educational philosophy behind a university curriculum yet keep those feelings in check while carrying out the daily work of lectures and grading. An individual may seek to imbue daily practice with his or her beliefs in small ways but is also capable of abstracting some tasks out of context and simply getting them done. This is certainly true among the responders and planners with whom I worked. The person designating police patrol schedules may feel dismay at increased homeland security patrols that diminish police presence in other areas. However, he or she is not paralyzed by the discord. There is a schedule to complete, a shift to finish, and a paycheck to earn.

The processes I examine took place and continue to take place in a political context. There is no question that the choices people made and the guidance they sought were freighted. I acknowledge that context but seek to keep it from obscuring the actions of the people working within it. Furthermore, readers must be aware that, as Sahlins reminds us, "these people have not organized their existence in answer to what has been troubling

---

2. The word "response" is used throughout generally to refer to emergency responses of various sorts.

3. The limitations incumbent on an anthropologist in this role are discussed in more detail in chapter 4.

us lately" (1999, 406). The people with whom I conducted this research simply did not spend time discussing the latest presidential speech or congressional debates. In the immediate aftermath of 9/11, many people did not have time to talk about these things at work, even during the "down time" I spent with them. They were busy trying to understand what might affect their organizations. Their conflicts, negotiations, and struggles were often highly local, and these are described in context in the ethnographic chapters. The information of most interest to them came not from interpreting national debates but, more often, from back-channel discussions with regional representatives of federal agencies, state officials, and one another. It is likely that some practitioners did not feel comfortable discussing their interpretations of national politics around me. However, given the wide range of things they did feel comfortable saying in my presence, I feel justified in saying that most in the community were not spending much time on the macrolevel debates that consumed so much public energy at the time.

I suppose it would be possible to conclude from this lack of discussion that practitioners had completely absorbed the idea of homeland security, had been co-opted by the vision of quasi-military preparedness that worries many of us in academia. Although there was some degree of uncritical acceptance, I came to understand that their practices showed a degree of engagement, assessment, and manipulation not always visible from the more public vantage points from which these practitioners are often viewed. A different type of field study, perhaps with more structured interviews or surveys, might have shed more light on the internal struggles of practitioners with respect to national discourses. However, the power of daily action to shape the manifestation of homeland security is equally important to examine and leads to critical insights not otherwise available. Some of these are discussed in the final chapter.

I recognize that the decision to write about the nitty-gritty of everyday life, not tightly linking practice into a critical analysis of larger cultural trends, is, itself, a political as well as ethnographic choice. However, one of the enduring tasks of anthropology is to find the places where apparently monolithic institutions are created, maintained, and transformed through everyday actions. In helping people understand the everydayness of sweeping change or entrenched ideas, anthropology can make one of its most substantial contributions. In this book, I have tried to humanize homeland security, to show it on a scale where it becomes comprehensible and manageable, as something partially constituted in the patterned behaviors and innovations of people acting on the local rather than national stage. I hope this also shows it as something that is accessible to questioning and control by citizens acting at the local as well as at national levels.

THEORY

My purpose in this book is to provide an ethnographic and analytic account of human activity in one area of U.S. national security rather than an attempt to advance substantively a particular theoretical position. Consequently, theoretical discussions consume relatively little of the text. The study is part of a larger anthropological project of understanding national security as a socially and culturally constructed aspect of human life. As such, it is tied to so many branches of theory and critique that I could have written for hundreds of pages before getting to what people actually get up and do in the morning. There are future research possibilities in discourse analysis, work, identity, gender, conflict, negotiation, state power, militarization, and neoliberalism. There are particularly interesting lines of analysis to be done using the frames developed in organizational anthropology and popular writers on business and organizational practice. I acknowledge that some readers may miss these topics, our familiar analytic companions, as I missed them while I was writing. In the following chapters, they take a backseat. However, the fieldwork, as well as the analysis and commentary, proceeded from certain theoretical foundations that bear exposition. This section outlines the approach to practice and human agency that underlies both the ethnographic accounts I present and the comments and conclusions I draw from my observations.

Using anthropological tools for the study of military and defense institutions has been an important part of anthropology's efforts to "study up" (Nader [1969] 1974). In recent years, anthropology has produced studies of nuclear scientists, defense intellectuals and plant workers, special operations forces, and peacekeeping operations (Cohn 1987; Gusterson 1996; Rubinstein 1989, 1993, 1998a, 1998b, 2000; Schoch-Spana 1998a, 1998b; Simons 1997). This book is not in the tradition of critical ethnographies of the powerful that followed Nader's call. However, it is true to several other reasons to study up presented in her original piece—the need to be "as at home in studying a law firm as a secret society . . . in describing those unwritten customary behaviors that are completely indispensable for understanding, for example, what makes Congress tick," and the needs addressed in her section on democratic relevance—writing ethnographies for the "natives" of institutions and writing ethnographies that help citizens understand the institutions that shape their lives (Nader [1969] 1974, 293, 294). Each of these reasons contains within it an implicit need not only to assess critically and unpack the political discourses surrounding powerful institutions but also to understand their dailiness, practices, and unofficial processes. It is in these latter aspects of the tradition of "studying up" that this study is rooted.

PRACTICE, AGENCY, AND SUBJECTIVITIES. A homeland security practitioner with backgrounds in law enforcement, emergency medical services, and emergency management reflected on the first three years after 9/11.

There was nothing coherent, no national strategy that meant anything at the local level. You'd listen to what they were saying on the news, in the press conferences. Right. It was painful trying to rationalize the conflicting things, the idea, the goals they seemed to have, to be giving to the public. Absolute security and totally open borders and shipping. Meaningless. It had no meaning for any of us. We didn't pay much attention. We were too busy. People think some of us got carried away, but we were attacked. That did happen. We had to think, what if it happened here, would it be the same kind of cluster as in New York? We had to figure out what to do. I don't think very many of us had to be told that we needed to do something. That's our job. I don't mean we weren't influenced. The whole country was. But anyone who thinks there was some national program is hallucinating. Sometimes we thought there was pressure to do something in particular, but I don't think it was really there. You know? It was just us reacting. To each other, the press, rumors, whatever. Even now, [federal] homeland security, it's a holding company. It has no internal . . . consistency? Is that the right word? No message, not for the local level. It's not one thing. You don't squeeze it and little homeland security units come out.

To understand the account of practice presented here and the degree of individual agency involved in what is presented, one must first understand the intensely messy and fragmented nature of the attempt to create homeland security. Preexisting conceptions of national security and the national debates that took place after 9/11 were powerful constraining forces but were not the only aspects of culture shaping how Boston and other communities came to grips with this new/changed aspect of their lives. Ordinarily, one might expect legislation, policy, and plans to influence action, but in 2001–3, it was the absence of a coherent policy approach, the rapid changes and blank spots in policy, that became powerful shaping forces. As the following chapters show, the lack of consistent policy (or public opinion) opened up spaces for action on the part of local actors.

The plans and reassurances presented to the U.S. public in the first two years after 9/11 were like rain in the desert. They evaporated before they hit the ground. Informal discussions at recent anthropological meetings (AAA 2004, 2005, and 2006) suggest that some anthropologists believe that, beyond the concerns about militaristic and colonialist discourses flowing through national visions of security, there also was an institutionalized concept of homeland security that was imposed on local people or that they were swept up in the influence of a discursive storm. This is based on incorrect assumptions about the degree of coherence among national policymakers and the degree of autonomy of local actors. If there was any attempt from the Beltway to impose a comprehensive set of ideas, assumptions, and goals, it was not successful. Every local-level meeting and coffee klatch was full of contradictory rumors about what national policy was going to look like. Among the more astute practitioners, the rumors were about whether national policy was going to have any resemblance to what was possible to get done at the local level or if it would paint a rosy picture of seamless coordination and airtight security that would be impossible to carry out.

Through the following accounts of how local practice came to constitute what planners, responders, and the public understood to be homeland security, the reader will need to keep in mind the book's central metaphors of construction and thinking out loud. Within the context of the louder, larger political debates about national security, responders and planners were just making it up as they went along. They were reinventing what Geertz called "the informal logic of actual life" (Geertz 1973, 17). This book is an account of that reinvention, of what human agency looked like and what it created in a particular time and place, and of the potential consequences for this aspect of American life.

The project of examining the human ideas and actions loosely categorized as related to national security requires tacking back and forth between examining agency and the powerful forces that constrain and channel that agency, between intimate, particular accounts of human experience and anthropology's engagement in generating social theory and critique. The discipline has had something of a struggle to reconcile approaches that privilege the role of discourses and political-economic forces

4. For a concise history of this tension, see Ortner 2005.

with those that emphasize the particular, meaning, and agency.[4] However, recent writing has tended to call for both approaches (Abu-Lughod 2000; Keane 2003; Ortner 1997, 2005). Specifically, Abu-Lughod called for a continuing anthropological tradition of thoroughly local ethnography as an important grounding mechanism for studies of power and structure (Abu-Lughod 2000, 263, 266). This book is in that tradition, finding the contestory nature of social life not so much in individual acts of resistance as in the entire process of developing this area of security at the local level.

I deliberately privilege agency and practice for two reasons. First, as of this writing, much of what anthropological conferences and journals have had to offer on the topic of post-9/11 U.S. national security activity has privileged macrolevel issues and analysis or accounts of the impact of changes in national security.[5] Second, there is little ethnographic description available of homeland security at the level of practitioner action to inform more macrolevel discussions. My field site and the timing of my research provided me with unusual access to the daily work of planners and responders. I decided to make use of that access to provide description and analysis that would not otherwise be easily available to the discipline by presenting an ethnographic account.

The description and analysis in the following chapters is organized around the concept of practice described by Bourdieu and elaborated by others (Bourdieu [1972] 1999; Comaroff 1985; Comaroff and Comaroff 1992; Ortner 1984; Pellow 2002; Rubinstein 1998b; Sahlins 1985; Wicks 1998). The fundamental underlying principle of practice theory is that there is a reciprocal relationship between the larger patterns or structures of culture and the daily behaviors, ideas, and discourse of people. With Ortner and Giddens, I prefer a conception of practice theory that is a bit livelier than the structure-driven constraint of habitus proposed by

5. I do not wish to minimize the importance of these studies. I know of anthropologists who are working on contributions to understanding the impacts of new national security practices on different groups in the United States and abroad, on our spatiality, and on our conceptions of identity. Especially in the wake of Hurricane Katrina in 2005, anthropologists are doing excellent work in understanding the governmental actions and inactions that contributed to the effects of the hurricane and the problems with response and recovery. See, particularly, the special issue of *American Anthropologist* in December 2006. As a quick search of any anthropological database will show, there also have been many excellent publications and conference presentations related to national-level debates and macrolevel analyses and critiques. However, these works do not (and are not intended to) address the inner workings of the organizations crafting the security policies and practices in question.

Bourdieu (Giddens 1991; Ortner 1984, 2005). The structures of practice theory do not come into daily life unbidden like a superorganic wind. They are created, maintained, and transformed by those daily lives.

Of course, this stance about the importance of practice is founded on certain assumptions about human agency and subjectivities. With regard to agency, I presume actors who are at least partially aware of the social forces at play in their lives, even though they may not always see precisely how those forces constrain and shape their actions. In describing agency among Sherpas, Ortner wrote, "Neither submitting to power nor 'resisting it' in any simple sense, the Sherpas work through it and turn it to their purposes" (1997, 158). It is this complex relationship between individuals working on the world and the world working on them that I saw at play among planners and responders in Boston. Further, it was not simply a matter of individuals in a dance with institutions or power flows. Agency was something forged among them and manipulated by them, as suggested by Keane and Miyazaki (Keane 2003, 241; Miyazaki 2000, 44). This is the essence of agency that underlies my analysis. Not simply resisting or complying, the planners and responders floated, swam, surfed, and struggled—sometimes as individuals, sometimes with company—in the political and discursive forces at work. This approach also is aligned with past anthropological work stressing the importance of ambiguity and creativity within organizational frameworks, especially when the larger context of the organization is changing (Schoch-Spana 1998a; Schultz 1995; Strauss 1992; Wright 1994; Zabusky 1995).

Agency, how people attempt to work on the world and the cultural constructions that surround them, is in turn shaped by subjectivities, "the ensemble of modes of perception, affect, thought, desire, fear, and so forth that animate acting subjects" (Ortner 2005, 31). I assume subjectivities that both create and are created by cultural constructions. Although the data I gathered do not allow examination of individual subjectivities in this analysis, my assumption of their importance is the root of my emphasis on practice, on the ability of people to interpret and affect the shape of their world, even as they are tossed about by it, on understanding the reciprocal relationships inherent in all cultural action. One is unlikely ever to get to the bottom of things. As the joke goes, "It is turtles all the way down."[6]

6. Many versions of this joke exist. All are variations on a general theme of a "native" explaining that the earth sits on the back of an elephant, which stands on a cobra, which is coiled on the back of a turtle. When the interlocutor asks what the turtle stands on, the response is, "Well, after that, it's turtles all the way down." Although this joke makes the

This book addresses one range in a full cline of inquiry about homeland security. That cline runs from structures to subjectivities and all actions, discourses, and symbols in between.

AGENCY AND THE COMMUNITY. My focus on practice and agency also has significance because of the nature of my research community. They were not elites, not necessarily even people who wanted anything to do with national security. In this sense, they were somewhat different from groups previously studied. Cohn and Gusterson examined the production and maintenance of ideas about security and defense (Cohn 1987; Gusterson 1996). However, their work focused on elites in relatively controlled discursive communities. Areas of security activity that take place in civilian spaces within national borders, such as homeland security, blur the culturally constructed boundaries separating law enforcement, emergency management, and national defense, opening such communities to new influences. As discussed in the chapter on finding the community (chapter 4), this unbundling reflects some of the same interesting spaces for agency and transformation that scholars of globalization have discovered (Fidler 1996; Hannerz 1987, 1996; Sassen 1996).

The ability to define the problem and pose possible solutions to the perceived risks of terrorism traditionally has rested in the realm of senior policy planners of the defense and intelligence communities. People in these communities have had the cultural capital to monopolize the resources and information necessary for addressing terrorism (Bourdieu [1972] 1999). This domination is being unraveled by the inclusion of people from outside of the normal range of participants. As the following chapters demonstrate, new actors, firefighters, emergency room doctors, even members of the lobsterman's cooperative have become part of the conversation. Their practice is reshaping what national security means in the United States, unraveling the monopoly of defense planners.

Homeland security in the United States in the first years of the twenty-first century encompasses a large scope of practices, policies, power struggles, and shifting ideas and ideals that shape the way people in this country and elsewhere understand security. Expert discourses, in this as in other aspects of culture, imbue even local discourses with authoritative narratives of security (Keane 2003, 240). These narratives influence actions—paying attention to one type of "threat" but not another, sub-

rounds in science and policy circles, it has its anthropological roots as well. See Geertz's version in the *Interpretation of Cultures* (1973, 29).

suming existing categories of work under the homeland security mantle—but these narratives are not the only source of actor perceptions.

While the larger structures and ideologies associated with national security are powerful, they are not the only force at work. One of the fundamental tenets of practice theory is "that society is a system, that the system is powerfully constraining, and yet that the system can be made and unmade through human action and interaction" (Ortner 1984, 159). It follows, then, that any understanding of large-scale cultural phenomena requires attention to what Rubinstein has called "the smaller, ordinary activities of daily life" (Rubinstein 1993, 550).

The practices and process described in the ethnographic chapters constitute a great deal of what homeland security was for the Boston area. Ortner wrote of the influence of practice on structure that "change comes about when traditional strategies, which assume traditional patterns of relations[,] . . . are deployed in relation to novel phenomena . . . which do not respond to those strategies in traditional ways. This change of context, this refractoriness of the real world to traditional expectations, calls into question both the strategies of practice and the nature of the relationships which they presuppose" (1984, 155–56). The people in the Boston policy community were thrust into a new context that caused them to stretch their existing institutional orientations and models to meet new needs, both the need to incorporate new activities and concepts and the need to preserve flexibility of practice in the face of demands for codification and institutionalization.

For reasons described in chapter 3, I am constrained to write in much more abstract forms than I would prefer, something especially painful given my desire to show the importance of agency. However, the examples and analysis I present show the results of individuals with varying and changing opinions coming together to try to make sense of a new influence in their lives. While members of the community certainly contributed to the overall maintenance of ideas about the need and reasons for homeland security, they were not simply acting out models imposed from outside. In a sense, they enacted the kind of challenge to state authority described by Ferguson and Gupta in their recent analysis of the problematic relationship between the spatiality of states and growing models of transnational governmentality (2002).

If few of them were engaged in resisting the larger visions of national security that permeated American culture after 9/11, neither were they helpless automatons. In the absence of clear guidance from other authorities, local people transformed traditional structures of public safety, public health, and medicine to include homeland security. They transformed concepts of national security to include nonmilitary professionals. They successfully rejected pressure to codify and institutionalize relationships, knowledge, and patterns of practice, managing to hold on to a flexible system that allowed them to react to changing circumstances, whether in a response or in the policy environment. As described in the final chapter, their ability to influence the shape of homeland security also has had some less immediately obvious consequences, producing socially hidden processes, successes, and problems.

INTERPRETATION

My approach to the data has been largely interpretive. This is in part a methodological artifact. Participant observation does not leave one with surveys or recorded interviews to code and analyze. Informant confidentiality concerns made it difficult to present large passages of observational notes. However, it is also a reflection of the data themselves and the context in which I was working. Homeland security in the time period just after 9/11 was an interpretive process for local people, as it continues to be. They were figuring things out, muddling through, and I was right next to them. I wanted to preserve that experiential, experimental quality by writing largely from field notes based on my participant observation rather than incorporating media analysis or the thousands of reports on homeland security that have been issued in the last six years.

Because of my insider/outsider status, described earlier, I also am writing as a strange sort of "halfie," although not of mixed national and cultural identity as the term was defined by Abu-Lughod (1991). This status developed only gradually over the course of my field research and writing and, I believe, has had more of an impact on the way I arrived at the interpretations leading to my commentary and conclusions than it has on my presentation of ethnographic information. Although my research community was certainly powerful enough to represent itself, interpretive anthropology still raises all the questions of authorship and authority inherent in discussions of standpoint approaches and situated knowledge (Bernard 1998; Haraway 1991). Any representation I could make would be partial, difficult, and contestable. However, I cannot conceive of any other way I could have conducted the research and presented the data that would have been true to messiness of the situation as experienced by the practitioners and my own changing status among them. As always, it is difficult to enter any realm of anthropology without looking down to find Geertz's footprints already there. He wrote of contemporary field settings:

Anthropologists are going to have to work under conditions even less orderly, shapely, and predictable, and even less susceptible of moral and ideological reduction and political quick fixes, than those I have worked under, which I hope I have shown were irregular enough. A born fox (there is a gene for it, along with restlessness, elusiveness, and a passionate dislike of hedgehogs), this seems to me the natural habitat of the cultural . . . social . . . symbolic . . . interpretive anthropologist. (Geertz 2002, 14)

VANTAGE POINT AND LIMITATIONS

As will become apparent throughout the following chapters, the collection of people and organizations involved with homeland security was complex. There were many different perspectives and priorities. A researcher starting this study with people from law enforcement would have been able to provide greater insights into practice that focuses on people posing potential threats, surveillance, investigation, and, sometimes, criminal proceedings. That starting point also would have given more perspective on the investigations that sometimes take place in the aftermath of an event to gather evidence and build a case against an attacker. In particular, research starting from that vantage point would have been able to provide greater insights into the shifts in law enforcement, at local and federal levels, from post-event response and investigations to increased emphasis on surveillance and social control. In fact, a brief but interesting account from this perspective is now available (Bornstein 2005). However, fieldwork conducted from that perspective might have uncovered a little less about planning for and dealing with the consequences of an event. A study that took as its starting point hospital emergency rooms or state-level policymakers would have similar advantages and disadvantages of perspective.

I started with organizations that primarily deal with consequence management and spent most of my time with response and emergency management organizations. I was in firehouses and emergency management hideaways and in the consequence-management and recovery planning meetings. I spent less time with people concerned with figuring out who might pose threats and stopping them. I broadened my outlook at every available opportunity, but the overwhelming majority of my field experience was with the "consequence" side of the homeland security house.

People in these organizations are less involved with preventing disasters, accidents, and attacks than in mitigating against them, responding to them, and recovering from them. As such, they are also less concerned with who is causing problems and the geopolitics of terrorism than they are in figuring out how to clean up after it. This certainly made casual conversation much more comfortable, as I was not interested in engaging in discussions of the reasons for political violence. However, it also colored my perception of the community and my understanding of practice. Wherever possible in the text, I have tried to point out areas where I know that this vantage point has obscured something significant. Beyond that I simply have done my best to make use of the rich set of data I was able to access in this part of the community.

This vantage point also is a historical artifact. Initial ideas of what homeland security should be included many things that earlier would have been called emergency preparedness—mitigation, response, recovery. There is still some question among practitioners at all levels about whether these activities should continue to be categorized as homeland security or whether the category should be reserved for more traditional law enforcement and national security activities, such as intelligence, investigation, and prevention. The tension among various models of homeland security is discussed in more detail in chapter 7.

Finally, my status as a participant observer among these organizations at this particular historical moment led to constraints on ethnographic style and content. In brief, along with the normal anthropological concerns for informant confidentiality, respecting the confidences of the community, and preserving access, I also needed to consider real-world security concerns. My informants were well aware of the research done by the 9/11 hijackers and the person who sent the anthrax-laced envelopes that same autumn. We discussed how to balance the need to tell their stories with real and perceived concerns about providing information that could support other attacks. While my attention to these concerns created conditions of great access, it also has meant that I have been unable to discuss the content or participants of many activities. These constraints and the implications for field methods and ethnography in security settings are explored in chapter 3.

CHAPTER 2 // CONTEXT: POLICY AND GEOGRAPHY

Except for brief periods of immediate crisis, the public will continue to be dominated by the normal human tendency to avoid facing terrible possibilities, accompanied by scarcely acknowledged fantasies that are still less in touch with reality.

SPENCER R. WEART, *History of American Attitudes to Civil Defense*

POLICY

In societies where violent conflict takes place on domestic soil, the idea of large separate programs for defending the civilian population would seem redundant. After all, what is defense if not the protection of one's people, resources, and culture? Since its formation, the United States has been fortunate to have relatively few interstate conflicts play out on domestic soil. One consequence has been that ideas about protecting civilians became uncoupled from ideas of war and defense and border protection. In recent years, these ideas became so disconnected that it was actually possible to have public debate on the need to include domestic civilian protection in national security programs at all. The development of contemporary homeland security structures and policies has been and will continue to be informed by the history of civil defense programs in the United States. This section sketches the history of that context through the post–World War II era.

Civil defense garnered most of its public attention in the first three decades of the "nuclear age"—the 1940s, 1950s, and 1960s. Many in the

United States supported a vigorous military defense, but there was concern about what would happen if bombs got through. How was the civilian sector to be protected? Then, as now, it quickly became apparent that full protection was impossible, and even moderate protection was prohibitively expensive. Certain trends, such as public and private shelter building, came and went, but no coherent permanent program took hold. Then, as now, debates about the appropriate degree of connection between national security and civil institutions complicated the planning process (McEnaney 2000, 11).

Public interest in civil defense reflected and reinforced fears about "the bomb." As with weapons of mass destruction today, the potential consequences of nuclear explosions were not fully understood, and uncertainty fed public fears. Then, as now, scientists also were unsure. Some were concerned about chain reactions. Some debated the relative dangers of the blast, the heat, and the fallout from an explosion. Physicist Ralph Lapp described the impact of a bomb on an American city, predicting 100,000 casualties, with at least half of that number dead. Continuing U.S. and Soviet tests of nuclear and hydrogen weapons generated reports and rumors that shocked scientists and the public alike (Winkler 1984, 16).

EARLY YEARS. Government activity on civil defense initially drew on World War II models of public warning, such as air-raid sirens. The Office of Civilian Defense had been created in 1941 to prepare for potential attacks on U.S. soil. Never used and ridiculed for its emphasis on morale issues, the agency was abolished in 1945 (Winkler 1984, 17). In 1946 a board was appointed by the secretary of war to look into new provisions for civil defense. The group, called the Bull Board, was convinced that civil defense should not be a military responsibility and suggested that each level of government provide rescue training to small groups (Winkler 1984).

The secretary of defense established a new Office of Civil Defense Planning in 1948. The office was charged with developing a national plan for civil defense. The agency's Hopley Report, named for its director, suggested that responsibility for civil defense should be located in states and communities, with only a small national coordinating office (Winkler 1984, 16). Although little cited in current literature, this report lies in the background of many attitudes about current federal responsibility for homeland security. In contrast to the report of the Bull Board, the Hopley Report suggested that the national coordinating office be placed under the secretary of defense to facilitate coordination with defense assets (Blanchard 1980, 32).

This debate also foreshadows later discussions about the appropriate bureaucratic location for homeland security.

President Truman initially gave civil defense authority to the National Security Resources Board (in 1949), but Soviet tests and U.S development of the hydrogen bomb convinced him that a more permanent structure was merited (McIlroy 1997, 60; Winkler 1984). The onset of the Korean War provided additional incentive (Blanchard 1980, 40, 47). He established the Federal Civil Defense Administration (FCDA) in January of 1951. Executive Order 10222 transferred all responsibility for civil defense to the new agency. The responsibilities vested in the FCDA have passed through a number of organizational hands since then. These responsibilities, along with a number of other emergency-related tasks, were handed over to the newly formed Federal Emergency Management Agency (FEMA) in 1979 (Federal Emergency Management Agency 2001). This arrangement has stayed relatively stable until the Presidential Decision Directives of the mid-1990s began to rearrange institutional authority (National Security Council 1996a, 1996b, 1996c).

Civil defense under Truman was relatively quiet in comparison to later efforts. One fairly successful program was the National Industrial Dispersion Policy. The voluntary program encouraged businesses to move out of congested areas in the hope that dispersion of both industry and population would lessen the impact of a nuclear strike. A report at the end of Truman's term indicated that new defense plants had located in less densely populated areas but that efforts to disperse federal offices had not been successful (Winkler 1984, 17).

The Truman administration also initiated a limited shelter program, despite the protests of some who favored evacuation plans. Planners were primarily concerned with blast force at that point, since fallout dangers were not yet understood (Winkler 1984, 17). Then, as now, programs changed focus as new information about the threat emerged and as the public or politically influential groups became interested in a particular aspect of the threat. Blast-proof shelters proved prohibitively expensive on the scale required to protect the public in urban areas. Cost sharing between federal and state governments was recommended and the federal role was limited (Blanchard 1980; McIlroy 1997). Some states implemented the program; others did not. Some areas simply did not have the time, money, or interest to get programs off the ground (McIlroy 1997). Other areas, such as Southern California, urged building the kind of family shelters that provide so much popular amusement today but failed to institutionalize an overarching program (Winkler 1984, 17).

Gradually, there seems to have been a shift in emphasis from defense or protection to survival. Pamphlets, films, and TV shows emphasized individual action to survive. "Bert the Turtle" taught children to "Duck and Cover" to survive a blast during the 1950s. Other civil defense materials emphasized the importance of knowledge in survival. Citizens also were encouraged to believe that they would not need special training or protective equipment to survive (Winkler 1984, 18).[1] At the end of 1951, a convoy of trucks with dioramas of the consequences of nuclear attack toured the United States to encourage public involvement (Federal Civil Defense Administration 1950; Winkler 1984, 18).

Civil defense professionals of the time faced some of the same problems that homeland security practitioners do today — or at least they did so until the attacks on the World Trade Center and Pentagon in September 2001. Many people simply assumed that U.S. military forces could deter or fend off any attack before it affected the United States (Warren 1966; Winkler 1984, 18). Some felt the delegation of responsibility to state and local organizations indicated that the federal government did not take the issue seriously. Then, as now, state and local governments often were unwilling or unable to devote time and resources to civil defense, leaving the country with a shaky and poorly understood structure (Funigiello 1990, 419).

EISENHOWER. The Eisenhower era brought a shift in political and public understanding of the threat of nuclear weapons and of how civil defense could work (Blanchard 1980). It became apparent that the only real defense against the new thermonuclear and hydrogen devices was to be nowhere near the site of their detonation. Evacuation plans proliferated. Some hoped that the Interstate Highway Act of 1956 would provide for easier, rapid evacuation of urban areas (Blanchard 1980; Winkler 1984, 16).

Beginning in 1955, there was a series of exercises designed to test American readiness. Even then, the exercises demonstrated the overwhelming magnitude of the problems that might occur and the need for improved coordination of agencies and levels of governments (Winkler 1984, 18). Forty-five years later the government is holding the same sorts of exercises, the TOPOFF series, so named because they are supposed to involve

---

1. This is echoed in the contemporary national "Ready" campaign that encourages citizens to assemble a simple preparedness kit, reassuring them that, "with a little planning and common sense, you can be better prepared for the unexpected" (Department of Homeland Security 2005).

the top officials in the country. These exercises are uncovering the same problems.

As shelter programs fell into disfavor, so did evacuation plans when more was learned about the effects and range of fallout (Blanchard 1980, 120). The problem of fallout was brought into the spotlight in 1954 when the crew of a Japanese fishing boat were affected by radioactive dust from an explosion eighty-five miles away (Winkler 1984, 18).

Physicist Ralph Lapp once again commented on the nature of the problem. Foreshadowing later fears about other weapons, he wrote that radiation "possesses all the terror of the unknown. It is something which evokes revulsion and helplessness—like a bubonic plague" (Winkler 1984, 18–19). The novel and movie *On the Beach* dramatized the terror of uncontrollable fallout. Later concerns about radioactive contamination of U.S. milk supplies served to heighten public fears (Winkler 1984, 19).

Public opinion had an impact on federal planning. Concerns that public fear would undermine foreign-policy options led some in the federal government to encourage less prominent civil defense programs (Vandercook 1986). The Eisenhower administration actually tried to convince the public that *On the Beach* was not an accurate representation of what would happen. A Civil Defense Administration official was featured in a 1953 issue of *Collier's Magazine*. He described the danger of public fear and encouraged various "panic stoppers" such as practicing defense drills at home, packing emergency kits, avoiding gossip, and having faith—classic examples of engaging civilians to give them a sense of control (Oakes 1994, 42; Zarlengo 1999).

The House of Representatives began to hold hearings on civil defense in 1956. A year later they concluded that programs were not functioning. They made recommendations to vest more authority in officials in charge, develop a national plan (again), and start a federally funded, nationwide shelter program. The Gaither Committee made similar recommendations to Eisenhower in 1957, but little was done. Eisenhower issued a National Shelter Policy, which made shelter the responsibility of individuals. It did provide authorization for some federal funding of state projects, but little money was distributed (Winkler 1984, 19).

The FCDA became the Office of Civil and Defense Mobilization (OCDM) in 1958. The agency continued its public outreach, focusing on showing people how to build fallout shelters. National magazines such as *Life* and *Good Housekeeping* published features on family shelters. By the end of 1960, the OCDM estimated that there were a million family shelters in the United States—largely owned, of course, by families in the middle and upper classes (Winkler 1984, 19).

KENNEDY AND JOHNSON. The early 1960s brought continued interest in civil defense. President Kennedy extended existing programs, encouraged continuing citizen activity, and pushed for increased federal funding (Winkler 1984, 20). His early concerns centered on public awareness of what they should do in an emergency. An appropriation of over $200 million went mostly to stocking and marking existing shelters. Kennedy also proposed a $3.5 billion project to build shelters for the entire population over a period of five years. The program never came to pass, and most actions in the 1960s continued to encourage individuals to take responsibility for protecting themselves rather than expecting the government to do it. Again, pamphlets and news articles emphasized the importance of understanding the threat, although these were among the last years of that emphasis (Winkler 1984, 20).

People had been alarmed by Kennedy's early initiatives, and the alarm manifested in many ways. Conversations across the American middle class turned to nuclear war and building shelters. Companies such as IBM offered loans for shelter building, adding to a commercial boom surrounding civil defense. Insurance agents and priests debated not nuclear war but, rather, who should be allowed to come into private shelters (Winkler 1984, 20). A special issue of the *New England Journal of Medicine* described how devastating a blast in Boston would be, even when destruction was figured using the government's own conservative estimates (Editor 1962).

Faith in civil defense programs declined after the early 1960s. People began to listen to the voices that said that all the federal programs were a diversion, deflecting attention to the true consequences of nuclear war. The National Committee for a Sane Nuclear Policy, commonly known as SANE, sponsored advertisements, rallies, and published literature describing the inadequacy of civil defense measures encouraged by the government (Winkler 1984, 24). Administrative commitment under President Johnson declined and, with it, so did funding (Blanchard 1980, 403). Subsequent efforts were more subdued.

The role of civil defense in larger defense initiatives was also debated. Some felt that an adequately protected population would help deter enemy attack (a position held by some involved with homeland security today). They suggested that if enemies knew that the United States could absorb a nuclear strike and move on, they would be less likely to attack. Others felt that civil defense programs might only encourage the arms race. They worried it might lead the Soviets to think that the United States was preparing to launch its own attack. On a more practical level, people could see that both expensive and cheap shelters frequently succumbed to problems far less severe than a nuclear attack, such as spring flooding and leaf-jammed air intakes (Winkler 1984).

Meanwhile, the efficacy of the weapons increased (Winkler 1984, 21). Public awareness of the increased threat may have contributed to the demise of civil defense. Subsequent emergency management and defense programs have been professionalized, perhaps because the public became aware that homemade solutions could not keep pace with weapons development. Middle-class Americans in the 1960s were overwhelmed by the impossibility of protection while simultaneously believing that something was being done to protect them (Warren 1966). Winkler called civil defense a casualty of the first steps to arms control (1984). People already exhausted from trying to figure out whether civil defense measures would work saw the Limited Test Ban Treaty of 1963 as removing the immediate concerns of fallout from tests.

LATER YEARS. There can be little doubt that civil defense campaigns during the 1950s and 1960s contributed to the normalization of ideas about nuclear war and to the acceptance of a role for the domestic sphere in military affairs (McEnaney 2000; Peattie 1984). Scholars and laypersons alike were concerned about the long-range impact of civil defense programs on the culture (Waskow 1965). The idea of personal involvement in national security no longer seemed so strange after the 1960s. The incorporation of such deadly discussion in everyday life had wide ranging consequences for U.S. social and cultural life, which are still being explored (Blanchard 1980; Brown 1988; McEnaney 2000; Mechling and Mechling 1991; Northcutt 1999; Peattie 1984; Waskow 1965; Winkler 1984; Zarlengo 1999).

Subsequent Cold War presidents continued to support civil defense in spirit if not in fact. Nixon, Ford, and Reagan all encouraged further research on surviving a nuclear attack (Blanchard 1980). Even into the 1980s, FEMA and the Department of Defense tried to develop programs that took new defense programs, such as the Strategic Defense Initiative, into account (Abrams 1983; Lamperti 1983; Leaning 1987; Leaning and Leighton 1983). These programs frequently failed to address consequences beyond the immediate crisis period and were also criticized for assuming a calm and obedient public (Abrams 1983).

Despite occasional public and political interest, no comprehensive effort at civil defense was ever made (Winkler 1984). It remained important as a symbol of national participation in defense, but priorities lay with military measures and civil defense was ultimately combined with other types of disaster-preparedness programs under FEMA in 1979 (Winkler 1984, 21).

With Soviet deployment of the first intercontinental bomber in 1954, the United States had lost its sense of invulnerability, but the attention did not last (Northcutt 1999). People built fallout shelters in their basements or learned where the public shelters were. Schoolchildren were drilled in how to hide under their desks, as though the ordinariness of the graffiti-scarred wood would protect them from the consequences of a nuclear attack. Still for most people, civil defense was passive during those decades (Blanchard 1980; Kerr 1968; McEnaney 2000; Mechling and Mechling 1991; Northcutt 1999; Waskow 1965; Zarlengo 1999).

The last gasp of U.S. interest in civil defense issues was in the 1980s. By then, public and official interest had waned, programmatic funding declined, and organizational priorities shifted. There seemed to be a collective embarrassment in the public and government agencies about having gotten so exercised about something that ended up being unnecessary and having bought into a militaristic vision of personal safety. This led to a bias against things associated with civil defense that created problems throughout the development of post-9/11 policies and programs. A report from Gary Hart and Warren Rudman, well known for their frankness about emergency preparedness, addressed this issue:

Emergency preparedness can save lives—potentially a lot of lives: During the Cold War, the prevailing view among most Americans was that civil defense measures were futile—even self-defeating. Nuclear war was viewed as Armageddon, and preparations to survive a nuclear strike were seen as making nuclear war more probable because they eroded the presumed deterrence value of the "balance of terror." The contemporary security environment mandates that we put this anti–civil defense bias behind us. (Hart and Rudman 2002, 16)

Of course, this assessment itself uses the same arguments and language about the "contemporary security environment" that were made during the Cold War, a line of reasoning that is less likely to be successful a second time.

According to an informant in public health, in 1996 FEMA ended its program of funding states to help communities maintain and calibrate their radiation-detection equipment. Community interest had clearly ended much earlier, as evidenced by this informant's collection of vintage batteries, which he had removed from the Geiger counters that communities began bringing to him for repair shortly after 9/11. However, in an interesting example of how substance often expires before its symbols, the official civil defense logo was not retired until November 30, 2006, nearly three years after the formation of the Department of Homeland Security (Dunlap 2006).

RENEWED INTEREST IN THE 1990S. During the 1990s, the government of the United States began to increase its attention to the possibility of unexpected attacks. This increased attention resulted largely from two related factors. The first was growing concern among security planners in the defense and intelligence communities about the capacities and mobility of perceived terrorists (Banks 1999; Carter, Deutch, and Zelikow 1998; Falkenrath, Newman, and Thayer 1998). Technological developments and the increasing ability to communicate and move afforded by globalization created a situation in which more nonstate actors have the capacity to pose significant threats (Banks 1999, 1; Smithson and Levy 2000, 4). The technologies of nuclear, biological, and chemical weapons have become smaller, more portable, easier to use, and less expensive (Falkenrath, Newman, and Thayer 1998, 96; Zilinskas 1999, 25). Communication by telephone and computer facilitates access to materials, as well as planning and coordination. Ease of travel (and the openness of borders that is maintained by the pressure to facilitate global commerce) makes training and operations far less complex than they were during the Cold War era. Activities of groups categorized as "terrorists" pose significant problems for a security apparatus that was designed primarily to cope with state actors. Nonstate actors, even if state supported, are not geographically confined and may not be susceptible to the same kinds of deterrents, diplomacy, sanctions, or coercion that would be effective with states.

The second factor provided a social context in which funding for increased counterterrorism efforts could be made more acceptable. In the decade preceding the 9/11 attacks on the United States, there were a number of small but highly publicized terrorist attacks. The bombings of the World Trade Center in 1993 and the Oklahoma City federal building in 1995 moved the idea of terrorism from foreign airports and distant cities to the American heartland. In combination with the 1995 deployment of a chemical weapon on a Tokyo subway, these attacks opened public discourse about the possibility of a biological, chemical, radiological, or nuclear attack at home. In a manner reminiscent of reaction to Soviet intercontinental bombers, the American public began to feel like its borders were permeable. Popular media—novels, movies, and sensationalist journalism—latched on to the idea of weapons of mass destruction terrorism, furthering the public's sense of unease (Smithson and Levy 2000, 1–2).[2]

These incidents provided the context for a series of Presidential Decision Directives (PDDs) that addressed terrorism and preparedness, setting the tone for much of what followed (Banks 1999, 5; Smithson and Levy 2000, 2).[3] Presidential Decision Directive 39 outlines three elements of a national strategy for combating terrorism: (1) reduce vulnerability and take action to deter attacks; (2) respond to and manage the crisis, while pursuing responsible parties; (3) manage the consequences, especially with regard to restoring capacity to deal with public health and safety issues (Cordesman 2000, 1; National Security Council 1996a). The directive also set out some of the specific roles and responsibilities for federal agencies and provided the basis for future directives addressing national security.

Presidential Decision Directive 62 clarified specific missions of various agencies and set out a more systematic approach to preventing and mitigating the consequences of attacks with weapons of mass destruction (Cordesman 2000, 2; National Security Council 1996b; Office of the Press Secretary 1998). Presidential Decision Directive 63 was targeted at critical infrastructure protection (including cyber crime) for both government and private sectors. The directive aimed to establish interagency work relationships and programs leading to national security, economic security, and public health and safety (Cordesman 2000, 2; National Security Council 1996b; Office of the Press Secretary 1998).

Presidential Decision Directives 39 and 62 are the elements of policy that led to the structural division between crisis management and consequence management. The FBI was designated as the lead agency for crisis management and FEMA as the lead agency for consequence management. As defined by the General Accounting Office, crisis management addresses stopping the attack, arresting the terrorists, and gathering evidence for

---

2. Examples in popular culture of the time include the movie *Outbreak* (Peterson 1995), Richard Preston's books *The Hot Zone* and *The Cobra Event* (1995, 1997), and Ken Alibek's memoir, coauthored by Stephen Handelman, *Biohazard: The Chilling True Story of the Largest Covert Biological Weapons Program in the World—Told from Inside by the Man Who Ran It* (1999).

3. These directives are classified. I rely on unclassified abstracts made available by the National Security Council and on secondary sources that analyze the directives.

prosecution. Consequence management encompasses all that might follow (Cordesman 2000, 2; National Security Council 1996a; Office of the Press Secretary 1998). This division between crisis and consequence management informed subsequent legislation and programs for many years, even after it was clear that the distinction was not useful. As explained in the following chapters, the distinction proved untenable in actual operations at the local level and in the types of planning required.

By far the most significant piece of public legislation of the 1990s, in terms of local impact, was passed in 1996. Title 14, the Defense against Weapons of Mass Destruction Act, of the National Defense Authorization Act for Fiscal Year 1997 established the Nunn-Lugar-Domenici Domestic Preparedness Program, commonly known as Nunn-Lugar (Smithson and Levy 2000, 2). The act made the Department of Defense (DoD) the lead agency for implementing the Nunn-Lugar program of improving domestic capacity to respond to terrorism at the federal, state, and local levels. The program included training programs, development of national-level response teams, and conducting exercises to test preparedness (Falkenrath, Newman, and Thayer 1998, 262). The DoD was expected to work in cooperation with the FBI, Department of Energy (DoE), Environmental Protection Agency (EPA), Department of Health and Human Services (HHS), and FEMA (Cordesman 2000, 3). Nunn-Lugar became a reference point for many subsequent ideas on homeland defense and homeland security. Communities still refer with pride to their participation in its programs, seen as a mark of their attention to homeland security before 2001.

Concerns about possible gaps in public health response also generated a great deal of legislation. In 1998 President Clinton sent a budget amendment proposing funds for the creation of a civilian antidote and vaccine stockpile, improved public health surveillance, equipping and training states for chemical and biological weapons response, and expanded National Institutes of Health research into therapies that might prove useful against biological agents (Cordesman 2000, 3). Subsequently, fiscal year 1999 appropriations (PL 105-277) included $51 million for the Centers for Disease Control and Prevention (CDC) to begin developing stockpiles for civilian populations. The request for fiscal year 2000 for HHS bioterrorism efforts was $230 million, of which $52 million would go to the CDC for continuation of the stockpiling programs (Cordesman 2000, 3).

Total counterterrorism funding (including force protection) increased from $6.5 billion in 1998 to $9.3 billion (requested) in 2001 (Monterey Institute of International Studies 2001). Two days after the September 11 attacks on the World Trade Center and Pentagon, Congress approved $40 billion—half for recovery and half "to launch the war" against terrorism (Drehle 2001). Four years and a 195 percent spending increase later, it has become nearly impossible to track the funding streams associated with homeland security (de Rugy 2005).

AFTER. The first news story I collected in my early morning news scan on 9/11 was the following from the Glendale/Burbank edition of the *Los Angeles Daily News:* "Should City Prepare for Terror? City Considers Large-Scale Emergency Plan," announcing a public meeting to debate the merits of developing a plan for dealing with acts of terrorism and the possibility of setting up a metropolitan medical response system (Gao 2001).[4] In the course of a couple of hours, the discussion in cities across the country went from "should we have such a plan?" to "why didn't we have one before now?"

The policy context after 9/11 for people involved with homeland security at the local level was chaotic. As the following chapters demonstrate, much of the frenetic activity of federal agencies and the Bush administration failed to trickle down in usable form. There are several excellent works available that discuss the post-9/11 policy process and context (Banks 2003; Brill 2003; Maxwell 2004). Here, I will simply provide an outline of the major shifts that provided some of the operating context for my research community.[5]

October of 2001 saw the creation of the Office of Homeland Security within the White House and the beginnings of national debate about whether an office in the White House was sufficient to coordinate the substantial shift in security priorities that seemed likely. The same month saw the passage of the controversial United and Strengthening America by Providing Appropriate Tools Required to Intercept and Obstruct Terrorism or the USA PATRIOT Act, commonly known as the PATRIOT Act. The act was introduced and passed in less than three days. Some aspects of the act were not especially controversial, such as increased payments to

4. Metropolitan Medical Response System (MMRS) programs were designed to allow major metropolitan areas with dispersed medical and health response assets to plan and purchase equipment and stockpiles as a region. Although the program has been moved about within the changing federal bureaucracy, the national MMRS program continues to be one of the few sources of federal dollars that obliges recipients to plan and operate regionally and on an interagency basis.

5. All acts are available on the congressional legislative service, http://thomas.loc.gov/, unless otherwise cited.

the families of public safety workers who died in the line of duty and the ability of the FBI to hire more translators. However, there were provisions in the bill, ostensibly to streamline the ability of investigators to gather and share information on potential terrorists, that caused concern about domestic spying and infringements on civil liberties (Banks 2003; Eisgruber and Sager 2003; Maxwell 2004).[6] Also in October of 2001, President Bush issued the first in a series of a new type of Presidential Decision Directive, the Homeland Security Presidential Directives (HSPD). However, the first of these to be widely recognized throughout the local and state levels of homeland security did not appear until 2003.

In November of 2002 after much debate, President Bush signed the Homeland Security Act of 2002, which authorized the creation of the Department of Homeland Security. The agency attempted to consolidate agencies perceived to have a significant homeland security mission, along with some of the many independent homeland security–related programs that had been developed in isolation from one another over the years. It combined the following agencies and programs into its four directorates:

- Customs Service
- Immigration and Naturalization Service (partial)
- Federal Protective Service
- Transportation Security Administration
- Federal Law Enforcement Training Center
- Animal and Plant Health Inspection Service (partial)
- Office for Domestic Preparedness
- Federal Emergency Management Agency
- Strategic National Stockpile and the National Disaster Medical System
- Nuclear Incident Response Team
- Domestic Emergency Support Teams
- National Domestic Preparedness Office
- CBRN Countermeasures Programs
- Environmental Measurements Laboratory
- National BW Defense Analysis Center
- Plum Island Animal Disease Center
- Federal Computer Incident Response Center

6. For a detailed treatment of the surveillance implications of the USA PATRIOT Act, see Banks's 2003 legal analysis.

- National Communications System
- National Infrastructure Protection Center
- Energy Security and Assurance Program

It also took over the Coast Guard, the Secret Service, and certain other aspects of the Immigration and Naturalization Service as independent segments that would not be subsumed in its directorates (Department of Homeland Security 2004a). When the department officially opened its doors in March of 2003, it meant that one out of every twelve federal employees worked for the Department of Homeland Security (Transactional Records Access Clearinghouse 2003).

Between February and December of 2003, the White House issued three HSPDs that had a significant impact on the state and local levels. While I was still in the field, HSPD 5 was issued, mandating the adoption of a national incident management system starting in 2005 (Bush 2003a). This was an attempt to codify and standardize the incident management systems in play throughout the country and to encourage those not using incident management systems to adopt them.[7] It also included other provisions, less widely understood at the local level, regarding resource management, preparedness, and information management among other things.

This directive remains controversial. Organizations already using incident management systems are reluctant to modify them to a national standard. Those not using such systems remain disinclined to do so. However, the HSPD was implemented with a financial aspect. Eventually, those states, towns, or organizations not complying can expect to see funding streams cut off (Department of Homeland Security 2004b).

Homeland Security Presidential Directive 7 set federal agencies the task of identifying and planning for the protection of critical infrastructure, a task that involved state and local collaboration (Bush 2003b). Homeland Security Presidential Directive 8, the National Preparedness Goal, set the stage for a substantial reorientation of federal involvement in the development of state and local homeland security (Bush 2003c). Through its dictates, the Department of Homeland Security has started to assume responsibility at a much greater level of detail for the conceptual and prac-

---

7. Incident Command Systems and Incident Management Systems are described in more detail in subsequent chapters. In brief, they are systems used to organize the main functions of an incident (operations, planning, finance, and logistics) into a form that is not agency specific, making information flow and control more predictable and manageable.

tical work of defining what homeland security should be, something that was a significant part of the work of the local planners and responders with whom I spent my time. Under HSPD 8 the federal government has started to develop lists of target capabilities and sets of scenarios to which communities and states should be able to respond. These are still being revised and are the subject of much speculation among those who will be charged with implementing them. The standardization is welcomed by some, but mandates for certain types or levels of capacity will always be greeted with skepticism by those who have to engage those mandates with local realities.

As of this writing, the Department of Homeland Security continues its seemingly perpetual internal reorganizations and maneuverings. In the aftermath of the 2004 hurricane season and the brutal impact of hurricanes Katrina and Rita in 2005, there have been discussions about more substantial reorganizations, such as making FEMA independent or increasing the role of the military. Rumors abound about renaming FEMA or relocating its responsibilities to a new, "fresh slate," organization. This type of reshuffling is known among many practitioners as "same tree, different monkeys."

Programs that are implemented locally move from agency to agency within the Department of Homeland Security, sometimes leaving locals with little understanding of new rules and new players. Rumors and questions fly at the local level. Will this office stay in FEMA or will it be moved over to the Office for Domestic Preparedness? Who has control over the programmatic funds that were appropriated before the last move? What is so-and-so's latest cell phone number? Apparently, with all the changes since 9/11, some things, including the disconnect among federal, state, and local organizations in homeland security, remain the same.

The degree to which federal response assets will be available to locals is one of the major outstanding questions. Law in the United States (primarily the Posse Comitatus Act of 1878) establishes a general prohibition on the use of the military in domestic law enforcement and supports a nonlegal tradition of hesitating to use the military for any domestic mission (Drycus et al. 1997; Trebilcock 2000). Although the National Guard has picked up missions that support homeland security activities in many states, responsibility for homeland security still falls primarily to civilian organizations (Banks 1999, 6, 20; 2004). As the structure is currently arranged, involvement of federal organizations and resources must come at the request of the state government, unless that government is incapacitated (*Robert T. Stafford Disaster Relief and Emergency Assistance Act* 1988;

Department of Homeland Security 2004c). Each state has a different policy structure for planning and response with which federal assets must integrate on arrival. In terms of actual operations it is local people—firemen, police, clinicians, and so on—who handle the initial phases of any incident. They notify local officials, who notify state officials—either the governor or the state's emergency coordinator.

In practice, most locals assume that some incidents, such as a terrorist attack, would produce a monumental federal response very quickly and that the niceties of notification and request would likely be taken care of as time allowed rather than as a precondition for federal involvement. The more pressing concern for most planners is what to do when expected federal assistance is slow to arrive. Current unofficial planning guidance suggests that towns should be capable of handling an incident for forty-eight to seventy-two hours on their own or with state assistance.[8] In a significant national event, the time frame might be much longer, especially if finite federal resources, such as pharmaceuticals, are required in many locations at once. Despite all the changes and supposed improvements in the federal approach to homeland security, locals still face the very real possibility that, in an attack or natural disaster, they may be on their own.

LOCAL COLOR

The complexity of Boston for homeland security is illustrated in all that follows, and my choice of it as a field site is addressed in chapter 3. However, there are some geographic and circumstantial aspects of Boston that are appropriate to mention in a chapter on the context of homeland security practice. The city of Boston occupies a central position in the Massachusetts Bay area. The 2000 Census reported 589,141 residents spread over just under fifty square miles (Boston Metropolitan Area Planning Council 2004). It was founded in 1630, a fact that is given daily testimony in the labyrinth of narrow streets and alleys, in old tunnels and basement connections, and in the shifting foundations of buildings that were built on landfill before people understood what that would mean. It is a popular site for historical tourism, especially for those interested in the Revolutionary era. It draws a significant part of its livelihood from the prestigious universities in the area, including Boston College, Boston University, Harvard, and MIT. It also has a thriving financial district and a busy port.

8. Unofficial in that it is suggested by field representatives of federal agencies but not yet codified.

TABLE 1: Inner Harbor Town Demographics

Town Name	Land Area in Square Miles	Population	Median Income[a] ($)	Percentage of Population Identifying as[b]			
				Black	Asian	Latino	White
Boston	49.55	589,957	39,629	25.3	7.5	14.4	54.5
Chelsea	2.19	35,116	30,161	7.3	4.7	48.4	57.9
Everett	3.39	38,037	40,661	6.3	3.2	9.5	79.7
Winthrop	2.01	18,303	53,122	1.7	1.1	2.7	95.5

[a]Boston Metropolitan Area Planning Council 2004.
[b]Massachusetts Department of Housing and Community Development 2004.

As in most of New England, there is not much open space between Boston and its neighbors. Other communities ring the port and have significant economic and social interests in its operation (as well as concerns about the inhibiting of port operations due to security concerns). Table 1 illustrates the differences in population, race, and median income among the four towns that occupy places on the inner harbor section of the port. Each has its own government, laws, financial priorities, and sociocultural patterns, making coordinated operations much more difficult than they would be for a city that dominates its geography more completely, such as Los Angeles.

Regional arrangements in Massachusetts to smooth cross-jurisdiction planning and operations are inconsistent. After 1997, five of the state's fourteen counties were abolished as wasteful. Three more have reorganized as Councils of Governments. The remaining six counties still exist (League of Women Voters 2005). This inconsistency is merely one layer in a complex arrangement of regions, each with its own purposes and boundaries. The Boston Area Metropolitan Area Planning Council (which includes Suffolk County as well as parts of dissolved counties) contains 101 cities and towns and is a forum for state and local officials to collaborate on planning issues. The Massachusetts Emergency Management Agency has four regions for emergency planning. The state also has five Emergency Medical Services (EMS) Regions to enhance coordination among ambulance services, responders, and hospitals. The state's Department of Fire Services had six regional hazardous materials teams and now also has five training districts set up by the Firefighting Academy. Many areas have

Local Emergency Planning Committees (LEPC), set up in response to the Emergency Planning and Community Right-to-Know Act in 1986, that mostly deal with the chemical hazards posed by industry but also now take an interest in more general emergency planning. Communities have come together to create mutual aid agreements among towns for emergency services that are not necessarily mapped out along any of the other regions. Metrofire, the largest fire mutual aid system in the state, has thirty-three towns in its jurisdiction and also includes the Massport Fire Rescue service associated with the Massachusetts Port Authority. Hospitals were trying to work out enhanced mutual aid agreements while I was in the field. Regional reconfiguration and creation of new types of regions continues. A list of possible ways to slice up the state or even just the Boston area would be very long. This richness of regions creates many opportunities for people to develop affiliations and build relationships. However, it also sometimes puts people in competition for homeland security resources or makes it politically and practically difficult to determine which regional template makes sense for a particular project.

Finally, no account of the context of homeland security could be complete without an explanation of the single biggest barrier to everything in the Boston area, the Big Dig. The Big Dig is the local term for what is locally believed to be the largest highway project ever undertaken in the United States (Wilmsen 1998). The idea was to remove a poorly conceived central highway that cut through downtown Boston, put it underground, and create, as well, better access to Logan International Airport, which is part of Boston but separated from downtown by the harbor. Studies of the problem began in 1969, and official planning started in the early 1980s. Construction began in 1991 and has been a local nightmare every since. Enormous construction fences block sidewalks, roads that are open one day are gone in a haze of machinery the next, signs reflect how things were last week, and the traffic jams were legendary. As one National Public Radio host put it one morning, there were jams of "biblical proportions." Almost as legendary were the cost overruns, which by the time I arrived were simply referred to as being in the billions (McGrory 2005). Even the most knowledgeable drivers got lost. I only truly began to realize the impact of the Big Dig when, while riding with a very experienced fire chief, he slowed at a fork in the road. I didn't understand why he was going so slowly, almost stopping. He gazed at the mishmash of signs in front of us as traffic parted around his official vehicle. He looked over at me and said, "I have no fucking idea how this is set up today. We're

FIGURE 1. Navigating the Big Dig: 2003 Big Dig sign. (Randy Heins, Harvard University—University Information Systems. Used with permission.)

just going to have to drive around." This took place within a mile of his firehouse.

While I was there, a decade after construction had started, one of the most eagerly awaited sections was opened, the connecter from downtown to the airport. Radio commentators giggled at the seven-minute trip that had once taken over an hour. Those of us who regularly had to use the route giggled along with them. (Of course, the new stretch was soon backed up at rush hour by people feeding into or out of other sections of the project that were not finished or by the periodic floods that came about due to the mysterious leaks and falling ceiling blocks in the brand-new tunnel.) Some area residents, including many responders, made a kind of sport out of knowing the twists and turns of each day's changes and of learning back streets around the worst of the mess. Unfortunately, no matter how light-spirited one was about it, it made an already crowded, complex operating environment nearly impossible. There was simply no way to know what was best. One just had to set out on a course, taking what little one had gleaned from various sources, and make the best of whatever routes and obstacles you ran into. For responders and emergency planners in the Boston area, it mirrored the complex national and local policy landscapes they had to navigate after 9/11. For me, it became a metaphor for the methodological twists, turns, jams, and unexpected access points, described in the next chapter, that came to make up the project. For all of us, it was very good training for what it would mean to become involved in homeland security.

CHAPTER 3 // MUDDLING THROUGH: METHODS, ETHICS, AND WRITING

Topics related to producing ethnography do not separate out as easily in practice as they do in scholarly papers or conference debates. However, in this chapter, I introduce the research context and set out what I feel to be the more significant issues of method, ethics, and writing that I have faced in this research. The first section presents brief descriptions of the research site and community. The next addresses the methodological challenges of studying a network in flux and sampling practice. Practical ethical concerns are addressed in the third section. The fourth describes the benefits and challenges of participant observation as a primary data-gathering method. The challenges of writing up from data drawn from participant observation are discussed in the final section. This material is intended to serve as background for an understanding of the nature of the data I gathered. However, I also hope it will be informative—sometimes cautionary—to others conducting research within this topic.

THE RESEARCH SITE

I selected the Boston area as my research site for a number of reasons. As a major urban area, Boston is home to regional offices of many of the federal organizations involved in homeland security. It was also geographically close to the bases of two important military participants: the National Guard's First Weapons of Mass Destruction Civil Support Team and the training division of the Soldier Biological and Chemical Command. In contrast to many smaller cities, Boston had already started planning and training for terrorism preparedness and was, therefore, already in the process of trying to sort through the problems identified in training exercises prior to the September 11 attacks. Unlike other larger cities such as New York, Seattle, and Atlanta, Boston had not had a large-scale act of terrorism or a significant terrorism scare when I made my selection in 1999.[1] Finally, Boston's political and economic position as a major city of the eastern seaboard, its active international air and water ports, and its proximity to several facilities of military significance—such as Hanscom Air Force Base, Lincoln Labs, and MITRE's research operations—were believed to make it a likely site of terrorist activity, although perhaps not in the way that actually happened.

As an older city, Boston presents challenges to any emergency operation. Many streets are narrow and their layout labyrinthine, making the movement of emergency personnel and vehicles difficult even under ordinary circumstances. Under the streets is a complex maze of utility and subway tunnels, some of which have been in disuse for long enough that they are known to few. Routes out of the greater urban area are indirect and often congested, suggesting that any large-scale evacuation would be a problem. Many of the medical facilities capable of handling large numbers of emergency admissions are clustered in a small area along the Boston-Cambridge border, a situation that makes consultations convenient but would be disastrous if that area was near the center of an attack. Interestingly, this situation was noted in 1962 as a significant problem for crisis and consequence management in the event of a nuclear attack on Boston (Sidel et al. 1962).

As described in more detail in later chapters, the tensions among public and private, as well as federal, state, and local participants in the area's homeland security, were demonstrated quickly after 9/11. Although regrettable and sometimes frightening, these schisms added to the appropriateness of Boston as a research site.

---

1. In the late 1970s, the Boston area experienced several smaller instances of domestic terrorism. In 1976, a group called the United Freedom Front (later known as the Ohio 7) bombed the Suffolk County Courthouse (Howe 1989; Regan 1993). In 1978 a plane at Logan Airport, a Newburyport courthouse, a post office, and National Guard property were bombed by members of the Fred Hampton Unit (Associated Press 1977a, 1977b).

THE RESEARCH COMMUNITY

This study was rooted in the hypothesis, now supported, that homeland security in the Boston area was practiced within what Shore and Wright (1997, 15) call a "policy community"—a community of varying types of ties that emerges through the directives of policy and the indirect influences of that policy on social life. Although the participants in a policy community may not all know one another through face-to-face interactions, they are joined in networks by the relationships entailed in or otherwise made necessary by policies. The policies and the networks they engender in turn produce sets of power relationships that further influence the community.

The community is described in greater detail in chapter 4, but a few remarks are needed here. The people who form the homeland security policy community in the area come from an astonishing variety of institutional backgrounds and levels of government. It is convenient to think of the institutional backgrounds in the following categories: public safety (including law enforcement, fire services, and emergency medical services), emergency management, medical/hospital, public health, military, including the National Guard services, governmental/administrative, charitable/nongovernmental, and private sector. Public safety and emergency management formed the bulk of the early community due to the initial policy directives (National Security Council 1996a), although this quickly began to change to include more people from public health and clinical backgrounds (Henretig 2001). As people began to conceptualize what homeland security was going to mean, the importance of planning emerged as a critical community function alongside response. This led to the inclusion of more people who held planning and training roles in their disciplines.

It also is useful to conceptualize the levels of government as federal, regional, state, and local, although a particular agency often has actors operating at more than one level. The FBI, for example, may have personnel from a local task force, a regional bureau, and the federal home office all operating in the same area. Some organizations, notably the National Guard, may switch their level of government affiliation depending on political decisions and the nature of the task at hand. The affiliations along lines of institutional background and/or level of government are discussed in chapter 8. This multiorganizational, multilevel structure provides an unwieldy number of participants for any planning, training, or actual operations. It was no less unwieldy for research. The process of finding the policy community and gaining entrée is discussed in more detail in chapter 4.

NETWORKS AND PRACTICE

In this project, I investigated human practice in the context of an emerging, multisite, social network.[2] The work was multisited in the sense that there are real people in many real, physical spaces who have the relationships forming the network. The network, however, was not spatially based except in the sense of having its focus (but not all of its activity) within U.S. national boundaries. Rather it was based in policies coming from all levels of government and providing sometimes conflicting or unrealistic objectives and instructions.

The overt common goal of the people generating the policy and those expected to enact them is the internal security of the United States. Ideas about what that goal looks like and how to get there are far from harmonized. No social network was ever as tidy as the diagrams look, and that of homeland security is no worse or better. It is not a wholly new network of fresh-faced individuals ready to enact government directives. It is, in part, a network being created from segments of existing networks connected in new ways or at new levels of intensity of relationship.

None of this should be news for anthropology. Classical network theory recognized the difficulties of capturing such fluid arrangements (Bott 1971; Epstein 1961; Mitchell 1969; Wolfe 1978). Contemporary social network analysis includes the idea of investigating specialized networks, based on a subset of relationships, as well as more traditional full relational networks (Trotter and Schensul 1998, 713). Ethnographers also investigate networks made up not of individuals but of communities or organizations (LeCompte and Schensul 1999, 53–54). The range of social network theory is too broad to cover here. Suffice to say that there is an ample literature on which to draw.

It may seem new to tangle with a social network as it emerges, rather than one we presume already to exist in semi-static form. This obstacle is purely one of disciplinary terminology. The idea of social networks has become common enough that we tend to think of them as being concrete

---

2. Although I was not able to do a formal network analysis, the networks concept was important in guiding my fieldwork.

things that can be observed and measured. The reality is that "social network" is a concept we use to describe a process through which people interact with one another and get things done in their daily lives. Sometimes these arrangements of relationships have been functioning long enough that they can encounter significant contextual bumps without exposing any rough edges or falling to bits. This makes it easier to create an illusion of the network as a static thing, but it is still inaccurate. In the case of homeland security, the whole network is still rough edged and every bump creates problems for the people trying to use it.

What was somewhat more perplexing was the lack of clear spatial boundedness. However, there is an old military aphorism that applies: every crisis is local. Although the policies that help generate a network are sometimes abstract, every activity takes place in a location. Some of the activity of homeland security takes place in existing spaces—firehouses, training fields, and conference rooms. The mix of organizations and people in these places is changing, and that affects how these spaces are understood and used—changes that are another source of information. Some activity takes place only on paper or electronically, through websites, e-mail, and telephone calls. In fact, some parts of anthropological research on this kind of network have to take place in these forms, something that is a difficult methodological adjustment after over a century of spatially defined anthropological fieldwork. These spatially attenuated kinds of relationships may be relatively new terrain for anthropologists, but they exist regardless of our comfort level. There is no such thing as a fully formed or finalized social network, and this includes space as well as number and types of relationships. Investigating practice in a network while it is still forming forces attention to its processual aspects and, perhaps, generates new knowledge about social networks in general.

So then how does one see that process of network formation at work when there is no equivalent of the veranda from which to observe? How does one capture it ethnographically? More important for the purposes of this project, how does one investigate practice that is both enmeshed in and simultaneously helping to create a changing and disquietingly ephemeral context? It would have been reasonable to study only a manageable fragment, focusing on power relationships or gender or race. However, such an approach would not confront the social phenomena of practice within large, nonspatially based networks. I also had the option of retreating into abstractions drawn from transnational theory such as Appadurai's scapes and flows (Appadurai 1990). Analyses based solely in text or discourses available in conveniently accessible news stories and government documents are also possible. While they might produce a more polished result, none of these approaches appealed to me when dealing with an institution like national security, so often perceived as monolithic and impenetrable.

At the one extreme, tidiness of results is purchased at the cost of masking the complexity of the network as a whole. At the other, one loses understanding of human agency and how the network is formed, maintained, and transformed. It is too easy to use abstract concepts to mystify power and complexity further rather than to understand their operations. Both reductions and abstractions can lead to poorly defined understandings of problems, yielding simplistic results (Rubinstein, Scrimshaw, and Morrissey 2000, 45). Following Rubinstein (1984, 7–11), I believe that anthropology need not choose between these two extremes but, rather, is uniquely suited to develop complex models for complex realities. Rubinstein also has argued persuasively for the importance and feasibility of multilevel accounts of social phenomena (1984, 93; Rubinstein, Scrimshaw, and Morrissey 2000, 45). It is this full engagement with complexity in the face of its inherent messiness that I have sought to preserve throughout the project.

I had planned to use a targeted sampling strategy to capture as much of the spectrum of human agency as possible. I believed the strategy of deliberate sampling for heterogeneity was the best option, given the multiorganizational and multilevel nature of the policy community. As described by Johnson (1998), this form of sampling involves targeting types of groups to represent a range of such groups found in the population. I also expected that the "snowball" technique, having each interviewee identify future leads based on certain criteria, would supply some leads (Trotter and Schensul 1998).

Despite all the chaos and rapid organizational change following the attacks in 2001 and despite my choice to abandon most of the rest of my research strategy, for many months I continued to cling to my original sampling ideas. Old habits die hard. I made grids and checklists to keep track of the organizations I had visited. I tried to spread my contacts across disciplines. I found myself frustrated that I was always at interagency meetings and exercises and training sessions rather than spending "quality time" with an agency as it went about its daily business.

It was only after I had to defend to my anthropological colleagues my intention to study actual practice rather than the national political debate that I realized the flaw in my approach. If my purpose was to observe the practice of organizations coming together to figure out homeland security, then perhaps I should be sampling practices, not organizations? Perhaps I should be looking at *how* the network was used rather than trying to diagram it? Once conceived in this way, the idea of sampling seemed to move much more in line with my research goals than it had been in the original research design. I knew that there were some local homeland security activities to which I would never have access, such as actual responses to attacks, intelligence gathering, and criminal investigations. However, the very interagency activities that had been frustrating me constituted a great deal of the practice I had come to investigate. I devised a simple categorization for interagency activities to which I might conceivably be given access and tried to spread my participation among them as much as possible.

For each of the nine categories below, I distinguished between official meetings or events and those that were unofficial or informal.

1. Security Initiative—large and small meetings in which participants try to develop direction, policy, and procedures related to the security of a specific geographic area or topic, such as port security or security of fuel tankers.
2. Exercise Development—meetings to design exercises and drills that allowed security plans to be practiced and/or tested, excluding the meetings in which exercise evaluation and reporting were discussed.
3. Exercise—the actual playing out of exercises to practice and/or test security plans.
4. Assessment—tours of a particular geographic or topical area to assess targets, hazards, vulnerabilities, available protections and response resources, and response options.
5. Operation—nonresponse activities involving rolling equipment, such as escorting a tanker through the harbor.
6. Training and Education Session—classroom and practical sessions designed to teach a set of students about a particular issue or protocol or to help them learn how to use/remain skilled with equipment.
7. Demo—demonstrations of capability by one organization for other organizations (but not necessarily the public); demonstration of equipment by vendors or by an organization considering purchase.
8. Planning Session—a loose category including meetings to refine or update plans, coordinate plans among agencies, determine the appropriate response to a newly identified situation, or plan

how an event would be handled—for example, planning the public safety and health presence and operations for the Boston Marathon, deciding how to react to an increased national alert level, reviewing different agency plans for handling a hazardous material spill in the port.

9. Reporting—meetings in which reports on assessments or exercises were designed and written.

These activities, together with the kind of informal discussions that take place in transit or over lunch and the back-channel decisions of policymakers, were some of the key venues in which the community figured out what homeland security was going to mean. Although I could not formalize this sampling procedure as much as I would have liked for this study, it proved to be a valuable approach, as it enabled me to focus more on how people were coming together rather than on the institutional backgrounds that might have kept them apart. I expect that this type of activity-based sampling may be a necessary component of any research study on a policy community.

So, although networks were a critical component of my research methods, there is little mention of them in the ethnographic chapters of this book. This is merely a stylistic choice on my part. Instead, I use the words "community" or "policy community" and "relationships." By doing so, I hope to avoid conjuring up expectations of network diagrams and weighted relationship scales, which I would not have been able to create amid such rapid change even had I thought they were useful. I wanted to focus attention on, among other things, how people in the community used their relationships to conceptualize homeland security and get work done.

ETHICAL CONSIDERATIONS

There is no chance that an anthropologist working on project involving national security would go unchallenged on ethical grounds. For this project, there were three primary ethical considerations, each of which is discussed below. One, concern about the research topic itself, was of little personal concern but was kept alive by colleagues. The second, concern about the secrecy, has both ethical and ethnographic implications for any research in this topic. The third concern is the vulnerability of research results, more a long-term consideration for the discipline than an immediate practical problem.

One of the earliest ethical concerns to be raised about my project by colleagues was that of anthropological research relationships with national security organizations. The distinction between a project that is partially based on the study *of* these kinds of organizations and a project that is based in study *for* these organizations is not always a comfortable one. The discipline has had an uneasy past with the federal government, so the concerns are understandable. I think, however, that the recent work on military and national security topics should reassure most that it is possible to conduct this kind of research without being inadvertently used as a spy (Bogdan 1980; Brosius, Goode, and Thu 2002; Guillemin 1999; Gusterson 1996; Hunt 1984; Masco 2002; McNamara 2001; Miller 1999; Pogrebin and Poole 1988; Rubinstein 1998a, 2000; Schoch-Spana 1998a; Shore and Wright 1997; Simons 1997, 1999). I am not suggesting that such concerns should be dismissed, only that they should be clarified. Recent disciplinary debates and the formation of an ad hoc commission to investigate relationships among anthropologists and security organizations, discussed in chapter 1, point in hopeful directions.

Secrecy also is a great concern within the discipline and was a particularly difficult issue throughout my research and writing. There were three interlocking issues that have led me to write with somewhat less ethnographic richness than I would have preferred. The first issue was actual security. Publicly exposing real vulnerabilities in Boston-area security was a concern. Although some security issues were resolved while I was in the field, there are many difficult problems that may take years to fix, if it is feasible to fix them at all. It is easy to forget, after several years without a successful attack, that security issues are still a concern. In fact, however, even under the rosiest scenario, it seems unlikely that all the domestic, foreign, and transnational groups and individuals who have considered using violence against U.S. civilians and property have lost interest in doing so. Providing detailed descriptions of what was discussed at meetings or of solutions developed posed the possibility of giving these groups and individuals information or leads they otherwise could not access. I addressed this in part by having a particularly trusted informant, who also had an academic background, review the examples I planned to use, and I revised the manuscript according to her suggestions.

The second issue was balancing academic transparency with the desire to respect informant requests and maintain access to the community for future research. Although I did not have to obtain any official security clearances for my work, in the chaotic environment after 9/11, I was exposed to information and situations that would now be categorized as "security sensitive" or "sensitive, but unclassified." Some of this information falls into the category above, protecting legitimate security concerns in the area from exposure to those who would exploit them. However, as discussed in more detail in the ethnographic chapters, some information was downplayed or hidden to cover up incompetence and other problems. If I was asked to refrain from discussing something or if that request was implicit in my access, I have treated that information with the respect any anthropologist would accord to his or her informants. This was a difficult process. However, I concluded that I am an anthropologist, not an investigative journalist or pundit. My greater access to the community comes at the price of living up to reasonable informant expectations. I have maintained this uneasy balance between secrecy as a topic of analysis and secrecy as a fieldwork necessity. In conferences and conversations, I have been accused of contributing to unnecessary government secrecy about security. Scholars seem to understand the uses of secrecy for preserving rapport and protecting informant confidentiality in traditional research projects. It is more difficult for them to feel comfortable when the research community is involved with U.S. national security activities.

The third issue related to secrecy was the normal anthropological practice of protecting informant confidentiality. Elite security planners and policymakers may, in some circumstance, be considered public figures. However, very few of my informants in this project could be categorized as elites within their context. They were working-class men and women with promotions and retirement benefits to lose. The ethnographic issues this raised are discussed later in this chapter. Methodologically, the challenge was to be sure that informants understood what I was doing and how information would be used.

Many security professionals are accustomed to dealing with interviews and research requests from the press. They are used to certain journalistic conventions of acceptable use, such as "on background," "not for attribution," and "on deep background."[3]

3. Data collected under "not for attribution" ground rules can be used, so long as the exact source is not identified. The bulk of my field data falls into this category. "On background" information is intended to provide guidance for further research. The basic information can be used so long as the source is carefully protected. "On deep background" information cannot be used immediately and may not be able to be used at all. Its purpose may be to spur further research or stop or delay it. My field data from this category are either not recorded in writing or are stored in encrypted files with limited backup copies.

Accordingly, I decided to adopt the definitions used by the *Kansas City Star*, a commonly accepted source for these conventions (American Society of Newspaper Editors 2001). The conventions allow an interviewee to give a reporter enough background to understand a particular topic (or why he or she should avoid a particular topic), without being named. In some cases, the reporter cannot use the information at all, except as a stimulus for further research and source development. Informal conversations with possible informants at the federal and regional levels indicated that research participants in my study might interact with me in these terms. It was not realistic for me to expect them to learn the anthropological standards for information use. Rather, I needed to be ready to interact in terms they understand. I did not always offer the option of interacting in these terms but felt it was important to have decided on standards in advance. Doing so ensured that the acceptable use of information could be clearly determined if questions were raised in journalistic terms.

Informant expectations regarding information use form the background for the more important third ethical concern. One of the most significant considerations for an anthropologist is maintenance of informant confidentiality over time. Institutional human subjects review boards require that researchers obtain "informed consent" from research participants in written or verbal form (Fluehr-Lobban 1998, 185). Researchers are expected to explain the nature of the project, the possible risks of participation, and the actual level of confidentiality of anonymity that can be expected. Often the trust between research and participants is crucial to successful completion of the research project (Fluehr-Lobban 1998; Rubinstein 1998a). My human-subjects protocols were approved in August 2001 and included significant assurances of confidentiality and risk reduction. I made assurances verbally when written consent was not possible.

At the time that I made these assurances and filed my human-subjects protocol, I was unaware that notes and raw data from federally funded research may be subject to release under the Freedom of Information Act, or FOIA (National Science Board 1999). While it is unlikely that anyone would go to the trouble of filing for access to my field notes, some anthropologists make a point of using the FOIA to conduct research on national security, the military, and intelligence agencies (Price 1997). With Gusterson, I believe that I have an obligation to respect confidentiality even when my personal political opinions may coincide with those who would seek to breach that confidence (2003, 26). Informants gave me information that, under journalistic conventions, was too sensitive to be published but that provided context or leads for usable data. In a sort of strange cross-eyed panopticon arrangement, these security professionals might be able to protect certain unclassified information in their filing cabinets from FOIA access by citing national security interests, but once they have given it to me, I cannot. I do not even have the socially accepted (although not legal) standing of a journalist protecting sources (Reporters Committee for Freedom of the Press 2001). Available information from the National Science Foundation and the Code of Federal Regulations does little to clarify how vulnerable these documents actually are. Current anthropological wisdom on this topic is that the Privacy Act would trump FOIA in the case of field notes. While this is somewhat reassuring, this is not quite the sturdy protection I believe the discipline should seek.

Again, it seems unlikely that anyone would have an interest in subpoenaing my notes (although somewhat more likely in the context of increased academic and public concern over new government secrecy measures). I chose to destroy all copies of certain field records, a step it is unlikely other researchers would need to take. However, as anthropology continues to study large institutions, engage in controversial topics, and develop the applied aspects of the discipline, issues of data ownership and privacy will continue to arise. These concerns intersect with human-subjects protocols in ways that have the potential to be damaging to research participants, despite the best intentions of the anthropologist. They also are linked to concerns about the problematic roles anthropologists might play in field research that is linked to national security or how anthropologists might be employed in ways that violate the ethical standards of the discipline. Recent work in the discipline to clarify the AAA Statement of Ethics and the discipline's relationship to different kinds of engagement with national security–related organizations have started this process but are a long way from completing it (1998, 2004; Brennis 2004; Peacock et al. 2007). It remains to turn these positions into practical guidance and protocols.

PARTICIPANT OBSERVATION

Ethnographers set out to show how social action in one world makes sense from the point of view of another. Such work requires an intensive personal involvement, an abandonment of traditional scientific control, an improvisational style to meet situations not of the researcher's making, and an ability to learn from a long series of mistakes. The language of the received view of science just doesn't fit the details of the research process very well if you are doing ethnography.

MICHAEL AGAR, "Speaking of Ethnography"

I had intended, as so many anthropologists have, to use a clearly defined set of methods. As with all anthropological projects, it is questionable how much of that research strategy could have been maintained under normal circumstances. The events of 9/11, just as I was beginning to make my opening forays into the community, sent me into confusion. It may be difficult for those who were not in an East Coast city during the months that followed the attacks to understand just how profoundly they altered life for people who had any interest in safety or security. Even people with no connection still looked up when a plane flew low over the city. Subway commuters eyed each other's backpacks and shopping bags with embarrassed suspicion. Sikhs and others in danger of being erroneously associated with the perceived threat of Islamic fundamentalism wore flag pins and other patriotic paraphernalia prominently. Police on new protective details looked exhausted. Firefighters, restricted by the commissioner from joining their New York City colleagues in digging at the World Trade Center site, looked shell-shocked. After the anthrax attacks, the thousands of white-powder calls stressed public health and safety organizations to the breaking point. Those of us with a healthy appreciation for what the U.S. retaliation might mean held our breath.

Should I give up my research topic? Try to do something else or at least change locations to a place not so exhaustively involved in reconfiguring itself? I found the idea of leaving intolerable. I wanted to see what happened. I wanted to understand how people in these organizations made sense of all this. I also knew that I had an opportunity to see something that no other anthropologist was going to get to see. I didn't know exactly how I would turn it into something I could share with the discipline, but it seemed foolish to throw away such an opening. Having decided to stay, I had to figure out what to do. Should I try to keep going with my planned sampling strategy and interviews and see what happened? Somehow it seemed profoundly arrogant and unethical to expect people to find time in their days to sit down and do a formal interview with me. It would have been ridiculous to expect them to allow me to tape-record anything when nobody knew yet what information was now going to be considered sensitive. I also did not want to be underfoot. In public safety and public health, people who had already faced demanding jobs were now working even longer shifts under great but vaguely defined pressures. I needed to find a way to watch and learn without being too much in the way. Ultimately, I went to my primary informants and said, in essence, "I am going to be here for a year. My discipline has a tradition of learning by doing. I have two hands. Put me to work."

I ended up going along with people as they worked, met, and investigated. I corresponded with them and talked to them on the phone as they tried to work out what was going on. Gradually, I became familiar and somewhat accepted at community events. I took notes, wrote up to-do lists, helped people figure out what the key points were in decisions they needed to make. I passed along my observations and analyses when I thought they might be helpful or when asked for them. I became engaged with the same issues facing my informants. I started trying to solve the problems, not just study them. At one memorable event, a small exercise, a member of a public safety organization had the group officially adopt me, amid much laughter and jokes about tribes.

In my initial research conception, I distinguished between systematic observation and participant observation, with the former being a more distanced practice and the latter giving greater access to the tacit dimensions of practice (Bernard 1994, 137; Dewalt, Dewalt, and Wayland 1998, 260). I assumed that I would be able to do more systematic observation than actual participation, not realizing how chaotic things would be and also not understanding how much of homeland security practice would be on the planning side of things rather than actual operations or responses. When I realized the participatory quality of the opportunities my informants were offering, I followed Bernard in believing that this could only improve the validity of my research (1994, 140–41). In short, I gave myself over almost entirely to participant observation.

In doing so, I began a process that gave me excellent access to the community but also raised a number of issues, each of which is described in more detail below. It became difficult to maintain a distinction between participant observation and applied anthropology. The kinds of data that can be gathered through participant observation, given ethical limitations, made it hard to determine appropriate styles for writing, providing evidence, and presenting material with authority. I am still struggling with these concerns and may continue to so long as I work within this topic.

HELPING THE COMMUNITY

Many anthropologists try to help their research communities. That help may take many forms, taking a turn at grinding millet, providing medical supplies, or offering political intervention. Similarly, the goals of such assistance vary and may overlap in actual practice if not in how they are reported. There are actions that can be usefully categorized as participant observation, a standard field technique. More systemic involvement with helping to solve community problems can be called applied anthropology or advocacy, depending on one's perception of the political weight of the actions. When the assistance is granted outside of the anthropologist's culture or social group, it can be easier to leave the aided community behind and draw boundaries between participant observation, applied research, and advocacy.

Erve Chambers wrote of applied anthropology:

Applied research . . . does not generally derive from a theoretical base, but rather from those assumptions and perceptions of need which have been identified as having policy significance. These perceptions of need may be influenced by social science theory, but they are not dependent upon it and are typically also influenced by ideologies, political and commercial intent, hunches, and raw guesses. . . . The goal of collaborative inquiry is generally to help decision makers select from alternative strategies for implementation and to measure the effects of their choices. It is important to keep this in mind—that the major objective of applied research is not to challenge the most basic assumptions which underlie a policy stance, but to help figure out how to translate ideas into action and then to determine the impact of those actions on the real world. (1989, 141)

George Marcus completes the picture by complicating it with his observation that "anthropologists find themselves in collaborations rather than create them out of their defined and controlled field projects" (1998, 241). I believe that the most accurate characterization of the collaborations I formed would be "action anthropology," as characterized by Rubinstein, in that I came to hold both research and solutions to my research community's problems as coordinate goals (1986). I distinguish this from applied anthropology as I had no contract, paid or otherwise, to assist with a defined problem. I also distinguish my assistance to the community from advocacy, first, because I had no call to intervene with higher levels of government on their behalf until after my fieldwork was complete and, second, because of the association of advocacy anthropology with support for a community's political endeavors.

I have found that participant observation gradually transformed itself into action anthropology, as both the need for assistance and mutual confidence in my ability to provide assistance increased. It is not easy to tease apart the concepts when much of the practice of my informants centered on answering questions very similar to my own. The line between asking, "How are they going to figure this out and what are they going to do?" and "How are we going to figure this out and what are we going to do?" gets a bit blurry when you spend every day with the people asking the latter and very little time with those who are asking the former.

Although this book cannot be applied directly to a discrete real-world problem, the data in it came from working on such problems. Such utility most commonly took the form of carefully defining a problem with which they were grappling. In such a rapidly changing environment, people rarely took the time to spell out what they meant by a particular concept or goal. The gap between the way things were and the way people wanted them to be needed to be filled with more than rousing political speeches intended to inspire effort.

In looking at the community with anthropological tools, I was able to develop realistic definitions or frameworks for decision makers. In developing these, I was able to incorporate sociocultural influences in ways that were acceptable to the community. Perhaps the most striking example of this is in introducing the idea of tacit knowledge and relationships as things that should be counted when assessing resources or trying to build capacity. There was local knowledge of the important role tacit knowledge and relationships play in getting things done, but they were rarely discussed as a formal part of the structure or as an asset to be maintained (see chap. 8). By giving these concepts names and demonstrating that they could be discussed as part of overall capacity, I brought them into the discourse of the groups with whom I worked as they tried to assess what was necessary for post-9/11 responses and what it would mean to be prepared.

I also must admit to a certain amount of "going native," which I discussed in more detail in chapter 1. Before heading into the field, I had read Hortense Powdermaker's assertion that "being alone . . . gives a greater intensity to the whole field experience than living with company, and frequently provides more intimate data because the field worker is thrown upon the natives for companionship" (1966, 114). When I chose my field site, I was both thankful and worried that I would have some access to my friends and family, in nearby New Hampshire, while at my field site. I wanted the intensity of the field experience, but I also am very place-centered and relished the idea of going home to recharge my batteries. As it turned out, Powdermaker's words were more relevant than I imagined. Although I could occasionally visit "home," I found that my need to stay focused on security and terrorism was isolating. When I had little to discuss other than the fact that the most recent smallpox vaccination guidelines were unintelligible to responders, it was easier to stay with my informants who shared my interest. Likewise, I spent little time with "the public" in Boston, preferring to be with people from the policy community or alone. At the end of my fieldwork, the identification had become strong enough that I took a job in preparedness and security planning rather than staying in a Harvard fellowship.

THE LIMITS OF PARTICIPANT OBSERVATION

There is no question that this approach to the project gained me unprecedented access to the community. No structured interview can give you the same flavor of what is really going on that you will get from being stuck in an hour-long traffic jam with a fire chief who needs to vent. Unfortunately, there are problems with the information one gets with that kind of access. The first is that it is not a systematic technique either physically or intellectually. Physically, I could not always write things down when I wanted. There were situations where it would have violated the sense of rapport, such as when people chose to unburden themselves in my direction. There also were situations where it was mechanically impossible to write, such as when I was clinging to the side of a police boat on the choppy harbor.

I created mountains of notes, just not necessarily about anything that I had intended. Taking notes for people in meetings became a blessing as it allowed me to write down observations as well as minutes without making people feel uncomfortable. E-mail and telephone calls back and forth became gold mines of information about what people viewed as homeland security work. For the rest of it, I listened, tried to remember, and spent a lot of time typing up my memories, impressions, and insights as soon as I got to a computer. The exigencies of daily practice rather than research design dictated what I got in my notes. I got some comfort from the historical moment in which my research was taking place. No study in my community during 2001–3 would have yielded replicable data. The pace of change was too great. I had to focus on the hope that the analysis I developed using an interpretive approach would be useful. As others have found when examining security-related issues, in cases where secrecy and security levels are not always predictable, one takes what chances one gets.

More understandably, but more problematic for the purposes of writing up data, my participant observation meant that I often heard and saw things that would not have been available to a complete outsider.

Sometimes there were security concerns for the area. My informants were understandably concerned that their resources and vulnerabilities not be precisely identified in a public document. Certainly some of this was cynical covering up of gaps and incompetence, but much of it was sincere. My informants saw the results of the research done by the 9/11 hijackers and the person(s) who mailed the anthrax-laced letters. The country as a whole was still debating how to balance security concerns with the public's right to know, and my informants were not certain how that debate would end. The ethical issues associated with this were discussed in the previous section, but it is worth discussing the methodological and ethnographic implications, which were significant.

There were times when people admitted to concerns that could have cost them their jobs if they came out in the press. Others expressed political opinions that their colleagues might find reprehensible. Sometimes it was just a matter of an off-color joke that brilliantly captured some absurdity of homeland security but would have made the teller look like she did not take her job seriously enough. This kind of information is particularly problematic when relying on participant observation for the bulk of ethnographic data. Interviews preserve a context of research and distance between researcher and informant. Participation begins to mask that context. Prolonged participant observation, such as my fieldwork provided, can make it difficult for informants to remember the research project. No matter how perfect the example or illustrative the anecdote, I had to consider the context in which I was given access to it. Was it because the person(s) were having one of the moments when I was part of "us" or were they still thinking about the fact that they had a researcher in the room?

Anthropological methods and ethics still seem to rely somewhat on shields of geographic and economic distance for their effectiveness. It is one thing to provide ethnographically rich passages about a poor community far away. Despite some anthropologists' concerns about government misuse of anthropological information, many writers seem comfortable in the knowledge that it is very unlikely that enough people in their research communities will read their publications to cause any problems. I have no such distances on which to rely.

The idea that anthropological methods yield different results in different settings is not news. However, the settings in which anthropologists will be increasingly called on to work should stimulate more disciplinary attention to methods than seems to be the case if recent disciplinary meetings are any indication. Clifford Geertz recently wrote that the world was moving "toward fragmentation, dispersion, pluralism, disassembly, -multi,

multi-, multi-. Anthropologists are going to have to work under conditions even less orderly, shapely, and predictable, and even less susceptible of moral and ideological reduction and political quick fixes" (2002, 14).

As more researchers "study up" or study "-multi, multi-," producing information where geographic and economic distance cannot provide an additional scrim of informant protection, it would be useful to revisit the standard tool kit with an eye to what kinds of data can actually be produced using these methods. It also would be helpful to have conventions of writing, evidence, and authority that work for those of us who have to communicate what we have learned in such settings. Projects disconnected from geography and complicated by collaborative relationships still have the "muddling through" quality described by Marcus as he called for innovations in research design to handle such topics (1998, 234, 244).

For me, the limitations meant that writing up data from participant observation would be a fundamentally interpretive task. I had to draw insights and check on them in a less than systematic way. I struggled with the difficulty of providing examples and stories that would not compromise informants. At the same time, the choice of method had significant benefits as well. People recognized that I had made a choice to try to help rather than make a quick name for myself with a tell-all exposé, and many of them respected me for it. I have permanent research relationships in the Boston area and among homeland security and national security practitioners throughout the country. It also has meant that I was able to apply anthropological concepts to community problems and try to make a tiny bit of difference in one area's homeland security. And, yes, I have left out significant things, but what anthropologist does not?

Of course, in a perfect world, I would now seek funding to go back and do more systematic and focused research. In reality, I do not regret the method I chose. It has enabled me to apply my analyses to policy in a far more direct and timely manner than would otherwise have been possible and helped build a permanent connection to the community. If it has made writing the book difficult, I find the trade-off acceptable.

WRITING UP OR THE "UNCERTAIN CONDITIONS OF ITS PRODUCTION"

I have chosen to err on the side of caution when writing concretely about my research community and individuals within it.[4] Given the tremendously vulnerable circumstances of many communities in which anthro-

4. The phrase "uncertain conditions of its production" is from Marcus (1998, 247).

pologists work, it may be hard for some to imagine what risk anthropological writing could pose for community largely populated by middle-class Americans. There are, however, levels of danger. As described above, few Boston-area homeland security practitioners were elites, secure in their professions, or public figures at the level where exposure is an occupational hazard. They have promotions to be denied. They have fragile working relationships that can be destabilized. Each person gambled to speak with me and to allow me to participate and/or observe.

With a relatively small community composed of a small number of representatives from each organization involved, it does not take much description before a knowledgeable reader can identify specific people. Homeland security activities take place in a politically charged atmosphere. An honest admission of error, an off-color joke, even an acknowledgment of the overwhelming nature of the job facing the community, any of these things could cause problems for a community member's career. They also could damage community networks, many of which have delicately constructed architectures to allow motion around politically sensitive issues or relationships.

Where such danger might reasonably exist, I have tied to present examples from the community in one of two ways that minimize the potential for harm. In some cases, I remove a quotation or paraphrased opinion from its context, setting it within the larger community. In most cases, I write about a community activity or structure in abstract enough terms that the individuals are masked by the larger group. While neither of these strategies is ideal for ethnographic writing, each provides some way of bringing the community into the analysis. This abstraction has been disheartening, as it must be for many who have to hide the identities of the people who helped them and whom they came to like and admire. I want the reader to see the slow smile and raised eyebrow on the face of a particularly helpful fire chief's face when I caught his eye during an especially ridiculous meeting. I want to be able to describe what made everyone go silent in the middle of an otherwise boisterous vulnerability assessment tour. I want to tell the story of the thoughtful and articulate commander who discussed cultural models and the impact of neoconservatism on security policy with me in an old warehouse. I want to paint pictures of the physical spaces the community used and bring their work alive with anecdotes. Doing so would not be acceptable.

Overall, I have tried to organize information that will give the reader an understanding of what the homeland security policy community was while I was in the field, the kinds of work that people in the community did under the rubric of homeland security, and the means they used to get that work done in the face of uncertain policy and ambiguous political, economic, social, and cultural contexts. If it seems a bit messy, then I have done my job in not making things any tidier than is necessary for understanding. It was messy and confusing and not ordered according to anthropological themes.

CHAPTER 4 // FINDING THE COMMUNITY

The community engaged in WMD preparedness is at best fragmented. The chal-
lenge our office continues to face includes identifying the partners engaged in
this cooperative effort. Unfortunately, there is no single document that details the
various organizations/agencies. Our office would be interested in reading your
paper when completed.

The sentences above were written in response to an inquiry I sent out
early in my research looking for guidance on the key players in homeland
security.[1] The response was from an official in what, at the time, was supposed to be the key coordinating office for preparedness in the country.[2]
Things didn't get any clearer as time went on.

Some early reports made attempts at lists. Two of the most widely available immediately following 9/11 were a much-reproduced chart from the
Monterey Center for International Studies, created in 2001, that showed
the massive tangle of federal involvement (and which was never intended

---

1. Throughout this document, I will refer to homeland security efforts or homeland security activities; these are catchall phrases I use to encapsulate a range of daily activities,
including planning, negotiating, meeting, political maneuvering, researching, performing public safety or health duties that overlapped with homeland security, dealing with
resource allocation, training, exercising, learning, and responding.
2. The organization no longer exists.

to be used to show state and local relationships) and the U.S. Department of Justice's (1998) list of domestic preparedness personnel:

293,000 firefighters
699,000 licensed practical nurses
1.5 million firefighter volunteers
1.31 million nurse's aides
704,000 police officers
18,000 ambulance drivers
50,000 911 operators
98,000 water/waste personnel
150,000 EMTs
47,000 electric power personnel
560,000 physicians
83,000 rail transportation personnel
64,000 physician's assistants
156,000 critical infrastructure managers
1.97 million registered nurses
TOTAL PERSONNEL: 7.7 million

Both had significant limitations. The Monterey chart was useful for illustrating how complicated things were "even at the federal level," but there was no equivalent diagram to show how complex and variable things were closer to the ground. The Department of Justice's list clearly had some issues, somehow managing to leave out even key players, such as emergency managers, the entire field of public health, and the National Guard. After significant, fruitless documentary research, I expected that one of my first and most useful tasks would be coming up with an operating definition and parameters for the homeland security community. Such goals seem hopelessly naive in hindsight.

I arrived in Massachusetts with a carefully constructed research proposal, which was quickly upended by the events of 9/11. In the aftermath, I had to tread lightly in the field to avoid being perceived as an added burden. It was a stressful time. I knew that any attempt to get uniform, systematic access to a tightly controlled sample of organizations would be doomed by the confusion and increased workload faced by the people in those organizations. I made the rounds of different agencies, talking with people informally and trying to get a sense of the best way to gather information about homeland security from each organization. I still hoped that I might be able to impose some form of research structure on the situation.

This approach was made difficult by the constantly shifting membership of the community. The people involved in homeland security activities come from an unexpectedly large range of backgrounds. There were the traditional public safety professions: police, fire, and emergency medical services. There were the military organizations one might expect, the U.S. Coast Guard, the National Guard, and the occasional special branch of the traditional military. Health organizations, such as public health departments and hospitals, played a role. Of course, the familiar American Red Cross and Salvation Army were often involved. The federal presence was a combination of the more obvious Customs, Immigration and Naturalization, Border Patrol, Federal Bureau of Investigation, the Centers for Disease Control, and the Federal Emergency Management Agency, and the less obvious partners, such as the Bureau of Alcohol, Tobacco, and Fire Arms, the Department of Energy, Navy intelligence and divers, and the Agency for Toxic Substance and Disease Registry.[3] Yet, there were other, less familiar, identification cards that appeared at security checkpoints. School administrators, water resource managers, transit authority representatives, inspectional service officers, security personnel from large facilities, public information representatives, and community leaders. It seemed that every event caused some new group to be added to the list. The airplane attacks of 2001 made people realize that air traffic controllers and the Federal Aviation Association would need to be in the loop. The anthrax incidents later in 2001 brought postal service employees to the public's attention. They are in the spotlight again, in the role of responder rather than victim, as plans are developed to see if they could be used for medication distribution in a large-scale health event. Ultimately, in a case that will be discussed in more detail below, a representative of the lobsterman's cooperative became the final straw in my attempts to compile a list of organizations involved at the local level. Planners had similar problems. There was no preexisting organization or policy that could encompass federal agents and lobstermen.

Thinking that perhaps the critical organizations might be documented, I also began trying to get copies of emergency plans, a task that had proved impossible to accomplish given normal archival methods. Most organiza-

3. Customs, Immigration and Naturalization, Border Patrol have now been combined within the Department of Homeland Security.

tions hold their emergency plans fairly closely. There are good and bad reasons for this. There are real security concerns. Familiarity with an agency's response plan could allow somebody to disrupt it and potentially cause additional harm. Unfortunately, these concerns are sometimes used as a smokescreen to conceal plans that have not been updated in years or that were written to allow the agency to check off a regulatory requirement rather than to actually develop a workable plan. While the plans are technically available to the public, they do not have to be easily available. Also, some plans are kept in perpetual "draft" state, and this is given as a reason for not releasing them. Especially after September 2001, agencies were reluctant to let people see their plans, particularly if they believed that the gaps in them might be revealed in print.

Gradually, I was given access to agency plans and started to ask questions about how they meshed with the plans of other agencies and other jurisdictions. I had conversations about how people planned to integrate homeland security into their existing plans and procedures. The more I asked, the more I began to realize that not only was there no agency at any level that had a sense of the whole landscape in which homeland security was taking place, but there was also no agency that had the mandate to go out and get such a picture.

The context in which they were operating did little to encourage the interagency work being demanded by politicians and the press. Funding was largely stovepiped, predesignated for a particular type of agency and activity, leaving no flexibility to allow interagency sharing or planning. A common complaint from my informants was that grants only allowed them to purchase equipment and pay for training for their staff. Unfortunately, they did not allow two agencies to combine funds to purchase a better or more appropriate piece of equipment. In such a zero-sum system, no planner or head of department wanted to be put in the position of suggesting that a piece of equipment or a program might be of more benefit to the community if it was located elsewhere. This atmosphere did not encourage anyone to truly take the plunge into interagency efforts. There was simply too much to lose at the organizational level, and the broader benefits were not well defined or well funded.

Schedules were overbooked and hectic. In the initial rush to do something, anything, after September 2001, there were still relatively few people in the community who knew enough to carry the work on their shoulders. Each agency might have a hazmat tech or a special operations unit or just a person interested in emergency management, but these individuals could not spend all their time in meetings trying to figure out what homeland security was supposed to look like.[4] They had to respond to actual events as well. While organizations did increase the numbers of staff they sent for preparedness or terrorism-related training, there is a learning curve in emergency preparedness and it takes time to move along it. Also, much of this training was oriented toward response, not planning. As will be discussed in chapter 7, much of the work of homeland security during the first few years ended up being the work of thinking through what to do and how to do it, not actually responding to events.

Another factor in the apparent local muddle was the lack of national consensus on what the United States was going to do about this new idea of homeland security. As suggested earlier, no effective guidance was available from the national level to help those who might have been motivated to develop a more systematic and considered approach to building interagency homeland security practices. A number of federal players had departments or divisions that tried to provide some leadership. The FBI had its National Domestic Preparedness Office. The Department of Health and Human Services had its Office of Emergency Preparedness. The Federal Emergency Management Agency had several initiatives. Unfortunately, these attempts at leadership were hampered by a lack of coordination among federal players before guidance was provided (a situation that continued even after the formation of the Department of Homeland Security). Nothing is so stifling to local innovation than getting apparently conflicting messages from those who control the regulations and the purse strings. There also was collective holding of breath regarding what the Bush administration would do in terms of federal reorganization. Local organizational traditions and "turf wars" played a role in keeping agencies isolated, although less than one might imagine, as will be discussed in a later chapter. The crux of the problem was that nobody was quite sure which way the wind would blow.

Organizations and politicians did try to address the confusion at the

4. The terms "hazmat tech" and "special operations" warrant clarification in the context of this study. A hazmat tech is a person with special training in handling hazardous materials incidents. This training is sometimes specific to the needs of a particular discipline. For example, a firefighter and a police officer would receive different training appropriate to the kinds of roles they would fill at a hazardous materials incident. Many public safety agencies are developing special operations sections or units. People in these sections have specialized training to allow them to respond to a range of missions that are perceived to be somewhat outside of normal operations. Examples of special operations missions include hazardous materials response, terrorism or hostage situations, and confined space rescue.

state and local level. As in other places around the country, Massachusetts saw a post-9/11 flowering of "homeland security" and "counterterrorism" offices, task forces, and advisory councils, as new organizations or as new departments within existing agencies. Intradepartmental efforts were sometimes successful in helping individual organizations answer the question "What do we do right now until the larger issues sort themselves out?" However, these new groups were hampered by the same stovepiping and turf issues as their parent organizations and could do little to paint the broader picture of homeland security in the region. Also, there was sometimes rivalry among the agencies regarding development of new units and capacities. Why was Agency A developing a Weapons of Mass Destruction Unit if Agency B already had hazardous materials units trained to handle weapons of mass destruction? Who would get the resources for training and equipment? Who would handle responses? The media was full of reports of a windfall in federal dollars for everyone who could lay claim to homeland security activities.

There also was an element of prestige involved in who would be most closely identified with homeland security, having the special units and the authority to speak for the broader response community. The post-9/11 boost to the cultural capital of firemen was not lost on other agencies.[5] In this case, firefighters and, to a lesser degree, police officers were able to use the perception of them as the heroes of 9/11 to exert great influence over the formation of public and political discourses of homeland security. Few politicians would stand up at a press conference to discuss homeland security without uniformed members of the fire and/or police services on the podium. Holiday parades always featured marching groups of emergency managers or public health officials. The images of firefighters and police officers from the 9/11 response were powerful. These agencies were the "face" of homeland security for many in the public. This, in turn, played into a perception in the political and responder communities that the public was most likely to trust local responders.[6] This influence contributed

5. Throughout, I use the term "cultural capital" as employed by Bourdieu, who described it as "the means of appropriating . . . the field of cultural production" ([1972] 1999, 184).

6. Although subsequent studies have done some assessments of public opinion, these were little known among practitioners while I was in the field. Two recent documents with worthwhile discussions and reference sections are the New York Academy of Medicine's report *Redefining Readiness* and materials from the University of Pittsburg Medical Center's Center for Biosecurity's materials from their Working Group in Governance Dilemmas (Lasker 2004; Working Group on Governance Dilemmas in Bioterrorism Response 2004).

to material and political advantages for public safety organizations over their lesser-known siblings.

Some broader efforts were reasonably successful. The State Attorney General's Office created its nationally mandated Anti-Terrorism Task Force (ATTF) under the guidance of a highly motivated individual who gradually built it into a mechanism to bring together many work groups of public and private stakeholders. These work groups served not only to solve problems but also to orient agency representatives to the activities and plans of other organizations. In many other cases, efforts to coordinate broad security planning were made difficult by preexisting authority structures. Massachusetts Governor Swift created an Office of Commonwealth Security, hiring an experienced and respected retired FBI Special Agent in Charge to be the director. Although the director had the ear of the governor, his authority to convene state and local agencies was not clear, and he was given no budgetary authority. Ultimately, it was through the personal efforts of the staff rather than the structure they inhabited that anything was accomplished prior to the office being absorbed by the larger Executive Office of Public Safety.

The movement of state homeland security responsibilities into a public safety agency echoed the problems created when any existing agency tried to develop a homeland security department. Nobody was quite sure where homeland security belonged. Some argued that the safety was the appropriate place due to the connection with first responders. Others argued that this placement neglected homeland security's health aspects, ranging from bioterrorism to critical incident stress management to handling the health consequences of infrastructure disruption, such as contaminated water or air. Yet there was no organization within the local and state health departments that could or wanted to take the lead for overall homeland security activities. Still others worried that a public safety focus might neglect broader emergency management and critical infrastructure issues in favor of first response and investigation. In fact, as discussed in chapter 7, developing the parameters of homeland security became an important aspect of the work of those in the response community.

Emergency management agencies might have made a likely resting place with their broad spectrum responsibility, including prevention, mitigation, response, and recovery. However, their ties with organizations like FEMA and the Red Cross were stronger than their connection to the response community. Many emergency management agencies have focused more on natural disaster mitigation and community recovery than on response and management of an incident, supporting the response agencies that take command. Placing homeland security in emergency management also seemed to neglect the intelligence gathering and prevention aspects of homeland security.

A final blow to the prospect of emergency management agencies as a home for homeland security authorities and funds was their history. In Massachusetts and several other states I visited, there was a perception that emergency management agencies were heavily weighted with patronage positions. There was a persistent sense that, as one informant put it, the only explanation for the employment of some of the people you met in emergency management was that the person "must be somebody's nephew" or "must have [compromising] pictures of somebody." I have no evidence about the truth of this one way or the other, and many of the emergency management people I met were highly dedicated and creative. However, in Massachusetts, the perception combined with some lingering planning problems within the state agency to kill any immediate prospects of them becoming a coordinating force. At the local level, Boston's Emergency Management Agency (BEMA) was a division of the fire department, usually led by a fire chief at a rank that precluded his or her being able to represent the organization at interagency meetings with the mayor. Being saddled with issues of rank made it difficult for them to act as objective brokers among response agencies.

Having crossed off the three big public welfare structures—health, safety, and emergency management—there were few other options open for anyone wanting to develop a coordinating authority for homeland security operations in Boston or the state. In a time of economic upheaval and looming recession, nobody except the federal government was interested in doing a complete reorganization to create a new homeland security entity. There was also a sense of the country wanting to wait a bit to see what the new federal structure would be. Nobody wanted to institutionalize new structures that would be incompatible with a new federal system. For over a year, Boston, and Massachusetts as a whole, lurched along with a Rube Goldberg structure before deciding to move state homeland security into public safety and much of city homeland security into the mayor's office. For the duration of my fieldwork, the community did not have even the comforting illusion that somebody was developing common goals for them to pursue. The fact that they accomplished as much as they did is a testimony to the ability of people in the community to form unofficial networks and manipulate existing structures to get work done.

My ability to learn about overall homeland security through traditional interviews was hampered further by people's understandable reti-

FIGURE 2. Interagency work at a "dirty bomb" drill at Logan Airport. Photo by Jim Gaffey.

cence to speak about security gaps and interagency problems. On the one hand, people wanted to recognize their organization's attempts to build interagency relationships and have me acknowledge the obstacles they faced. On the other hand, they did not want me to write an exposé about the difficulties they were having in "getting it together." There was also the difficulty that nobody quite knew what "it" was supposed to look like when they got it "together." Even when they were ready to talk, people had difficulty figuring out how to express their experiences and ideas. The common discursive envelope for homeland security had not yet been formed.

It quickly became apparent that I would get no more than a fragmentary view of homeland security practice by visiting individual agencies. Fortunately, in between these sparsely scheduled agency visits, I took every opportunity to attend meetings, ride along with people, help with small projects, observe drills, or come to training sessions. Gradually, I became a familiar face. People asked me to take notes, I corresponded with them, talked on the phone, tried to help them make sense out of what was happening. My circle of meetings and committees and events grew, and I gradually realized that I was finding what I would not see by visiting each agency in turn. I was inside the "inter" part of "interagency."

IN THE "INTER"

The first time I saw the lobsterman at a port security meeting, I knew that I was fortunate to have been kept away from my expected research methods. I was attending a meeting of a large interagency group that met as part of a U.S. Coast Guard initiative to help figure out what securing Boston Harbor meant and then try to find a way to put that definition into practice. The meeting was full of all the usual suspects, police, fire, Coast Guard, INS, Customs (this being just prior to the formation of the federal Department of Homeland Security), and the Massachusetts Port Authority. There also were some faces I was only beginning to find familiar—industry representatives, local businessmen, the state's Environmental Police, and staff from the Water Authority and the Transit Authority. One man, however, seemed out of place in his hooded sweat jacket and heavily bearded face. I knew he must have given the Coast Guard facility gate guards some satisfactory credential, but I could not figure out what it might be. At the end of the official presentations and reports that started the meeting, he was recognized to speak. He identified himself as a member of the Lobster Cooperative in the port. Lobster boats go everywhere in the harbor, and their crews are alert to changes in their territories, whether unusual boat activity or strange things taking place on the shore. He had come to offer the services of cooperative members as watchers and to find the appropriate channels for reporting something suspicious.

There were a few things that were interesting about his presence at the meeting. First, his was a group most would not have anticipated as playing a role in homeland security in the Boston area. Second, although many in the community made unofficial use of knowledgeable locals, people at the meeting were clearly at a loss as to how to make the relationship official. Third, the case crystallized something I had been seeing but not identifying as a trend: new organizations standing up and asking that their relationship to homeland security be acknowledged by the more easily recognized public safety community.

Some meeting attendees were being presented with an entirely new face to consider for group membership. Others were simply having their ideas about the role of the Lobster Cooperative broadened into more active participation. All were being confronted with the need to articulate and make visible a resource and a communication channel that had previously been unarticulated and largely invisible.

Had the Lobster Cooperative representative approached any individual agency, the likely outcome would have been that the agency would have offered to provide a conduit for information rather than inviting the cooperative to the table. Of course there are exceptions to this, but that kind of compulsive liaising was commonly reported to me. Some argued that it came from turf protection, others that it was just more efficient to keep the number of active decision makers in the community small. Some suggested that it was simply a courtesy to keep somebody from having to attend yet another meeting. Regardless of the source, its effect was to keep potential members away from the table, an exclusionary process to be discussed in more detail below. However, gradually more and more organizations approached interagency meetings and task forces directly. In doing so, they offered themselves as community members and helped create a generative mess of organizations and knowledge that broadened the possibilities of homeland security in the area.

A partial snapshot of that community a few months into my fieldwork would have included the organizations shown in the appendix. However, there are things missing from this table, as there would be from any attempt to capture such a system or its relationships. It does not include other towns that might be stakeholders in some activities (such as port security) but not in others, except as part of a mutual aid network. It does not include county organizations, such as the Sheriff's Department. It does not capture preexisting interagency affiliations, such as the position of State Police Troop F at Logan Airport. Most significant, it does not drill down to show all the sprouting and changing offices and units and task forces created within and among organizations as they tried to figure out what shape would best fit the demands of this new area of practice. Many of the organizations listed in the table have been renamed, moved, reconfigured, disappeared altogether, or taken on new roles. Every chart I made was immediately covered with Post-it notes and correction fluid. Every meeting involved at least one instance of somebody saying something along the lines of "or whatever they call themselves now" or "What do you mean they don't exist anymore?"

This process of figuring out what needed to get done, how to do it, and which hands would share the work was something that could not be seen in any individual agency. It was only between the official structures that the procedures and lines of communication were loose enough to allow rapid (and possibly temporary) additions, where new ideas and roles could be tried out without fear that they would become permanent. The community that was forming to handle homeland security in the Boston area and much of the work it was doing became ethnographically visible only in the "inter" part of "interagency" work.

As described above, the people involved in homeland security in Massachusetts come from a broad and rapidly changing mix of organizational backgrounds and levels of government. To discuss and write about the interagency process and the initial relationships that helped form it, I found it helpful to use the following conceptual groupings, which I will introduce briefly below: (1) categories, (2) axes of affiliation, and (3) core group and floaters. Categorizing the groups makes it easier to think without endless lists of organizational titles. Looking at the standard and novel lines of affiliation helps make visible some of the patterns of communication and activity. Finally, understanding the presence of a fluid, but recognizable, core group and the existence of "floaters" moving among the various activities and gatherings makes it easier to understand how the community held itself together amid the political turmoil of homeland security in the two years following 9/11.

I found the following institutional background categories useful in my own conceptualization and in discussions with community members: public safety (including law enforcement, fire services, and emergency medical services), emergency management, medical/hospital, public health, National Guard, governmental/administrative, charitable/nongovernmental, and private sector. At the start of my research, public safety and emergency management formed the bulk of the community due to the initial policy directives (National Security Council 1996a), although this rapidly changed more people from public health and clinical realms, as well as other backgrounds (Henretig 2001). Also, as the attacks on the United States in 2001 demonstrated, it became necessary to be alert to groups, such as air traffic controllers and postal workers, who may be drawn into homeland security as national risk assessments change. It also was useful to categorize the levels of government as federal, regional, state, and local, although a particular agency often has actors operating at more than one level. The FBI, for example, may have personnel from a local task force, a regional bureau, and the federal home office all operating in the same area. Some organizations, notably the National Guard, may switch their level of government affiliation depending on political decisions and the nature of the task at hand.

Over the time I was in the field, it became increasingly important to distinguish people involved with planning and management functions from those more involved with response functions. Sometimes this distinction could be made among agencies, but often it was necessary within individual agencies. As described in chapters 5–7, it became apparent that a great deal of homeland security activity would not be actual response but, rather, planning, thinking, conceptualizing, limiting, negotiating, and managing. While responders and response-based organizations, such as traditional public safety agencies, continued to play key roles, those a bit removed from "the front lines" became increasingly important. I found it helpful to keep this distinction in my mind as I assessed the contributions people were making and tried to break up activities into types of work.

Affiliation is addressed in more detail in chapter 8. For the purposes of understanding how interagency relations work, what is important is that individual actors and some groups will have multiple affiliations. To take Adams's concepts for multilevel analysis somewhat out of context, these persons and groups may develop their ideas and roles through participation in several different "operating units" at different "levels of articulation" (Adams 1970). For example, a policewoman's networks will be developed as she works at the level of her precinct but also at other levels of articulation as she participates in homeland security preparations as a part of "law enforcement," in contrast with "emergency management."

These affiliations can be quite complex, given the diversity of institutional background and position of those involved with homeland security. I know of no local or state agency in the Boston area that had a person specifically tasked to deal with homeland security immediately following 9/11. The people who became engaged in the policy community did so for a variety of reasons. Some people were officially designated by their agencies. Others had enough autonomy and interest to become involved on their own. In some cases, they had been working on related issues — terrorism or mass casualty incidents — and were the logical choice for their organization to send because of their existing knowledge. Some people were designated to attend meetings or keep track of homeland security for their organizations because they were well known and respected in the field and would bring a certain degree of personal power to any negotiations. Some were tapped for a role because their superiors made a connection between some aspect of their background (sometimes as little as one training session in terrorism awareness) and homeland security, although the designee might not see the connection in quite the same light. Some organizations developed one person as their "go-to guy" for all things related to homeland security. Others tasked people based on the topic at hand—preparations for medical care in mass casualty situations might be one person, while developing plans to deal with potential attacks on privately owned chemical facilities might be another.

Volunteers or conscripts, they similarly came from a range of ranks or status positions. It was not uncommon to see one fire jurisdiction represented by an assistant or deputy chief (quite high in rank) and another by a lieutenant (the lowest officer rank). Status was similarly distributed across other organizational types. The reasons for this diversity were rooted in a combination of the content factors described above and the degree of importance an organization placed on homeland security in general and a meeting topic in particular. These backgrounds and ranks had some impact on people's ability to develop affiliations, although I was surprised at the willingness of most in the community to get past rank and organizational distinctions.

Lastly, it was important to be able to talk about those members of the community who were involved in most homeland security activities, the "core" group, in contrast to those who "floated" in and out of direct, visible participation. As with everything about this community, people's positions over time were dynamic. However, there was a relatively stable core group of organizations (and to some degree individuals) involved in homeland security activities. Most were from traditional public safety and emergency management organizations. Others appeared and disappeared according to the needs and aspirations of their organizations. For example, representatives from the FBI were named on many committees but generally showed up only when their presence was requested for a specific discussion. In contrast, the Radiation Control Program from the Massachusetts Department of Health seemed to be everywhere. This may have been an artifact of its historical relationship with Civil Defense efforts but probably also was an indication of the program's hope to establish itself as one of the key players in weapons of mass destruction planning and homeland security in general.

I am specifically not setting up a core-periphery relationship in this last conceptualization. Non-core groups had a range of power positions within the community. They simply did not always participate in (and sometimes were not welcomed in) the activities of the core group. It is also important to recognize that these organizations were conducting their own homeland security activities, just not as visibly in the "inter" part of interagency homeland security in the Boston area.

THE POLICY COMMUNITY

The "inter" aspect of work done by the people in the Boston planning and response community is not simply an abstraction. It has become a significant part of the social apparatus used to manage this new idea of homeland security. Homeland security in the Boston area consists in what Shore and Wright (1997, 15) call a "policy community"—a multisited community of varying types of ties that emerges through the directives of policy and the indirect influences of that policy on social life. The community is multisited in the sense that there are real people in many real, physical spaces who have the relationships that form the community. However, the community is not spatially based except in the sense of having its focus (but not all of its activity) within U.S. national boundaries. Rather it is based in policies coming from all levels of government and providing sometimes conflicting or unrealistic objectives and instructions. It may seem strange to use this construct in a situation where policy was often absent or vague. However, the community was formed around these voids as much as it was by the few policies that existed. It also was based in the perceptions of practitioners about what policymakers and the public were likely to want.

The concept of a policy community allows analysis of human organization that does not have the benefit of easily visible spatial constraint. It also provides a device for focusing on and writing about interactions among people and groups rather than among predefined bureaucratic positions. Finally, drawing attention to the people along with the positions they inhabit facilitates investigation of policy-based relationships and actions not only in terms of imposed governance but also as they are used as a means of maintaining and contesting existing (or proposed) forms of social organization.[7]

Although the participants in a policy community may not all know one another through face-to-face interactions, they are joined in networks by the relationships entailed in or otherwise made necessary by policies and perception of need. The workings of these networks in turn produce sets of power relationships that further influence the community. As suggested by Shore and Wright, understanding such a community involves identifying and tracing the everyday interactions and problems among

---

7. I use the term "governance" in the sense of a power system that works both on and through individuals (Foucault 1982; Gordon 1991).

the different levels and sites of the processes generated by the policies (1997, 14).

In this case, the policy is vague and the indirect influences are many. I entered the area as the country was debating whether to reorganize a sizable part of the federal government to form a new agency to manage homeland security. Nobody knew exactly how that debate would turn out. As a consequence, the shape of the community, its parameters, networks, and tasks, was crafted largely by its members. This is consistent with other studies of community formation that have found that the definition of the community was often drawn from the daily practices of its members, not only its common geography or symbolism (Pellow 2002; Rubinstein 1998b).

Community members drew on existing organizations and relationships, as well as their own understandings of what homeland security would mean in the Boston area and the nation. For example, the powerful position of public safety meant that many members initially talked primarily in terms of response and their existing mutual aid agreements with other towns or agencies. It was only over time, as more voices were heard in the community, that other viewpoints—such as the need to think more about community readiness, risk communication, and recovery (still a neglected topic even after Katrina)—came to be more widely shared.

Practitioners were also influenced by the omnipresent possibility that the "policy" part of the policy community might become much more solid and prescriptive at any moment. Community members hovered somewhere between fear and hope about the influence of federal policy on their practice. While people dreaded the thought of an ill-conceived, top-down structure that would make their work more onerous, they also hoped for more guidance in forming the structure of homeland security and performing its tasks. The everyday interactions of community members as they tried to identify and solve problems ultimately created the policy community. The flow of influence, resource, and consequence was as nuanced and shifting as the social convolutions in a Jane Austen novel.

As it took shape, the community served an important function beyond simply allowing its members to get work done in the absence of national guidance or structure. Because it was an informal organization, it allowed its members to maintain flexibility of relationships and practices. As will be discussed in more detail in subsequent chapters, this ability to try things out without institutionalizing them served a critical need given uncertain hazards and uncertain politics. Also, the persistence of the core group allowed something similar to "institutional memory" to develop that made it possible for both individuals and organizations to fade in and out of active participation without the continuous loss of information and relationships that plagued interagency efforts prior to 2001.

The complexity of community membership was not only a difficulty for people who make charts or for anthropologists trying to develop a sample set. It represented a real confusion about the scope of homeland security and how to define the community of people who work on it. Cultural and financial capital were at stake in being included as a homeland security practitioner, as was a great deal of responsibility for new duties. While most organizations were happy to accept the former, some were less interested in the latter part of the package. Of course, after September 2001, many focused on "first responders," a vague construct of people who rushed in to save lives. There was a great deal of prestige associated with being called a first responder and many in traditional public safety organizations resented when others were put in this category. They felt that broadening the group to include emergency room physicians, support resources, emergency mangers, and so on weakened their position. I doubt many would have disagreed. There is a material difference between coordinating assets to support responders and walking into a burning building or defusing a bomb. However, defining first responders as the primary players in homeland security meant equating the degree of danger faced or the time of involvement with the perceived value of the contribution to homeland security and emergency response in general. Even this equation was fuzzy. For example, an emergency management official might be on-site before the hazardous materials specialists arrived, but the specialists were far more likely to be grouped in as first responders than the emergency management official. Using danger and time as criteria for inclusion did not account for the critical need for incident management, planning, recovery, investigation, and all the many other areas of work that were gradually becoming understood as part of homeland security. There needed to be a way to disentangle the prestige associated with first response from that associated with homeland security, a way of including other contributors to the process that would not encounter resistance from first responders.

People associated with homeland security made a variety of attempts to come up with new terms to describe those involved in homeland security. Some have seemed genuine attempts at inclusiveness. Others appear to be attempts to associate a group with the first-responder glow. I have heard the term "first receivers" used to describe emergency room staff. My suspicion is that this will cause the same problems in the health field as "first responders" did in public safety, as it does not account for the contributions of those who are not just inside the emergency department doors. Many, myself included, simply dropped the word "first" and began discussing "responders." It also became more common to talk about "responders and planners" to include the need for supportive policies, plans, and procedures.

Despite all this emphasis on the "inter," there were attempts to disassociate organizations from homeland security. Private industries in particular often wanted nothing to do with attending meetings or being involved in the decision-making process. They did not want their facilities, security, and emergency plans scrutinized. The resistance was in part due to concerns about information security. Once written up in a report by a government agency, the information was susceptible to Freedom of Information Act requests from the press, the public, and competitors. However, another part of the resistance was a reluctance to be saddled with expensive improvements or to be officially knowledgeable of, and therefore liable for, preparedness gaps. In one particularly disturbing case that I became aware of after my fieldwork, a Boston-area hospital administrator refused to meet with a policy analyst about preparedness because a lawyer counseled against admitting gaps in the hospital's ability to handle a bioterrorism event or mass care. To admit being aware of gaps meant that the hospital might be considered liable if it did not repair them,

The discussions surrounding postal carriers provide an example of the difficulty of in-group definition. As described above, the position of postal workers in relation to terrorism and security was unclear in the national discourse. Some listed them among responders because they were directly affected by an attack. Yet they were not truly part of a response, so others categorized them as victims. Still others pointed to the willingness of carriers to continue their work in the face of an unknown, invisible threat and commended them on their bravery, comparing them once again to the responders—conflating bravery and heroism with deliberate involvement.

There also was always the question of jurisdiction. Who counts as somebody operating at the local level, as opposed to "the feds" or some other group perceived by community members to have concerns somewhat less connected to ground-level realities? Only those who work for a town or city? What about the regional representatives of state agencies? What about the people at the field offices of federal agencies? What about people from other towns? What about industry representatives? Local may mean different things in different places. "Local" in a small town in western Massachusetts could probably have been confined to those people working within the local government or business. In a larger town or a city, such as Boston, the definition was less clear. The governmental level of an FBI field representative may have been federal and his jurisdiction a large section of the Northeast, but his concerns were often drawn toward local issues in the city that was both the largest population center in the area and the location of his headquarters. During my fieldwork, the importance of being a local as opposed to somebody with other masters to answer became less critical. What seemed to matter most to people was the behavior of individuals and the stances of their organizations when it came to getting things done. I came to operationalize my definition of local not based on geography or level of government but by the degree to which people or agencies involved themselves in the workaday concerns of the community.

These may seem petty questions, but they have significance when people in the policy community have to decide who gets invited to the decision-making table and they matter when federal planners choose how to package the security funds to states and towns. Certainly such categorizations matter to those people in organizations outside the public safety core who have vested interests in being included or, as in the case of some private industry and hospitals, an interest in being excluded and therefore absolved of responsibility.

The appearance of the community also depended on the task at hand. One informant described this as the Rubik's Cube effect.

It's complicated. You don't know which combination of colors you are going to need. Every situation is a little different. Sometimes you want more red than blue. Sometimes you need yellow. Sometimes not. And anytime you change one face, it changes all the others. And you aren't seeing those sides, so you don't know what's happening, what effect it is having. Anyway, you know what I really want? What I really want it for somebody to tell me what my little square is supposed to do.

In a community made up of many faces, many possible combinations can be present depending on what side you view. Depending on the task at hand, a researcher would see variations in in-group composition. Because much of my work ended up being oriented toward the Port of Boston, I saw much more of the U.S. Coast Guard (USCG) and Massport Fire

Rescue than I would have had my opportunities presented themselves in the downtown area. The business of defining the conceptual boundaries of the field of action, and consequently the actors, is addressed in more detail in chapter 7.

THE VISIBLE COMMUNITY

The ethnographic visibility of the policy community existed largely in meetings and operations. Since my safety and the safety of the operation would have been compromised by my presence, my operational experience was extremely limited. My ability to make ethnographic notes on those occasions was limited either for security reasons or physical ones, as on one notable occasion when the police boat was simply going too fast for me to do anything other than hang on. I came to view these infrequent opportunities as chances to gain insights that would help me understand the meetings and gatherings that were the more routinely accessible aspects of the community.

From my field notes on an interagency port security meeting:

I arrived early for the port security meeting. This was partly because I wanted to be respectful of the people who were allowing me to attend. But, truth be told, I wanted to take advantage of the unheard-of bonus of being part of the meeting—free parking in Boston's North End. As other early morning drivers cursed and honked, looking for parking spots on the street, I cruised up to the gate of the Coast Guard station feeling like some sort of royalty. I picked up my visitor's pass and made my way through the security checkpoint to nestle my truck among the official vehicles already starting to accumulate on the pier. It was gorgeous out. The sun lit up the harbor like a postcard. The rigging shackles on pleasure craft made their little wind-chime noises, giant tankers roamed like dinosaurs barely visible farther out in the harbor, little ferries scooted across between Logan Airport and Rowes Wharf in the middle distance. The tide was in (for once!), so the air smelled of salt and seaweed rather than whatever that low-tide smell is in the harbor. I had a vantage point that few Bostonians get to have, an unblocked view out into the harbor with no tourists shoving and no vendors yelling. This is why some practitioners don't complain about having to go to so many meetings. It gets them away from their computers and into this. I took my time making my way through the lot, noting the side conversations already taking place as people made their way across the pier toward the meeting room. Fire chiefs from Everett, Chelsea, and Massport Fire Rescue were huddled next to one truck, deep in conversation. V. gave me a shrug and eyebrow wiggle. I suspected them of trying to come up with a unified position on how to handle the LNG [liquefied natural gas] tanker issue before it came up at the meeting. The National Guard's Civil Support Team Commander chatted with a Coast Guard officer. I knew the officer tended to control the agenda for the meetings and wondered if the commander was trying to get her to add or remove something. I saw [two state officials from usually warring agencies] coming across Commercial St., in deep discussion. I went inside and sat toward the back, knowing that, as always, more people would come and talk with me as I sat alone than if I approached them. The room was set up like an auditorium, with chairs in rows facing a podium. But, no fools, the Coast Guard had set it up in a room with an unusually large mingling space in the back where they had stationed the refreshment tables. I still like meetings at the Civil Support Team facility better, but USCG does a good job and it's closer for most folks. As is always the pattern, local public safety and a few "crusty old dogs" from Customs and INS showed up first and talked out a ton of issues ahead of time. Then the suits began to show up—industry reps, federal agency representatives, and state officials. Small groups, shoals of fish, formed, broke apart, and re-formed according to what other businesspeople needed to conduct and what relationships they wanted to affirm. Gradually people began to make "let's get this show on the road" noises, even though the show had clearly been under way for some time. People took their seats and official reports and presentations began. . . . At break, I was ambushed coming out of the women's room by a chief who wanted to know if I had heard anything about something called the daily threat matrix. He had heard that the president got it every day and thought maybe he was supposed to be reading it, but was afraid to ask. . . . After the meeting officially ended, industry representatives went off to a small table and began to talk. V. suggested a cup of coffee, and those of us assigned to the consequence management group casually headed out to the parking lot. We spent the next half hour leaning on one of the trucks enjoying the sun on the harbor and trying to figure out how to find a balance between the Coast Guard's need for specific protocols with the more flexible approach of the fire services and the Civil Support Team.

The policy community was the visible part of homeland security not only for me; it was the visible part of homeland security as well for many of the people involved. In the absence of any official structure or clearly defined goals or parameters, the primary mechanism available for working things out was meetings. During this time period, it was not uncommon for people to spend all day in formal and informal meetings. The focus of these meetings might range from some broad topic, such as "port security," to something more concrete, such as hammering out an interagency cross-jurisdiction concerning equipment interoperability in the continuing absence of federal guidelines. Informal meetings sometimes concentrated on a topic and sometimes were simply to share information, gossip, and rumors. Some meetings were half-day affairs involving many people. Others were brief, often less than an hour.

People held meetings to get work done. They held them to try to figure out what work should get done. They held them to ensure that all perspectives were understood and to make sure people felt included in the decision-making process. Some meetings were large performative affairs involving speeches by important officials. These were the meetings that would later appear in press releases to demonstrate to the public the interagency efforts under way on their behalf. Some were clearly designed to allow information sharing (formal and informal) and networking rather than to accomplish any particular task or display anything to politicians or the public. The meetings of the Maritime Incident Resource and Training Partnership (MIRTP) were an example of this type. A voluntary association of organizations, MIRTP took an interest in the Port of Boston. Their meetings often involved demonstrations or presentations on equipment or capacities available in the port area, as well as updates on projects and news. However, the most important aspect of the meetings was that they allowed people a chance to build and maintain relationships and keep each other informed about plans and activities.

Other meetings were smaller and focused on working through a particular problem or strategizing about the region as a whole. Sometimes these working groups were formal, but often they were informal, just a few people meeting over coffee to figure out how to revise a procedure, choose a training program, or coordinate their planned activities in particular types of response.

The community also was created and maintained by the flow of private and small group communication by e-mail and telephone. A sampling of subject lines from my archive includes the following: "well this explains a thing or two," "Big Talk, Little Will," "what a cluster, as usual," "why incident command doesn't work now," "organizational question," and many variations on "have you guys seen this [news story/policy/report/rumor]?" and "does anyone have a copy of [usually a policy or resource document rumored to exist]?" Some of this was geared toward specific problem-solving initiatives, but a great deal of what passed back and forth seems to have been information on the larger planning and operating context. People shared news stories about what was happening in Washington, D.C. They passed along information on equipment with their concerns about how standardization was going to occur. They asked each other, and me, questions about whether one agency in Boston or Massachusetts was going to take responsibility for coordinating homeland security in a meaningful way. However, without access to the phone calls and e-mail records of a wider range of community members, I have had to rely on my own participation in this flow and the general sense of that background communication that permeated everyday conversation.

Toward the end of my fieldwork, I could tell that people were getting better at making the most out of meetings. They held meetings before the meetings and sometimes after the meetings. These prefixes and suffixes to the more inclusive meetings served important purposes. The pre-meeting meetings allowed the core people involved in a task to strategize, develop manageable agendas, warn one another of potential tensions or land mines, and generally make sure that the rest of the meeting went smoothly. If you know that one of the attending fire chiefs has just been forced to close two of his firehouses due to budget cuts, you may decide not to ask him for resources today. The postmeeting meeting or meeting suffix allowed people to sort out what needed to happen as a result of the larger group discussion. If people at the meeting decided that a survey of plans might be a good idea, a few key people had to figure out how to get the plans, which organizations needed to be included, how they would be distributed for comment, and what would be done with the comments that people provide. If people in the meeting showed frustration about the actions of a particular individual, a few community members might step aside to figure out how best to go around the problematic individual or change his or her behavior.

When I first began being included, these smaller sessions would sometimes be held in place of the larger meeting, a practice that, while more efficient, reduced the chances that the group would adequately address all concerns and also decreased the buy-in on the part of agencies not invited to the table. As these problems with smaller meetings became more apparent, people began having them in coordination with the larger meetings, but at different times. This helped to some degree, but still alienated those who were not in the core group. Holding core group discussions as prefixes and suffixes to the larger meeting served both practical and political purposes. It reduced commuting and scheduling issues, as people in the core group had to travel only once rather than three times. It made it possible to include others in a more organic manner, without it appearing that they were being singled out to attend special meetings.

It also made the entire process appear more transparent. It is common for some people to show up early and/or leave a little late when attending an interagency meeting. The times immediately before and after the functional part of the discussion serve important social, political, and practical purposes. It seems natural that people might linger and chat. Even if excluded organizations knew that these chats involved decision making, they could choose to ignore it because it was adequately camouflaged. They did not lose face at having been excluded from the main meeting and, because the smaller groupings were not hidden, there was always at least the appearance that they could join in.

Meetings and submeetings were also a way of seeing how new people were recruited into the core group of policy community stakeholders. According to my informants, before 9/11 there were relatively few people in the Boston area who were interested in terrorism, weapons of mass destruction, or response to catastrophic incidents. There was a lot of work to be done, but the pace and scope of activity were largely self-determined. Immediately after the attacks in 2001, there was a great upsurge in interest. People were willing to make sacrifices to learn more, to attend training, to get plans in place, and to build bridges to other agencies. During my time in the area, this interest was already beginning to wane. People became burned out on twelve-hour shifts and endless streams of new information to absorb. Families and physicians began to warn about the effects of the pressure. Union contracts reasserted themselves. Some people simply went back to their old interests. Gradually, the greatly increased weight of homeland security was falling back on the same few shoulders that had been holding it up before 2001. There was an intense physical and psychological need for reliable new players to start sharing the load. Meetings were a way for the "old-timers" to pass on knowledge, creating continuity in the community. It also provided them with an opportunity to "infect" others with their sense of interest, commitment, and pride in playing a role in their country's security.

Background communication was an important community-building activity, but it was in meetings and operations that people could try out new terminology, definitions, and stories that defined who they were as a group, as opposed to a collection of unrelated organizations. These processes are discussed in more detail in a later chapter. For now it is enough to understand that it was in meetings and operations that the generative processes of the policy community and its potential power in determining the meaning of homeland security in the Boston area were manifested.

THE POLICY COMMUNITY AND GENERATIVE PRACTICE

Learning about the policy community was an exercise in seeing old institutions and understandings stretched and transformed as people developed the new area of practice called homeland security. It also meant watching people striving to become part of something new and shared while simultaneously trying to reinforce and promote their existing institutional backgrounds. The tools needed to interpret this kind of practice are similar to those developed to handle the fluidity and multisited or "trans-" nature of transnational and global phenomena.

Sassen's discussion of the transformation of sovereignty through globalization, *Losing Control,* provides one frame for understanding the homeland security policy community (1996). Sassen describes how state sovereignty is not being lost so much as it is being "unbundled" (1996, 29). As she describes it, sovereignty formerly associated with states is being displaced into international institutions, both public and private. States then become caught in a web of international and private legal codes that constrain their actions, if they wish to be perceived internationally as playing by the rules. Sassen is not necessarily heralding the demise of the state, but she is suggesting that its role is being substantially reconfigured. With Hannerz and Fidler (Fidler 1996; Hannerz 1996), I would tend to take the less extreme position: that some aspects of the state are being stretched and that the eventual outcome is not yet predictable.

For my purposes, what is interesting about the concept of sovereignty being unbundled is how it can shed light on the changes taking place as the United States reacts and reconfigures itself in response to perceived threats of terrorism. In the decades preceding 2001, there was a tendency to look at security activities in terms of monolithic institutions. Vague terms such as "the national security apparatus," "the military-industrial complex," and "the defense/intelligence community" were commonly used to describe the bewildering number of people and organizations involved. Attempts to create a shared set of ideas and practices labeled homeland security led to a situation in which the sovereignty of these groups over security activities is no longer complete. In this case, "unraveling" or "attenuation" might be more apt descriptions than "unbundling," as there are still many threads of power and communication extending from the traditional security organizations to those newly (and perhaps sometimes only nominally) in charge.

Following U.S. law and unofficial norms developed over the last thirty years, Department of Defense assets and most of the intelligence community were supposed to have very limited involvement in domestic affairs. However, immediately following the attacks in 2001, all possibilities seemed open. During the first year of my fieldwork, it was by no means certain how much involvement these agencies would have in homeland security, alongside the new players at the local, state, and federal levels. Gradually, it became clear that civilian organizations would control much of the homeland security domain, something now being called into question again. Although the policy geography became defined, people on both sides of the line had to think about how information, resources, power, and new areas of policy authority were going to be shared. This is not to suggest that traditional national security organizations are losing power. Inclusion of new partners does not necessarily undermine traditional power chains in large bureaucracies, as a recent study of health systems discovered (Nelson 2005). In fact, it may only cloud the links between power and accountability. I only mean to suggest that their direct influence in this new area of practice was limited.

This kind of reshuffling of authority is the same type of reconfiguration that Sassen describes, only on a different level of analysis. It has an impact on how people within the various organizations understand themselves and their roles. In the same way that the unbundling of state sovereignty may affect perceptions of the state, the movement of security activities outside of traditionally defined security organizations is altering larger cultural constructions of security as a social institution. Early on, people spoke about responders being "on the front lines" or as being defenders. Homeland security is becoming a distinct (if confused) new set of national security ideas and practices. This attenuates traditional ideas about and institutions of national security. It also brings some aspects of security processes into a realm where the actors are more visible.

However, this book is less about the transformation of old ideas of national security than it is about the creation of new ones. The homeland security policy community was a generative group. People from many different backgrounds had to come together not only to get work done but also to figure out what that work would be. That meant the melding and layering and filtering of many different perspectives. This part of homeland security work is described in more detail in chapter 7, but it is important to at least mention the conceptual tools that helped me to understand what the homeland security community was doing.

One of the most useful tools to come out of studies of transnational or global processes is the idea of creolization (Hannerz 1987, 1996). Blim has worked with the same ideas, although he articulates them more in the frame of localization of transnational processes (1992). Hannerz writes about creolization in a way that departs somewhat from traditional views of culture contact and change. He describes not a simple melding of elements of two or more cultures but a generative process, similar to the hybridity articulated in later studies (Ferguson and Gupta 2002; Gupta and Ferguson 1992; Jackson 1995; Nygren 1999). What is useful in this way of conceptualizing interaction and change is that it is not constrained by spatial ideas of culture contact. The contact is between actors and what they bring to the interaction. What they bring can be described in a variety of different ways, as habitus (Bourdieu [1972] 1999), as habitats of meaning (Bauman 1992 *in* Hannerz 1996, 22), as institutional orientations (Douglas and Wildavsky 1982), or as cultural models (D'Andrade 1992; Rubinstein 1989, 2001). These orientations or models provide frameworks for practice, but they do not form a rigid structure. Rather they are part of the mutually constitutive system of practice and structure, discussed in chapter 1 (Pellow 2002; Rubinstein 1998b; Wicks 1998). People use these orientations, learn, make changes, keep what works, and sometimes what doesn't. These individual actions and decisions feed back into the models that are shared with others and into broader structures of meaning and action.

The homeland security policy community in Boston was a space that allowed generative practice in a way that a more official structure could not have. Its unofficial status, fluid membership, and ability to shift with the tides of policy made it possible for people to do the things described in the next few chapters without the constraints of institutional rigidity. For example, it slowly became apparent that the idea of "weapons of mass destruction" was not the most useful term around which to organize practice. A formal organization that had designed itself around the wmd concept might have been in trouble. For the policy community in Boston, it meant only a small shift in the way people talked about things. As described in the following chapters, this flexibility was absolutely critical for a group of people trying to find its way through a very confusing transformation.

PART 2 What Is Homeland Security Practice?

CHAPTER 5 // A BRIEF INTRODUCTION
TO HOMELAND SECURITY WORK

[The agency] continues to move/stumble/move on, etc. One day we are building an organization, the next day we are deconstructing. Makes life interesting.

The next three chapters serve predominantly as a fieldwork-based account of what people in the homeland security community were up to in the course of their daily work. Here, I frame the subsequent chapters and introduce two important themes that run through them, coordination and information sharing/secrecy. I also provide a sketch of some of the questions with which the community was grappling while I was in the field.

The brief excerpt above—part of a chatty e-mail message from a man in one of the many federal offices that sprouted up to take on and coordinate homeland security work—captures the chaotic policy environment. It was a rich field site, full of power struggles, shifting discourse, changing traditions, and active construction of what security would mean for Boston. Consequently, each of the items listed in the following chapters could form the basis for its own book. The terms and categories and assumptions of the people in the community are all worth far more attention than I can give here. Each poses tempting theoretical tangents and suggests additional research. However, it is the purpose of this book to show how people *did* homeland security, how their practice constituted what homeland security came to mean in Boston, what they found on their desks in the morning, what they worried about, the kinds of things they struggled to understand and create.

Understanding the local homeland security is a fundamentally interpretive task. If you were a fly on the wall of a local agency said to be involved in homeland security, you would see meetings, maybe some new intensity to existing practices, a few new pieces of equipment, a few new training sessions and reference materials, and people would seem to be under more stress. You might have seen an increase in the number of back-channel e-mails and phone calls and early morning cups of coffee as people engaged in the process of "thinking out loud." However, much of what you saw would look a lot like regular public safety, public health, emergency management, or emergency medicine. Homeland security is an idea that was superimposed on organizations with other things to do. There was no organization at the state or local level that was allowed to devote itself entirely to homeland security activities. While I was in the field, the idea and practices of homeland security were finding their way into the community the way the fog would roll in off the harbor: hard to see when you were right on top of it but pervasive. Many old tasks were not so much changed as reframed and attached to new ideas. Rescue techniques and firefighting still have to take place whether a building is burning due to an electrical fire or a terrorist attack. An outbreak of disease requires investigation and treatments regardless of its origin. However, the significances of these actions changed slightly and they were regrouped by those who had to conceptualize homeland security for the area.

In fact, before the fall of 2001, few people would have thought of it as a new field of activity. Most people in my community thought of homeland security (or whichever of the many pre-2001 names it had) as a new issue in their regular work, more than as a neatly defined set of new actions, as is discussed in greater detail in chapter 7. It existed in new emphases or intensities, new complications, strange responsibilities and relationships, shifting sets of worries, and new people involved in conversations. It was the process of finding the right pace at which new ideas and activities could be incorporated and how much the community could actually accomplish, what one informant referred to as finding the battle rhythm of the community rather than trying to exist perpetually in the crisis mode that followed 9/11. Homeland security made its way into people's lives as they found their traditional roles occupying new places in local and national discourses, as they manipulated these discourses, as they learned to reframe their activities or create new ones, and as they interacted with others doing these same things to try to create what homeland security would be and mean in the Boston area.

In these three chapters, I attempt to frame what people were doing and thinking about and coping with in such a way that this diffuse thing called homeland security becomes visible, in the same way a streetlight on a damp night will make visible the haze. Any attempt to break this kind of phenomenon up into tidy structures will always be artificial, but it is a necessary evil if anyone outside the community is to get a sense of what it meant to be involved in homeland security. I have tried to minimize my natural tendency to try to impose order on everything, leaving as much of the mess in place as is practical. My choice of presentation is also an artifact of the reality that although I swam daily in people's attempts to find an easily explained structure in homeland security and emergency management activities (some of which are described in chapter 8), I never found one that held together in the face of what people actually do in their daily lives.

COORDINATION

Coordination forms a major theme in the following chapters. It remains a buzzword in the homeland security field. It is used to mean many things. Sometimes a person uses it to mean simple cooperation, sitting down with others to come up with a solution. Other people have used it to evoke a response capacity that is seamless across jurisdictions.[1] In my discussions, I use it to refer to a general set of activities in preparedness and operations that share a common goal—not getting in one another's way. If preparedness activities are not coordinated, towns or agencies can waste material and information resources duplicating what has already been accomplished or they may assume that another plan handles something that it does not. When locals plan for a mass care clinic, it is critical that they coordinate carefully with state mass care plans so that they are not expecting resources that will never arrive. The consequences of uncoordinated response plans and operations are more dramatic. If an incident commander decides to close bridges without knowing that the school superintendent has just decided to close schools and send the children home on buses, there may be busloads of children stuck on the side of the road with nowhere to

---

1. "Seamless" is a current buzzword against which the more practical people in homeland security struggle. To them it implies a uniformity that would impede action in the same way that a shirt with too few seams pulls and binds.

go. I use the word "coordinate" in this mechanical sense of planning and operating in harmony, rather than isolation or uniformity.

SECRECY

Themes of information control and secrecy also run throughout the chapters. My informants struggled with the lack of concrete information from federal sources and with the changes in information-classification rules that would allow them greater access. They worried about how to strike a balance between giving enough information to the public and giving so much that they would contribute to a climate of fear. They debated the merits of openly displaying security measures as a deterrent, as opposed to hiding them so as not to draw attention to what they were trying to protect. People maliciously or ignorantly used control of information to exclude individuals or organizations from discussions. Organizations and task forces tried to find ways to allow people to share information about day-to-day operations so that they could look for patterns without having to cope with an informational fire hose, the same overload problem cited by national intelligence agencies. Sometimes they just didn't know that some other organization needed information that they had, a problem described in more detail in chapter 8.

People tried to make sense out of what they perceived as competing demands for increased cooperation and greater control over information. They spent time talking about whether it was better to let the public know about all the security and response capacity improvements they were making or if that would just make it easier for potential attackers to identify gaps in the system, as they did when they learned the weak spots in aviation security. Even as I write this, states around the country are debating whether to make public the locations of their planned clinics to handle mass prophylaxis and treatment in the event of a health emergency or whether to keep them secret to minimize the chances of them being selected as targets.

This kind of "default to secrecy" attitude was and continues to be hotly debated among practitioners. Taking the example of the prophylaxis clinics, many argued that there was something fundamentally flawed in the idea of hiding a facility intended for public welfare. It would be like hiding a fire station or a hospital. Others pointed out such secrecy was a slippery slope. Where were the lines between the public's right to know and the need to keep information hidden from potential attackers? They also pointed out that the 9/11 hijackers took advantage of flaws in a system that required public understanding rather than one that had been unwittingly exposed. The more pragmatic debaters reminded everyone else that no matter what the official position was, most things related to homeland security response would end up public knowledge anyway due to the need to conduct preparedness exercises, site visits, and other activities that can never be fully hidden.

There also was the question of classification and "sensitive" information. Many, if not most, people in local homeland security policy communities did not have access to classified material, a situation with effects described in subsequent chapters. Little hard information was available about either how they could get access to restricted information or how, in turn, they could protect information they felt it was dangerous to release. Again, there were rumors about new ways of protecting information from release to the public. People began to refer to a new category, "security sensitive." The idea was that this designation would make it impossible (or difficult—the versions differed) for the public to get access.[2] As they always did, people in the community had different opinions. They had questions about the legitimacy of keeping certain types of information secret. Some felt that officials were using the national sense of emergency to hide things that would have provided more public benefit by appearing on the front page of the *Boston Globe*. The time period from 2001 through 2003 was full of unanswered questions about secrecy for people in the policy community. I have chosen to present these dilemmas as they appeared in daily life, enmeshed in the complexities of practice, rather than abstracting them as a separate topic.

QUESTIONS

A list of problems people in the community were trying to solve would be nearly endless. I present a few of them from here, largely related to response rather than prevention, to give a sense of the diversity and complexity of the issues facing the community, the issues around which tasks and processes were developed.

---

2. This category now is known as Sensitive but Unclassified (SBU). The degree of protection it affords seems to be in question. A 2004 study from the Library of Congress reported that "a uniform legal definition or set of procedures applicable to all Federal government agencies does not now exist. Regulations are reported to be under development in the Office of Management and Budget and the Department of Homeland Security" (Federal Research Division Library of Congress 2004).

How would we deal with an incident in the harbor that involved large numbers of casualties? How would we get them from the boat(s) to shore? What places on shore, largely privately owned, could be used?

If a dangerous cargo on a ship in the port was attacked or simply caught on fire, could we move the vessel? If not, is there enough foam across all the port jurisdictions to suppress a large fire? Could nearby communities be evacuated? How would they be notified? How would the environmental damage be handled?

If Boston needed to be evacuated, would the city's critical incident exodus plan work? Generally used for snowstorms when many people would leave at the same time, could the plan handle it if not only the commuters but also the residents needed to leave? Could the mass transit system handle the evacuation of people without private vehicles? Were neighboring towns aware of the plan and ready to handle the traffic and, potentially, shelter the evacuees? Who would determine how far people should go and how they would be told? Since shelters generally do not take pets and responders cannot care for abandoned animals, what should people be told about their pets? What would the police do if people refused to follow evacuation routes? How scalable were the response models from one or two small incidents to something widespread and of long duration? Did the Red Cross have the right resources in the right places to handle something of that magnitude, or did they only have enough staff and volunteers to handle one or two shelters? Who would stay behind and deal with the people who would not or could not leave? (Of course, all of these questions became much more pressing to all cities after the 2004 and 2005 hurricane seasons, but long before then, people were grappling with the seemingly intractable problems involved in figuring out how to move such a large number of people safely.)

In a major event, could the area rely on its responders to stay put and do their jobs? Will they be concerned about their families and leave? Is there any way to assess that realistically in advance, or will people report a higher willingness to stay on the job than they would actually feel? What can organizations do to ensure that responders feel comfortable about the status of their families during an incident? How should planners handle this variable when it comes to people outside of traditional response professions, such as bus drivers, who may be asked to perform emergency functions? What about the people who sign on to volunteer lists? How reliable is any plan that cannot answer these questions?

If there was an outbreak of an infectious disease in Boston, how would responders get vaccines or drugs out to the community? What if drugs had to be rationed? How would isolation and quarantine be handled if that was necessary to keep the rest of the population safe? Should people know in advance where the points of distribution will be located, or will that increase the possibility of those locations being targets? If an outbreak started in a particular socioeconomic or ethnic group, how would the city mitigate against that group being stigmatized and possibly targeted for violence?

In any incident requiring large-scale or long-term response, how would the area handle the needs of so-called special populations, people whose disabilities or socioeconomic circumstances made it impossible or difficult for them to take advantage of emergency populations, people whose backgrounds made them suspicious of government authority, people who did not read or understand any of the languages into which emergency information was translated, and so on? How much could be done in advance to determine and address the special needs of these groups without violating health privacy laws or unduly stigmatizing a group by special attention?

Given that any hazardous cargo arriving in the area by air, sea, rail, or road posed a potential target for attacks and accident risk, should certain types or quantities of material be banned? Who could decide such a thing? What would be the impacts on the economic life of the area? Was there any really solid information about how likely attacks were? Was there any good information on the possible consequences? What did it mean to make such things secure?

In New York City, after the attacks of 9/11, many who volunteered to help were unqualified. People pretended to be medical professionals and other kinds of specialists. How could Boston prevent such a thing, given all the different types of identification cards used by different jurisdictions and different agencies? If there was to be a standard identification card issued, who would maintain the database and issue the cards? How often would they check on the different kinds of certifications? What information would be included on the card? If digital information was to be stored in the card, as opposed to just the information that could be squashed onto the front and back, what technology should be used? Did anyone know if bar codes, magnetic strips, or radio-frequency identification chips were about to become obsolete? Did anyone, other than vendors, have the knowledge or time to study the issue?

How secure was secure? How much preparedness was enough? Was the public prepared to pay for staff and resources that might never get used? Was there any point to planning for things, like a large-scale infectious disease outbreak, past a certain scale? How honest could you be in plans about the limits of preparedness without losing your job or causing public panic? How honest could you be about things that you assessed to be non-issues but that had captured the attention of the press and/or the public?

Questions like these were not easily answered. Sometimes the hardest part was figuring out who could answer them or, as in the paragraph above, whether there was any point in answering them at all. Answers to one question often became entangled with other answers or other questions. The work and processes described in the following chapters was often done in response to questions like these.

CATEGORIES

There are two rough categories of homeland security work: daily task-oriented work and context building. The distinction blurs as tasks turn into the kinds of social opportunities in which social context creation takes place, but the separation is useful for highlighting those activities that bear most directly on social context construction. The subject of chapter 6 is the task category, the everyday activities and concerns that make up the meat and potatoes of homeland security. This chapter highlights some of the complexity that was introduced into seemingly mundane activities by the emphasis on homeland security. Chapter 7 addresses the things community members did through which they either deliberately or unconsciously created the social context in which homeland security was practiced. This chapter looks at some of the more conceptual issues with which the community had to grapple. It was in participating in this part of the work that I began to understand how people in the policy community were trying to create local homeland security. Chapter 8 addresses the processes and mechanisms the community developed or used to get the work done.

All of these activities—from the most mundane guarding detail or policy meeting to highly complex, meticulously negotiated interagency operations—took place within a shifting policy context and a funding structure that was not set up to accommodate this degree of local involvement in national security activities. They also took place within the normal twists and turns of American politics. Politicians continued to pursue agendas that made use of homeland security issues but often had little to do with actually creating sound policy. Political appointees looked out for their fiefdoms. Nieces and nephews received jobs for which they were not qualified. Decisions were made on the basis of too little time and too little information or as a result of being steamrolled by a shiny package deal presented by a smooth vendor. Well-intentioned politicians and government employees had differences of opinion about what was right and sometimes had higher priorities. Hearings and memos and working groups dragged on. As the country debated whether it would have a federal homeland security department and what the composition of federal involvement should be, people at the local level got on with their working days.

CHAPTER 6 // DAILY TASKS

Part of the work of homeland security lies in daily tasks. In most cases, homeland security is something that has intensified or added new aspects to things responders and planners were already doing rather than creating entirely new activities. In some cases, organizations took a systematic approach to rethinking their activities. More commonly it was a gradual shift in thinking among both rank and file and organizational leadership. The tasks described in this section may appear to be something of a hodgepodge, and in a sense they are. The framework I developed to understand this part of homeland security gives the reader a bit of structure, but I have deliberately tried to avoid giving the illusion that there was order to any of it while I was in the community. Tasks—the sometimes confusing reasons for the new emphasis they received, the vagueness of policy, and the blurriness of the boundaries among them—were all part of the muddle of trying to figure out what homeland security was going to be in the Boston area.

One significant distinction is between activities focused on preventing emergencies and those that dealt with response to, management of, and recovery from an event that had already occurred. Most of my participant observation and discussions took place on the response and management side of things—those people and units/divisions of organizations preparing for work that takes place once something has already happened.[1]

---

1. Although popular discourse sometimes labels people in these organizations as "responders," such labels are problematic because of the "first responder" debate discussed in

However, I did manage some observations and discussions related to prevention activities, such as intelligence gathering, watching, and guarding. I tended to spend time with people who were trying to manage those operations rather than frontline staff who would have been out doing them, so my observations are skewed toward the planning perspective. There also are disciplinary distinctions that are significant. Among the "after the incident" organizations, I spent the bulk of my time with people in the fire service and emergency management, as opposed to law enforcement, health, medicine, or private industry. The descriptions below are not comprehensive, but they provide a sample of the kinds of activities that were taking place and give some of the flavor of the community.

Many of the tasks described below were undertaken because of the perception among practitioners that the public and politicians needed to see that something was being done. While there undoubtedly was pressure from political figures and embarrassing press coverage of failures and gaps, some of the pressure may have been self-induced. I never saw any investigation into what kinds of things people wanted to see done (other than vague ideas about coordination and screening). I also never saw any poll that suggested the people were in any way reassured by the visible presence of security for its own sake. The one exception I would make to this was the presence of soldiers and military police in airports. I heard many statements to the effect of "I don't know how much they could do if somebody attacked, but I feel better seeing them here." In one terminal, I saw an older woman give her bags to her husband and walk up and kiss a soldier, saying, "Thank you. Thank you for being here. God bless you." Nevertheless, many of my informants would bemoan the need to expend resources on patrols or guards or barriers that were impractical in security terms but publicly or politically visible.

Some of the more visible activities associated with homeland security include shifts in intelligence gathering and processing; patrolling and other forms of watching; increased physical and behavioral guarding, which included escorting hazardous cargos, screening of cargo, vehicles, and people; and incident response, each of which is discussed in this chapter. All of these activities were interwoven with general orders (issued within organizations, not by a state or national directive) to be more alert, more aware of possible threats and vulnerabilities. Defining what it would mean

---

chapter 7. Here I am distinguishing between elements of organizations involved in prevention and those involved during and/or after an event. It is rare that an entire organization can be placed wholly in one category or the other.

to be more alert and assessing threats and vulnerabilities were negotiations that took place in some of the context-building activities described in the next chapter.

I have deliberately avoided using the term "surveillance" in naming the first two of the categories above. While surveillance activities are certainly a part of each, the term has come to connote something more sinister than the observation of a person or group. While I don't want to diminish people's concerns about increased surveillance of individuals and groups for perhaps less than laudable reasons, I also want to be able to talk about daily activities in the homeland security community without having to distinguish among the popular conceptions of surveillance, video surveillance cameras, and disease surveillance.

Many of the activities described below have the quality of increasing the visible presence of public safety. I have tried to categorize these along the lines of their stated purpose. For example, while both guarding and patrolling increase the visibility of the agencies involved, guarding tends to be focused on a specific location, object, or event; patrolling has a more open-ended goal. However, it should be understood that there are political dimensions to all these activities. As will be discussed in more detail in the next chapter, the decision about how to use scarce human resources was not always based on knowledge of a particular threat or vulnerability. One line of argument among practitioners was that visible security had both a deterrent effect and was reassuring to the public. Others countered that placing troopers in highly visible but operationally questionable locations, such as at public buildings, did little other than increase overtime bills and remove resources from more important but less politically expedient areas, such as community policing.

Activities in these categories also were responsive to new information about perceived threats. This became especially noteworthy with the advent of the color-coded homeland security system. This system consists of five colors, each of which is supposed to be associated with a particular level of risk that terrorists were planning to attack.[2] Green indicates a low risk. Blue means a "guarded state" or "general risk of terrorist attacks." Yellow indicates an "elevated" state of risk and, to date, appears to be the permanent resting color for the system. Orange alerts signal a high risk of attack. Red, not surprisingly, suggests severe risk or ongoing attack. These

2. To date, the system is still focused on terrorism, not reflecting the other emergencies for which the Department of Homeland Security is asking the public to be ready, such as natural hazards or pandemic influenza.

color levels were the butt of a great deal of national and local humor both because they did not seem to be tied to any particular set of activities and because it seemed impossible that anyone would ever take the political risk of lowering the alert state below yellow.

At the time I was in the field, most planners and responders had little or no idea what was supposed to change about their activities based on the threat level. Public safety and emergency management officials in Massachusetts and around the country complained that raising the levels, even if only for a particular location or economic sector, should be accompanied by specific, actionable intelligence so that they could deploy their resources accordingly. In the absence of such guidance, they did the best they could.[3] Intelligence gathering, watching, guarding, screening, and steps taken during responses might all take on slightly different flavors depending on what an official believed to be the best interpretation of what little information was offered from the federal level. As above, these decisions were not always made based on traditional public safety criteria. Sometimes politicians felt more comfortable at orange alert if the public was seeing more police cruisers, even if the intelligence showed no need.

INTELLIGENCE GATHERING AND PROCESSING

Intelligence gathering ultimately was the turf of law enforcement agencies. While people from other institutional backgrounds certainly contributed leads and hard information, the task of sorting rumor from possible fact and figuring out what to do with the information fell to law enforcement. Law enforcement at all jurisdictional levels participated in intelligence gathering and processing. These agencies were understandably reluctant to involve me in planning or operations related to intelligence gathering and sometimes were legally constrained from doing so.

The Boston Police Department, task forces such as the Joint Terrorism Task Force (JTTF), and local field offices of federal law enforcement agencies almost assuredly changed some of their practices, if only by increasing the intensity of them. Early in the autumn of 2001, Boston was named as one of the places where "sleeper cells" may have aided the people who hijacked the planes on 9/11 (Macero and Wells 2001). This was a public

3. The Office of Commonwealth Security in Massachusetts did ultimately develop a matching color system for state alert levels with more detailed information about actions and encouraged towns and organizations to develop their own protocols, but this had not been implemented fully at the time I was in the field.

example of the many leads received each week, each of which had to be investigated, few of which made it into the press. However, the general types of activities that were discussed did not change over the course of my fieldwork. People mentioned undercover work to try to gain information about potential threats and discover the whereabouts of people who were wanted by various law enforcement agencies. They used informants to gather the same kinds of information. The state set up and advertised a Terror Tip Line where citizens could call in with information. I assume that the stereotypical activities of warrant-legitimized telephone and computer tapping, mail reading, searches, and questioning took place, but they were not discussed in front of me.

Of course, the difficulty with intelligence is that it must be actionable. That is, it must be specific enough and credible enough that law enforcement agencies can either protect something or detain somebody. National level intelligence often filtered down to the local level in formats too broad to be of much use. If the Boston Police Department or Boston Emergency Management learned that there was a credible threat against Boston, that wasn't of much use to them. It is not physically possible to cover all vulnerabilities and be alert against all possible threats around the clock. A typical low-level and tongue-in-cheek discussion about ramping up security after receiving such intelligence might range over a series of self-answering questions, such as these jottings from notes I took on one meeting after Boston had received notice of a credible threat:

How many skyscrapers, historical monuments, political facilities, and economic assets might be vulnerable to a truck bomb? On how many streets must you prohibit parking to prevent such attacks? How many subways stations can you close for fear of chemical, biological, radiological, or explosive attacks? How many bags can you physically search at airports? Should we be testing everyone with flu symptoms to see if they have something more sinister? Do we even know how to do that? Should public events be canceled for fear that somebody will use them to stage an attack?

Even a partial attempt to respond to such a vague threat assessment would paralyze the area and deplete response assets that were needed for regular public safety activities, such as fires and crime. Those charged with deciding what *could* be done became discouraged. Promises to address barriers to information flow, such as classification, did little to help with immediate concerns.

I never asked to be included in intelligence-related discussions. To do so would have immediately changed my status from one who tried to be respectful of the constraints felt by my informants to somebody trying to get insider information I did not "need to know." At times, people would forget my outsider status and describe specific situations, but there was never a time when the policy or procedures of intelligence gathering were discussed in my presence beyond the larger, national-level issues that were in the press.

Some of these discussions revealed concern about how national-level pressures affected daily practice. There were questions about the USA PATRIOT Act. Among the law enforcement people to whom I spoke, the act was perceived to maintain their constraints but to speed the already existing processes by which those constraints could be waived. They were aware of and worried about public concerns about the implications of the act for civil liberties but did not know how to go about addressing those concerns. This was particularly problematic for some in the FBI who passionately believed that one of the main missions of the FBI was to protect civil liberties. One especially frustrated agent speculated, "I gave my life to this. To protect rights. Now nobody will ever believe me."

In the autumn of 2001, U.S. Attorney General John Ashcroft raised more practical concerns when he asked local law enforcement agencies to assist in conducting interviews with thousands of men from the Middle East currently visiting the United States. His request sparked debate over the constitutionality and civil rights implications of the proposed interviews. A few cities, including Portland, Oregon, refused to cooperate. People in the homeland security watched the situation in Oregon closely. Some supported Ashcroft's efforts; others were concerned about where such actions might lead. Many just wanted the country to sort it out so that they would have clear guidelines on which to operate.

WATCHING

Perhaps the most visible aspect of "watching" in homeland security is the presence of security cameras. While such cameras were already quite common in businesses, after 9/11 there was at least a perceived increase. My informants talked about there being more cameras on government buildings, as well as private ones, but I have no baseline against which to compare it. Although it may have just been my heightened attention, there did seem to me to be more cameras. Places that might only have had a guard before now had a guard and a security camera. I saw shiny new ones on the corners of buildings. Did they replace old ones or were they actually there for the first time? It was hard for me to imagine who might be watching the tape, given staffing shortages.

Again, the installation of some of these cameras may have been motivated more by a desire to show that the facility was doing something, if only putting up a camera, to increase the public's security than by any real intention of foiling a terrorist act. Some installations, however, were very seriously undertaken. One facility I visited frequently used to allow you to drive through the open-gated security fence and park, and then you were scrutinized via a camera at the door. One day I turned off the busy street into the gate at my usual speed only to be brought up short by a closed gate and a polite young man with a large gun. My identification and my vehicle were checked, and only then was I allowed through. Within a few weeks, a new, remotely operated gate topped with razor wire had replaced the old one. As a vehicle stopped at the gate, a person inside the facility could view and communicate with the driver through a sophisticated camera system. This was not one of the random efforts at watchfulness. It was designed not only to keep potential attackers at a safe distance but also to monitor anyone taking an unusual interest in the unmarked and rather nondescript facility. One informant told me that over the preceding months, they had seen three different men taking pictures of the facility. By the time they came out to investigate, the men had gone. After telling me about the photographers, my informant paused and then said, "Maybe they were just students, you know? But you just don't know. We're supposed to be careful."

Technological efforts might have been the showy answer to vigilance, but most increased watchfulness for homeland security had to be done the old-fashioned way, by soliciting human cooperation. Several attempts were made at the national level to enlist postal carriers, truck drivers, or the population at large to watch one another. All of these failed at least in part due to public outcry against the idea of "informing" on one another. In the end, most public safety watchfulness fell to law enforcement agencies. Other than the intelligence-gathering activities mentioned above, this took the more general form of patrolling. People living or working in especially industrial areas might realize that the streets near businesses using hazardous materials saw a few more passes by local police cars than previously. Residents with a view of the harbor might have noticed the Boston Harbor Patrol, the Environmental Police, or the Coast Guard vessels moving a bit more slowly as they did their rounds. As increased homeland security concerns were integrated into patrolling, the people in the patrol cars, boats, and aircraft, on the police bicycles, and on horseback needed to learn about what they might see that could be a clue to politically violent activity and incorporate that knowledge into their thoughts as they patrolled.

Other organizations also learned new things to watch out for and assimilated the knowledge into their daily activities. Firefighters and others at Logan Airport, for instance, suddenly had to wonder whether the traditional clam diggers taking advantage of the airport's rich clam beds were quite what they seemed to be. Park police needed to think more actively about whether the picnic and sports gear carried by visitors could contain bombs or man-portable air-defense systems, or MANPADs.[4] One organization that became more heavily involved in watching out for "suspicious activity" was Boston's Inspectional Services. Inspectors not only conduct routine health and safety inspections in the city; they also respond to the "strange smells" and "too many people in the building" and "boxes blocking the alley" calls. They investigate inside many nooks and crannies that public safety officials are unlikely to see. They have the very real possibility of being first on the scene of illegal activity. In the new work context after 9/11, inspectors had to consider that the "funny smells" might not just be the cooking of the new neighbors or a restaurant in need of health code enforcement. It might not even be something as dangerous-but-mundane as a drug laboratory. Instead, now they were expected to consider the possibility that the smell might be from the equipment being used to "cook" a chemical or biological weapon. Inspectors needed not only to learn about the clues they might see that should lead them to suspect such activity; they also had to know how to keep themselves and others in the area safe and who to call.

Medical facilities and public health departments also became involved in watching, although in a slightly different way. All states have reportable disease categories and disease trends for which they watch. Some conditions have to be reported to the national Centers for Disease Control and Prevention as part of national disease surveillance activities. With greater concern about possible covert bioterrorism attacks came greater governmental, organizational, and public demand for systems that would catch outbreaks before they spread. The intent was that hospitals, clinics, nursing homes, and other places where patients were seen would keep track of certain sets of symptoms and report daily or weekly so that aggregate statistics could be compiled and trends or unusual clusters identified.

Some thought also went into including pharmacies in disease surveil-

---

4. Man-portable air-defense systems are any shoulder-mounted missile system, such as the SAM-7s that almost destroyed an Israeli civilian airliner on November 28, 2002.

lance, as they could keep track of the kinds of over-the-counter medications sold and contribute to trend analysis. Less consideration was given to surveillance in shelters, soup kitchens, and other places where the uninsured might present with symptoms, despite the fact that impoverished and disenfranchised populations are known to be parasitized by emerging infections (Farmer 1996). Of course, these goals are more easily stated than accomplished. There is disagreement over what should be reportable— after all, not every cluster of "flu-like symptoms" is anthrax or severe acute respiratory syndrome, otherwise known as SARS. Several of my informants from public health departments said that compliance is also a problem. Hospitals were hesitant to release scarce staff to track symptoms, enter data, and send reports off to public health departments.

The type of watching that got the most media attention while I was in the field was screening. Screening is the process of checking a person, a vehicle, an object, or sometimes even a behavioral pattern to see whether she, he, or it represents a threat. In American public discourse at the time I am writing, screening is still used as a catchall phrase to describe both screening and inspection, and I use it in that sense here. However, while I was in the field, informants involved with cargo screening emphasized the difference between screening and inspection. Screening is the process that helps you determine which people or things to inspect and includes the use of luggage and cargo scans with X-ray or detection equipment. Inspection is the physical search. Although the process of determining screening criteria is often controversial, the practice of it generally is not, except in that it can cause delays. The practice to which most people and businesses object is inspection. The community ideal of screening is that a group of government officials (nobody is quite sure who) are supposed to sit down and make objective decisions about what threats and vulnerabilities exist and what observable characteristics can be correlated with likely threats. Of course, such processes are frequently political rather than practical in nature. In practice, people doing screening are often caught in situations where the criteria they are given, if any, do not make sense with their local knowledge or sometimes their prejudicial inclinations.

Airline screening got a great deal of public attention in 2001–2 as the federal government assumed responsibility for screening passengers and luggage (but not air cargo for some reason I have never understood), taking over for the private companies who were broadly believed to have been negligent in their screening and inspection. Airports were not the only place that people and bags were being screened, but they serve as a good illustration. As the transition to the newly formed Transportation

Security Administration began, airports also contended with the fallout from governmental and public debates about what were and were not acceptable screening practices. Discrimination against people from a wide range of backgrounds who "looked Middle Eastern" to screeners and airline personnel led to even stranger behaviors. Some airports appeared to develop quota systems to make sure no ethnic group, gender, or age group felt singled out (Branum 2002). In some airports, screeners began searching random passengers or every fifth passenger.

Law enforcement agencies tried to come up with checklists of characteristics other than race that could be used to identify people who might cause problems on a flight. These were called profiles and variously included everything from types of clothing to luggage contents, to national background and passport information, to behavioral patterns while in the boarding area. My informants often suggested that these profiles were not trusted by airport or airline staff, many of whom were still looking for nineteen "Middle Eastern" men, struggling to lock the barn door long after the horse was gone.

For a few months in 2001, there was a second official screening process as you boarded the plane in some airports. Some airlines even started trying to screen the people in the boarding area in advance of the first boarding call. In November of 2001 while waiting for a flight to Washington, D.C., I watched in a mixture of amusement and cringing as airline employees tried to add their own layer of watching. A small table had been set up to one side of the boarding door. Near it, an airline employee looked around, then loudly stated, "There's no profiles here. No profiles," as if she had been looking out for a separate species, *Homo profilensis*. Flight crews also took matters into their own hands, walking into the boarding area and looking over the people about to get on their aircraft. The lack of effective and acceptable standards made the process ridiculous.

Screening of things was somewhat less controversial, although much more complex in terms of governmental policies and business practices. At airports, enormous X-ray and sensor equipment required to screen baggage could not fit into existing buildings. With the airlines in economic trouble, few airport authorities or city governments felt that they could afford to build new facilities to house the equipment. Former employees of private airline security companies were required to take tests to see if they would be effective screeners. My informants debated the kinds of people who would be most likely to make good screeners. The young men and women who often applied were thought to be too distractible. The federal security director at one airport told me that what he really wanted was the

FIGURE 3. The Boston skyline, as seen from inside the cargo terminal. Photo by author.

kind of little old lady who could sit and knit for hours without dropping a stitch. The postal service debated how much screening and monitoring equipment could effectively be used in its sorting facilities. Owners of public gathering places such as theaters and stadiums felt comfortable telling people that all bags were subject to inspection leading to the inevitable feeling that they were only using security as an excuse to make sure that people did not bring their own food to avoid the inflated prices.

Cargo screening was another subject of media attention. Boston's largest cargo terminal looks like a giant's LEGO playground. Stacks of colorful modular containers are taken off ships and stacked to wait for the trucks that will pick them up and transport them to a rail facility or a receiver. The terminal is located less than two miles from downtown Boston as the crow or the radiation flies. As with terminals around the United States, cargo arrives in sealed containers from thousands of different shippers out of hundreds of different ports around the world. The trustworthiness of the shippers and of the foreign customs agencies that seal the containers was questioned by the U.S. Customs service and others in the community. The danger is twofold. Containerized cargo received by ship often arrives very close to large metropolitan areas, making it a danger as soon as it is offloaded.[5] However, many containers arrive and are loaded onto trucks bound for other areas of the United States without ever being opened, making them tiny pockets of "alien-ness" allowed into the country.

It is difficult to understand how much cargo is in the facility until you are in among the stacks. Visual perception plays some sort of trick, making the area appear smaller than it is. I came to the facility at the invitation of a Customs agent who wanted me to see what they were up against. Standing gazing up at the skyscraper-like stacks, it became clear what an enormous task they faced. With boxes moving in and out constantly, they had to develop ways to screen containers rapidly to identify likely subjects for inspection. In this case, inspection meant breaking the official Customs seal and manually going through the contents of the cases, a process that could take hours and would require mountains of paperwork. At the time of my visit, there was a not entirely formal system of giving containers from certain ports or shippers special attention. These ports and shippers were either known from past smuggling or other criminal activities or were located in countries on various governmental watch lists. The Customs officials working at the terminal had just received an X-ray truck through which they said all trucks leaving the facility had to pass. The process was very much like the screening of carry-on luggage at an airport. Screeners sat inside the truck, looking for any shapes that might indicate contraband or a bomb or other terrorist device. There were also sensors in the area, I believe for monitoring radiation, but this was not a question my guide could answer.

Cargo screening, whether at seaport terminals like the one in Boston or at the Canadian and Mexican borders, became a political football as the federal agencies responsible for borders, cargo, people, and transportation reorganized themselves. Politicians and pundits cited figures such as "98 percent of all cargo is screened" and "only 2 percent of cargo is inspected," both of which are true and both of which manipulated public misunderstanding about the distinction between screening and inspection.[6]

---

5. Containerized cargo is cargo that has been shipped in a standardized metal container that can be easily moved among transportation modes—for example, from a ship's hold, to a railroad car, to a tractor trailer.

6. This was common in news articles throughout 2002 and 2003, although it is impossible to tell when the use is deliberate and when it is simply a case of insufficient research. For an example, see the 2002 *Washington Post* special report on continuing problems in homeland security (Gellman 2002).

Officials sorted through their options such as trusted shipper registration, foreign port inspections and trusted port certifications, requirements for ships to send in their cargo manifest before reaching port, Coast Guard inspections before the ship enters the harbor, and screening technology at border points and in terminals. In the meantime, people working at checkpoints and in terminals were frustrated and sometimes frightened by the amount of interpretation they had to do in order to make policy work on the ground. In Boston, the Customs team had worked hard to combine policy and common sense into something that seemed to work fairly well, but so far as I could tell, that was largely due to the initiative and tacit knowledge of the people who happened to be there at the time.

GUARDING

Guarding can be distinguished from general watchfulness or vigilance in that it is associated with a specific place or event perceived by responders, politicians, or the press to need protection. These "targets" were sometimes high-profile locations, sometimes places where dangerous substances were kept, sometimes special events, such as the Boston Marathon or the Fourth of July celebration on the Charles River.[7] The amount of guarding activity increased after 9/11 and fluctuated with political winds, the changing of alert levels, or the presence of local intelligence suggesting a particular threat. Police, the National Guard, and private security personnel guarded fixed facilities, transits of people or things, and special events. Practitioners believe guarding activities serve as deterrents, as well as barriers between what is designated as both threatened and vulnerable and the perceived source of threat, such as terrorists. Building on ideas solidified during the Cold War, security planners believed that well-protected facilities would present a less appealing opportunity to potential attackers.

In the Boston area, travelers might have noticed that there was constantly a trooper parked at the entrance to the Ted Williams Tunnel, the new tunnel leading from the south end of Boston to Logan International Airport. Certainly, travelers at Logan Airport noticed an increased police presence on the access roads, near the parking areas, and inside the terminals. A piece of intelligence related to financial institutions might prompt an increased number of Boston police to be seen in the Financial District.

---

7. The process of determining what was a target and which targets required guarding is discussed in more detail in the next chapter.

For a time after 9/11, National Guard troops guarded Logan Airport and privately owned nuclear power plants. The large tanker ships that carry liquefied natural gas through Boston Harbor did so under the armed escort of a multiagency protection operation. The guarding of people was also important. When Richard Reid, the "shoe bomber" who was convicted of trying to blow up a transatlantic flight, was moved around the area, security was so tight that sometimes I did not even know that it had happened. Political convoys traveled along roads and highways, with police closing off cross streets and on-ramps before and behind them, helicopters traveled overhead, and additional police details guarded overpasses as the group of vehicles moved along like a bubble in a straw.

As people were still figuring out how to best manage protection "in the post-9/11 era," sometimes confluences of events would strain the area's resources to their limits as illustrated by this excerpt from my field journal:

Today President Bush visited the Seaport Hotel on a campaign stop for the Massachusetts Republican candidate for governor. A block down the street—shoe bomber Richard Reid was pleading guilty to the charges against him. . . . I got lost trying to avoid the presidential mess at the Seaport Hotel on my walk from South Station to Black Falcon [a cruise ship terminal where I was participating in an exercise-planning meeting]. . . . Up to Harvard with helicopters circling overhead as part of the security for former Vice President Al Gore, who is in town stumping for the Democratic gubernatorial candidate. Also the Zakim Bunker Hill Bridge, Boston's newest landmark and part of the Big Dig construction project, was dedicated with about 2,000 people in attendance, which made getting home fun. What an enormous mess. I can't even imagine the overtime bill for all the police details.

The situation had not much improved by the time of the Democratic National Convention in 2004. Many people from the response community (and the Boston community as a whole) complained about irrational security mandates, staffing issues, and constantly shifting objectives and guidance from the federal level. Even Massachusetts' neighbors got involved. New Hampshire had to hold planning sessions to determine how it would handle any possible migrations of people out of Boston if an attack occurred and, of more immediate concern, how it would transport special medical cases from northern New England to the hospitals in Boston when security personnel had been told to be especially suspicious of people posing as responders trying to enter the city and no uniformly accepted identification cards were available.

While some guarding involved officials patrolling or watching, some relied on physical barriers or information control. Aside from the seemingly endless public discussions of reinforcing airplane cockpit doors, physical barriers were also an important part of guarding on the ground. The most publicly visible version of this were the "jersey barriers," concrete rectangles that could be used to create a low fence around something, block a road, or create a slalom effect in a road to prevent rapid direct approach. These barriers were the source of a lot of humor. On a visit to an informant at a highly secured facility in the Washington, D.C., area, I remarked that all the barriers had the agency name painted on them. I thought it seemed like a lot of time spent on advertising what the barriers were supposed to protect. He laughed and explained that the reason had nothing to do with pride of place. In fact, the barriers were so in demand in the area that they would disappear. He suspected that federal agencies were stealing them from one another and the painted names were one way to lessen the temptation. Back in Boston, an informant working in a telecommunications hub joked about how he ate lunch in the world's safest Burger King. The restaurant was located on the ground floor of a building that also housed FBI offices. Consequently, it was one of many buildings housing government offices that were surrounded by fairly significant entourages of concrete barricades and orange mesh "no-go" zones. The barriers also gained public attention because of their ugliness. In Washington, D.C., many of them were replaced with brightly painted concrete flowerpots or pillars that were only vaguely reminiscent of the hitching posts they were supposed to mimic.

If Boston put any effort into that kind of beautification, I did not notice it. Where there were not concrete barriers, there were fences. Sometimes these were simply orange mesh safety fences of the sort one would see around a construction zone or hung up to block drifting snow on a highway. These were not intended to stop a determined attacker but, rather, to keep out random walkers and parkers so that a person too close to whatever was being protected could be spotted easily. These kinds of physical guards were to establish a "good-guy perimeter." If you were inside the perimeter you were, by definition, someplace you were not supposed to be and consequently subject to police attention. The other very common type of fence that was newly constructed or patched up and enhanced after 9/11 was the standard chain-link property fence. As people in Massachusetts quickly found out, however, these fences only work if you bother to shut the gate and/or post a guard. More than once, I arrived at a supposedly secure facility only to find doors and gates open with nobody monitoring them.

It would be hard to overstate how important these physical measures became within the first twelve months after 9/11. As people struggled to figure out what homeland security was going to mean in the Boston area and then to figure out what they needed to do to make that happen, they believed that the public and political figures wanted to see action. Physical guarding in the form of a jersey barrier or chain-link fence was far less expensive than paying overtime to a trooper but provided visible evidence that "something" was being done.

Ironically, guarding something with people or pieces of concrete also had the effect of highlighting it, of showing that there was something within worth guarding. Quite close to the highly secured fast-food restaurant mentioned above, there were two buildings that together housed a major hub of media and telecommunications. Damage to either, especially shortly after 9/11 when the northeastern communications network was still being rebuilt, could have had a major impact on the communications capacity of the Northeast. Only an unguarded alley separated the two buildings. However, an uninformed person looking for targets would have been far more likely to notice the security measures around city hall, the barricaded federal offices, and the guarded historical buildings around Faneuil Hall.

The idea of security through anonymity was not lost on people in the homeland security community. For their own facilities, many organizations decided that discretion was the better part of valor. While not exactly hiding their presence, they did not advertise it either. Fences were allowed to look old. Vehicles were parked behind anonymous brick buildings or inside large truck bays; physical addresses did not appear on business cards or PowerPoint presentations. Misdirection was also used. A city or state facility commonly used for some other purpose could easily hide the traffic and equipment associated with emergency operations. Practitioners argued that this type of security also provided relative security for the people and businesses near the emergency organization. The rationale was that if the organization was not a target, then the neighborhood was not a target. Of course, the case could also be made that people are best protected when they know what is in their neighborhoods and can plan accordingly.

Passive guarding was and continues to be used to cover inadequacies as well as capabilities. If you don't know where an emergency operations center is, you can't find out that it is only the size of a small conference room and has only one computer, that it is less a facility for supporting an emergency response than a place for people to get on one another's nerves. If an organization doesn't publicly acknowledge the location of its response-supply cache, it doesn't face public scrutiny for having located it in a place where it would be extremely difficult to deploy it during even a minor emergency. However, most of the time the intent was simply to protect a facility and the neighborhood in which it was located in the least expensive and most benign way possible.

Of course, this type of security also had its drawbacks. Facilities hidden in plain view often made use of old buildings, providing uncomfortable and inconvenient working space for day-to-day work. People who did not view their work as security sensitive found the arrangements somewhat embarrassing, especially when colleagues appeared to get a bit too much of a thrill from the self-importance imparted by secret knowledge. Civic-minded citizens, also known as nosy neighbors, might report suspicious activity at the facility and be difficult to calm down when no apparent action was taken. Activities taking place at the facility might seem in-explicable or frightening.

One such case involved the mannequin the Civil Support Team used in its training simulations. The mannequin was generally used to simulate a wounded or dead civilian or team member, sometimes dressed in civilian clothes, sometimes in military fatigues. I had heard, but never seen writ-ten down, its name, which I interpreted as Mendoughn. I assumed that this was an "in-joke" about somebody known to the team, until one day a member asked if I knew the story behind the name. The name was actually "Man-Down," a common term in military and response organizations to indicate when one of their number was hurt and disabled. They had given the mannequin the name after a woman walking in the woods near the facility saw a "man" in a uniform lying on the ground, while other men in uniforms raced about. Not knowing anything about the facility, her perception did not include the possibility of a training exercise. She called the police, who initiated a response appropriate to a man-down situation, much to the surprise of the training team members and irritation of the responding local police officers. While local law enforcement knew about the Civil Support Team's presence and, in fact, trained with them, they had not taken into account the fact that the woman did not have that frame of reference with which to filter what she had seen.

Discussion of these drawbacks and fumbles was lighthearted, but there was no question that it was also serious business. In New York City in September of 2001, the emergency operations center for the city was located in one of the World Trade Center buildings, a fact widely known to the public. Counterterrorism training sessions warned that attackers might attempt to increase the chaos caused by their attacks through destroying the locations designated as emergency operations centers or staging areas, removing the support and decision making for extended response. In fact, the reason this book does not have a chapter on space and place is that to write it would have been to expose the locations and configurations of places where many practitioners prefer to work unnoticed.[8]

INCIDENT RESPONSE

While the area around Boston was fortunate to have no large-scale homeland security responses during my time in the field, there were changes in incident response. Some of these had to do with the nature of the calls that came in, especially the number of "white powder" calls. Other changes had to do with who might show up at a response. Most involved operational changes, shifts in the considerations one might make when "sizing up" a scene or in what kind of equipment and techniques were used.

One of my earliest challenges in fieldwork was that I was not able to get good access to the community during the autumn of 2001 due to the constant responses people had to make to the calls about possible anthrax. In Boston, as in many areas around the United States, the cases of anthrax on the East Coast sent some of the public into a terrible state of fear. Information about anthrax powder was not easy to find, leaving people to worry about everything from talc to laundry detergent. Each person calling felt that they had a right to be taken seriously and the public safety community had to respond. Calls ranged from serious concerns about threatening letters received by public personalities to people who panicked when they saw a dusting of white powder under the baby-changing platform in a restroom. One case my informants discussed involved a woman who had reported white powder found in her home laundry room. (Of

8. Although I am constrained from detailed reporting on space and place, my ability to adequately observe the nuance of community formation and daily practices required close attention to the mutually constitutive nature of space and practice and cultural categories (Harvey 1996; Pellow 2001, 2002, 2003; Rapoport 1982). Anthropological approaches to space and place should become a fundamental aspect of methods training even for projects where it is not expected to be a main category of research. Fortunately, interesting discussions of the intersection of contemporary national security and spatiality are starting to appear in the literature (Denicola 2006; Low 2002, 2006).

course, some people gradually came to take these incidents too casually. In another state in 2004, a public official wishing to stop others from calling in a white-powder concern tried to convince them that the powder was sugar by tasting it. His reaction to what turned out to be a toxic cleaning chemical at least had the effect of ruling out sugar, and it certainly did add a measure of urgency to the response efforts.)

Boston's strategy for handling the overwhelming nature and quantity of the calls changed over time, but at one point it included sending a response-group type that came to be called the "three wise men," including one representative each from law enforcement, fire, and emergency medical services. Nobody ever explicitly stated the rationale for that composition, but I got the sense that it had more to do with public reaction and distribution of workload among the services than any sense that all three of those disciplines needed to be present.

As the community began to grapple with the idea that many responses might have homeland security implications, new faces began to appear at responses and old faces might appear in new or expanded roles. Air National Guard personnel based at Otis Air Base on Cape Cod found themselves called on to patrol the coast rather than just training over it. Law enforcement officers responding to fire calls had to consider that investigation at the scene might be more involved than it had been in the past. Medical responders and hospital personnel were sometimes more involved in criminal investigation than they had been a few months before. Smaller incidents became more likely to provoke a response from people in state and federal agencies, who also became more involved in planning and exercising. As described in chapter 4 and below, the entire concept of who counted as a responder or a member of the larger community involved with homeland security continued to change throughout my time in the field.

Although the types of responses and the people responding shifted somewhat, the changes most often discussed among my informants were those relating to how one approached response. As with so much about homeland security, these changes were already taking place before the term "homeland security" became commonplace, in response to perceived shifts in the risks one might face in a response. Industrial chemicals, dangerous substances associated with drug labs, explosives, and the possibility of terrorism were part of the response decision process for a small and growing group of responders. This group expanded rapidly after 2001. The most significant piece of retraining had to do with convincing responders, so focused on stopping the bad thing, to stop rushing into incidents. Responders began to be expected to take a great number of things into consideration before stepping into the danger zone of a scene.

The problem was popularly illustrated with the term "blue canaries." This nickname was applied to police who often arrived at scenes with little protective gear or detection equipment. They, like the coal miner's canary, unfortunately had the potential as an early warning system for later responders by succumbing to hazardous materials or secondary devices. One informant from a hazardous materials team put the joke a little more graphically when describing how to set up the hot (i.e., the really dangerous contaminated area), warm (a buffer zone, often where decontamination takes place), and cold (or safe) zones: "You know how, when we go into an incident, we're supposed to set up the zones, right? We're supposed to be pretty precise about laying them out. Well, when I come to the place where there are all the dead cops? That's where I put the hot-zone markers."

Although police got the nickname, the problem applied to firefighters, emergency medical technicians, and even emergency room personnel, all of whom might unintentionally harm themselves by moving into situations that have not been adequately assessed. Along with hazardous materials, secondary devices, deliberately planted to harm first responders and onlookers, have become a significant concern. I should note that every procedure I saw called for life-safety operations first. Ideally, responders should be protected to continue service, but they were allowed to take greater risks if there was a concern that victims could not wait for treatment. This was the case even in radiological incidents and was accepted as a normal cost of the job by nearly everyone to whom I spoke.

Although risk was accepted as part of the job, response agencies also began to expect their frontline staff to take more personal protective measures. This was part of a set of ideas, derived in part from the military, that came into the community under the term "force protection." Force protection is the effort to preserve response capability by not losing people, equipment, and supplies unnecessarily. All responders are increasingly expected to do a significant "size up" of the situation before moving into areas that might be dangerous. In a size-up, the responder or incident commander looks over the scene, getting a sense of what the hazards are and what the priorities of response should be, as well as what additional resources need to be called in. This was always part of standard response, but in the last few years, it has started to include new things to help prevent the blue canary syndrome described above. The size-up should now include the possibility of contamination from chemical, radiological, or biological weapons, devices deliberately set to disrupt the response, the possible need for enhanced criminal investigation personnel, whether this event has been staged to test the resources and response patterns of a community prior to a larger or more critically targeted attack, and other terrorism-related concerns.

While I was in the community, I watched the process of these new elements becoming part of the tacit knowledge (discussed in chapter 8) that allowed experienced responders to assess a situation quickly without appearing to work through the issues in a logical progression. The concerns also seeped into the minds of planners in the community. As I have become more and more involved in planning, I find that I have these things in my mind as well. A deserted backpack on a bench during holiday festivities on Boston Common was enough for me to drag my visiting family to the other side of the park. I see buildings in terms of their relative hardness or softness as targets. I view responses in terms of how they are staged to protect the ability to respond. An academic colleague working on issues of homeland security at the same time could not bring herself to get on the subway. I call it the "park facing out" phenomena, after my tendency to keep my tank full and park in such a way that I could pull out rapidly. Both practitioners and researchers, surrounded by these concerns daily, become a bit hypervigilant.

New measures also included things such as masks, "turn-out gear" or "bunker gear" with greater protective qualities, wearing plastic gloves to handle victims and evidence, and personal monitors, such as dosimeters.[9] There was resistance to all of these measures from some personnel. It can be difficult to explain to budget-conscious city officials why you need to wear such specialized gear in exercises. Many types of personal protective equipment (PPE) are hot, heavy, and make it difficult to move around. Some gear makes responders fumble during tasks at which they are normally highly competent, an embarrassment no one welcomes. Dosimeters and other monitors are hard to read through the plastic of your face mask. Sometimes radios can't be heard through protective hoods. As I write this, five years after 9/11, there is great concern that exercises are being held without forcing responders to try out their protective gear. As one experienced responder put it, "We know they can drag hose, for Christ sake. What we don't know is whether or not they can do it in their

9. Dosimeters are small devices that show the "dose" to which an individual has been exposed.

Level A's."[10] A response planner in another exercise echoed the concern by saying, "I don't doubt that they can direct traffic. My question is whether or not they can do it in what they would have to be wearing if the area was contaminated."

While some of the resistance to these measures was a practical response to financial and technical constraints, not all of it could be tucked away neatly into acceptable categories. Many of the people to whom I spoke talked about it in terms of responders being "old school" or "macho" or needing to appear tough. After all, if you are willing to run into a burning building, it might seem a little funny to suddenly have to be afraid of little tiny germs. A great deal of weight is given to the idea that there is a tradition of rushing into scenes, of being "an old fire horse" unable to stop responding when the bell rings. In the fire service, chiefs and/or the person serving as incident commander often wear white helmets. There is a running joke that this has nothing to do with visibility. Instead it has to do with being able to tell whether the chief has been closer to the scene than he or she should be by the telltale signs of smoke and soot marring the white surface.

People who define themselves as responders have to be given ways to explain hesitation, let alone reluctance. Most people I saw trying to train people out of the "rush in" behavior would use force protection as their central theme. They focused on ingraining the idea that you are of no use to victims or your organization if you are dead or incapacitated. This was not a new idea, but after 9/11 it did become a more powerful concept that trainers and supervisors could use to encourage their frontline staff to take precautions. If the precautions were taken for the good of victims or team members, they became acceptable and caused fewer worries about appearing less than perfectly brave.

As if personal protective gear and the need to restrain oneself from rushing in were not enough, responders also were increasingly expected to look beyond the immediate response. Beyond the initial scene, responders now had to consider the impact of their actions on later stages of the

10. "Level A's" refers to a level of personal protective equipment. The levels range from D to A. Level D indicates normal work clothing and universal precautions with no respiratory protection and little skin protection. Level A protection includes a fully encapsulating suit that protects against certain types of chemicals, as well as a self-contained breathing apparatus. Many people in response fields have come to refer to the gear by the name of the level in the same way they would refer to "turn-out gear" instead of naming the individual pieces of fire-resistant clothing.

response. Many training programs and exercise scenarios deal with concerns that responders may spread contamination through their desire to help victims.

In more than one exercise, I saw a medical responder to the scene of an explosion load up a patient without first assessing the possibility that the person could be contaminated by chemical, biological, or radiological material. Although the urge to help is understandable, doing so without first performing necessary decontamination would take the ambulance out of service for future victims and could end up shutting down the receiving emergency room. In a medium or large event, the loss of an ambulance or an emergency room could seriously compound consequences for the community. If the substance in question was an infectious agent or a particularly dangerous chemical, such as sarin, the consequences could be even more severe. The saving of that one life could lead to hundreds of other deaths. This sort of brutal calculation is not the sort of thinking that drew most people into response professions.

OTHER TASKS

These kinds of everyday activities—guarding, watching, and responding—tended to be the province of frontline staff. These are the first responders and other individuals who carry the bulk of visibility and physical activity on their shoulders. Figuring out how to arrange these activities and concerns into a coherent pattern of policy and practice is more likely to be the responsibility of somewhat more senior people and planners.

As discussed in more detail in the next chapter, these community members were more intimately involved in figuring out what homeland security would be than were frontline staff. They interpreted policy, assessed threats, developed necessary relationships, and other "planning-oriented" activities. While less likely to be out in a patrol car, these people were nonetheless occupied by practical concerns. There were grant opportunities to be discovered and applications to be completed. There were equipment options to be assessed, purchases to be made, and maintenance needs to be addressed. The interoperability of equipment and procedures had to be discussed. Budgets and schedules had to be reworked around new training, exercising, and operating realities. Union contracts had to be revisited to deal with similar concerns. There was new and confusing paperwork to be filled out and a shifting state and federal bureaucracy to track. Waiting on everyone's computer was the rapid proliferation of trade magazines, electronic newsletters, and regular news related to homeland security. Sorting through this information to find the pieces necessary to get through the day, let alone being able to get a broad picture of the larger national trends, was time-consuming. On top of it all, there also was the conceptual work of figuring out what homeland security was going to be in the Boston area and how the community could make it happen.

CHAPTER 7 // CONCEPTUALIZING SECURITY

The aspect of homeland security work that was of most interest to me was conceptual, although it served an extremely practical purpose. In the absence of clear federal guidance, people in the policy community were left to figure out what homeland security was going to mean in the area and then make that definition manifest. That work can be most easily understood by breaking it down into more manageable chunks of activities. I have tried to keep things as simple as possible, if for no other reason than that all these activities have become so politicized that it is sometimes difficult to remember that these are also things that people get up in the morning and *do*. I have tried to stay with categories that resonated with the people in my community, but they should not be construed as emic, merely as ways to impose a framework on a messy topic. In fact, there was a great deal of work involved just in terms of people figuring out what they needed to figure out. My purpose in this chapter is to use these categories as a way into this area of practice.

Defining what local homeland security was going to mean involved the following conceptual activities:

- deciding what hazards exist
- identifying likely targets and assessing their vulnerabilities
- deciding what it will mean to make something secure
- negotiating roles, responsibilities, priorities, and authorities (including jurisdictional and financial matters)

- figuring out how homeland security was going to fit in with existing understandings of the boundaries of emergency management, public safety, public health, and national defense
- creating and maintaining enough of a shared sense of community (symbolic, discursive, and practical) that efforts and discussions with the public were harmonized

The business of determining the conceptual and practical boundaries was coupled with the need to build a community of people who could reliably come together to make these decisions and act on them. This goal was in tension with, although not at odds with, the desire to resist institutionalizing relationships or roles (discussed in more detail in the next chapter). In a field where many organizations have had to deal with interagency operations in the past, homeland security may have initially looked like just another reason for interagency meetings and joint training. In reality, the scope, political fraughtness, and duration of homeland security as an area of practice necessitated more developed relationships, if not exactly official ones.

People worked these things out in the usual ways, informal and formal discourse, power plays involving resources and authority, posturing for one another or the public—all of which will make appearances in the discussions below. However, it is important not to lose sight of the fact that this was a deliberately cooperative venture in many respects. For every backhanded resource grab, I saw many more examples of people setting aside personal and organizational differences in order to get something resolved. My discussions with informants, as well as my own involvement in various projects, made it clear that "off-line" conversations were also an important area for this aspect of practice. However, the ethnographically visible venues for this aspect of homeland security practice were meetings, training, exercises, and responses. It was in these arenas, where people had to develop plans and procedures and assess available resources, that people worked out the common ground of local homeland security, solved some problems, and decided that others had to go in the "too-hard box."

For the purposes of this discussion, it is necessary to make a conceptual distinction between a hazard and a vulnerability. In fact, when discussing the need to determine what should be protected and how, many in the community talked about threat assessments, hazard assessments, target assessments, vulnerability assessments, and risk assessments interchangeably. However, as categories of practice, there are some subtle differences that are worth describing. Despite their conflation in common discourse, they represent points in a range of interconnected concerns that the homeland security community faced. Below, when I refer to a hazard, I am referring to a thing or person posing a danger to something of concern to the community, such as the presence of dangerous chemicals in a school laboratory. In complement, a vulnerability is some aspect of a potential target that makes it susceptible to that damage, such as the proximity of a subway station to fuel storage tanks. The distinction is important because it was much easier for the community to arrange their activities around vulnerability assessments than a hazard assessment, as will become apparent below. I also focus on perceived threats from terrorism at the expense of concerns about natural and industrial hazards. This does not necessarily reflect the relative weight ultimately given to these issues by people in the community. I have focused on terrorism only because that was the initial emphasis in discussions of homeland security.

DEFINING HAZARDS

Defining hazards is the work of figuring out what dangers are or may be present at a particular spot or time. The more common term for this area of practice is "threat assessment." I have chosen to avoid that term as it tends to anthropomorphize hazards rather than evoking the range of the topic. Hazard assessment is part of the planning process of every town and, hopefully, part of the tacit knowledge of an incident commander when he or she shows up on scene. For the people in the policy community, these questions were rarely speculative musings. They were both political and practical. They were political in the sense that once you have decided that there is a hazard, you may be held responsible for protecting what is threatened. You also may be able to access resources more or less easily depending on how hazards are constructed and described to those who hold the purse strings. Defining hazards was a practical endeavor in that knowing what hazards exist can help one decide what to protect and how.

Many people in the Boston-area policy community had long experience working out hazard assessments. For natural hazards, the picture was fairly well known. Hurricane season will run from roughly June through November. Blizzards will be a threat in the winter. Earthquakes are usually small to moderate in the area. Forest fires are not an urban issue except when smog from giant ones farther north or west drifts in to muck up the air quality. Industrial hazards were part of most people's assessments, although I always had the feeling that their approach to industry was somewhat less systematic than it was toward natural events. Nuclear power plants, hazardous cargos, fuel storage tanks, pipelines, and so on were all considered.

Terrorism was not a new idea, but the degree to which it needed to be considered in evaluating an area was ramped up as people tried to figure out what was expected of them in terms of homeland security. Since 2001, there has been much debate in the popular press and at academic conferences about whether there is a threat of terrorism, how much of one, who and what poses a threat, and who gets to decide. People within the response community also debated the relative merits of worrying about terrorists in contrast to hazardous materials spills. However, in the two years immediately following the events of 2001 and the subsequent attempted bombing of a transatlantic flight, it was hard to dismiss the possibility of a terrorist hazard.

The difficulty in incorporating terrorism into ongoing hazard assessments came from problems of risk assessment and, as always, information access. Many informants talked about how difficult it was for them to figure out not just what terrorists might possibly do but what they were likely to do as well. Was it necessary to plan for an attempt to smuggle a nuclear bomb on a pleasure boat? Could people truly make biological weapons as easily as some in the press suggested? Given that the anthrax attacks only killed a few people while the attacks using jet liners killed many, wouldn't it make more sense to worry about so-called conventional weapons attacks? Did anyone know what groups were interested in harming the United States or specific groups within it? Were they planning something for Tuesday? The answers or lack thereof to these types of questions had material consequences for the community in terms of staff hours, resources allocated, and plans created.

While I was in the community, there was not much widely available professional analysis from federal agencies about terrorist threats. Initially, much information about suspected terrorist activity was classified, and only vague warnings filtered down to the local level. In one case, an informant complained to me that he had lent a junior staffer to a regional counterterrorism working group where he had received a clearance to see certain threat analyses. Unfortunately, this junior staffer could not come back and tell his boss what he had learned because his boss lacked the appropriate clearance.

Sometimes the issue was not classification or clearance, but that necessary information did not flow where it needed to go. Practitioners told me this usually happened because somebody did not know it was needed or they simply did not consider passing it along to be a priority. There were times when it was difficult to understand how anything other than carelessness or malice could have interfered, but conversations rarely went in that direction except in jest.

The problem was not simply bureaucratic tangles. At high levels, security clearances require federal agents to go out and interview neighbors and family members. Even at lower levels, they take money and time to process, and the demand after 2001 was very high. Also, there was (and as of this writing still is) no single federal source for intelligence, so it was hard for locals to get a sense of what they might be missing or which agencies they should be asking for information. Even after the formation of the Department of Homeland Security, there was no single voice issuing threat assessments.

On the other end, there was no uniform receiver of information at the local level if a federal agency wanted to share. As indicated in previous chapters, the composition of the local policy community and the roles and relationships among agencies varied considerably from location to location. The formation of Anti-Terrorism Task Forces (ATTF) in the Attorney General's Office in each state in the fall of 2001 provided a coordinating mechanism that, while not perfect, did make it possible for some unclassified intelligence to be shared. Massachusetts' ATTF was very active, led by a man who saw the need for information sharing and collaborative planning.[1] He created a number of special-interest working groups within the ATTF, which further facilitated the flow of information and gave people a place to go if they were not sure what intelligence they should pursue.

Gradually, some locals in law enforcement received clearances, and some national organizations began to filter their information so it could be more widely distributed to those who needed it. It was not enough. Emergency management, fire, and health officials were still left in the dark. They heard about "threat matrices" and "counterterrorism briefings" but were frequently left watching the talking heads on CNN like the rest of the public. In one particularly disturbing case, I received a call from a local response official asking for my help in getting access to a set of threat assessments. He had heard of them and assumed he should have access to the ones associated with his city. This man, with all the resources of Boston's homeland security behind him, had to call a visiting

1. Massachusetts' ATTF is now known as the Anti-Terrorism Advisory Council (ATAC) and no longer serves the same functions, having become primarily a passive group that is briefed on basic information rather than a group of collaborative partners.

anthropologist to find out that the information he wanted was restricted to presidential staff.

In some parts of the community, this created resentment. Locals felt that the full burden of national defense within territorial borders had fallen on their shoulders without the accompanying resources, information, and political clout that the military enjoyed in its national defense mission. For most it was simply another frustration among the many daily hassles of overall emergency preparedness. As was so often the case in this policy community, people found ways to act despite the fact that they did not have full access to official channels and structures. In the absence of reliable information about this type of hazard, the community looked at assessing its vulnerabilities.

IDENTIFYING TARGETS, ASSESSING VULNERABILITIES

Many of my informants have told me that there was a lively discussion about target identification and vulnerability assessment going on in the public safety community long before 2001. As with hazard assessments, most communities had done some sort of work with assessing what places or people or things might be vulnerable to natural and industrial hazards. Of course, the thoroughness with which this was done varied from location to location and target to target. People prepared for the hazards they thought were likely. Hurricane-prone areas were more likely to have carefully developed vulnerability assessments for that type of disaster (although as we saw in 2004 and 2005, these assessments were not necessarily accompanied by a feasible response plan or mitigation activities). Places that had experienced a hazardous materials spill were more likely to have looked at what kind of damage such a spill could cause. My discussions with people in the Boston area and from other areas of the country also led me to believe that high-profile targets or those of interest to the powerful were more likely to receive a thorough vulnerability assessment than those with less political, economic, or symbolic clout. Over the course of my fieldwork, I saw several planners struggle to balance their concerns about the differential impact of disaster on the poor with the pragmatic realities of scarce resources and the need to be able to demonstrate that well-known targets were being assessed and protected.

Looking at targets and vulnerabilities in terms of a terrorist hazard had been less common. Some practitioners claimed to have been working on terrorism preparedness for years, and based on the literature, they were not alone (Advisory Panel to Assess Domestic Response Capabilities for

Terrorism Involving Weapons of Mass Destruction 2000, 2001; U.S. Commission on National Security/Twenty-first Century: Hart-Rudman Commission 2000, 2001). However, this perspective on target and vulnerability analysis did not have center stage. High-profile events—such as the first bombing of the World Trade Center, the Oklahoma City bombing, and the sarin attacks on the Tokyo subway—made many in government and response organizations look around them to see what could happen in their own communities. As described in chapter 2, there were a number of federal terrorism-preparedness initiatives already under way by the time I entered the field. The federal government had recently finished its largest and most public terrorism exercise, TOPOFF, in 2000. The exercise frustrated locals, who were not sufficiently involved in the planning, but it also pointed out serious gaps in response capacity and force protection measures, leading Gerald Arenberg of the National Association of Police Chiefs to say in relation to the current state of training of first responders, "We're all going to be dead ducks" (Vise 2000). The press coverage of the exercise and responder reactions to it increased the number of people who wanted to know how badly terrorists might damage their communities. Finally, the events of the autumn of 2001 and the subsequent political and social changes in the United States brought the terrorism issue front and center in any discussion of what a community should consider targets and what those targets' vulnerabilities might be.

It can be difficult to tease apart the ideas of target and vulnerability at the level of practice. We think of targets as being things that are chosen by an attacker. Because of the information restrictions described above, many of the people in the community did not have access to enough knowledge of potential attackers to make educated judgments about what they were likely to attack. Similarly, a thing is vulnerable only when paired with something or someone that may cause it harm. However, vulnerability assessments were not *as* reliant on knowing the intentions of a potential attacker. It is a little easier to look at a building or area or event and understand what could happen, regardless of whether it is intended or likely.

In practice, likely targets were identified using a mix of information. People certainly made use of whatever intelligence came their way, watered down though it might be. They looked at history and compared what had been attacked in the past to what they had around them. This was the case with public and/or symbolic buildings. They engaged in what came to be known as "red teaming," where people would try to "play terrorist." Sometimes red teaming was just a mental exercise for people trying to figure out what to protect. Sometimes organizations hired people to actually try to break through their security. Practitioners also looked at the hazards in their communities to see what accidents might be turned into intentional destructive acts. A tanker truck carrying what came to jokingly be referred to as methylethylawfylstuff is nasty enough when it rolls over accidentally. If such a truck deliberately rolled near a vulnerable site such as a school, the consequences would be magnified. Many planners assumed that terrorists read the same newspaper coverage as everyone else and might get some ideas.

So, a great deal of target identification was based on perceived vulnerabilities rather than known intentions. If it was vulnerable, you worried about it as a potential target. Of course, this had a political dimension in the same way that hazard assessment did. Potential targets that were of concern to people with influence received more attention than poor neighborhoods, although it is important to point out that many in the public safety and public health parts of the community worked very closely with poorer neighborhoods and tried to look out for their interests. Some of these choices also were pragmatic, at least initially. It seemed to make sense that you would worry less about an inner-city library than about the Prudential Tower, the most noticeable building in the Boston skyline. Of course, that position became complicated as the community began to look more at "hard" and "soft targets," as discussed below.

Assessing vulnerabilities was more of an art than a science. Having been out on a number of vulnerability assessment trips, I started to get a small sense of the unconscious/conscious process that goes on in people's minds as they do the assessments. I had extended conversations with people regarding what kinds of things they think about—other than whether we could get Bloody Marys on the boat we used for one harbor vulnerability assessment tour. The questions below from my field notes, articulated in more colorful language by practitioners, are the kinds of concerns that would be expressed in a typical tour.

How can the target be approached from each of the six directions?[2] Would an attacker need to be close by, or is there a way to attack from a distance? Could a means of attack be left near the target and do its damage without the need to breach the target's security? Can the target be disrupted by an attack on something else that is less well protected? Is there any way to

2. In these field notes I was using the word "target" here in the sense that it was used in the community, as a shorthand for a place, event, or thing that was in some way hazardous and/or vulnerable.

minimize the vulnerability or secure the target more completely? What is in the target that can burn, explode, vaporize, collapse, melt, run into waterways, or otherwise harm the target and its surroundings? How many people are in the target as potential hostages or casualties? What kind of social disruption would harm to this target cause? Is the harm that can be caused something that can be addressed with local resources, or would it exceed the response capacity? What do I think of when considering some other type of problem, such as drug smuggling, that could also be part of an attack? What am I taking for granted in this picture that can be used because I am not paying attention to it?

Vulnerability assessments included security measures that were already in place, although those often had to be checked. Many area businesses seemed slow to take security seriously. Their assertions in the media that their facilities or modes of transportation were secure could not be counted on as reliable information on which to base a vulnerability analysis. A particularly egregious example of this involved a business in the port area that received and redistributed a hazardous material. When local governments and public safety officials voiced concerns about the potential for terrorists to use this substance against the city, the company reassured everyone that its buildings, boats, and trucks were highly secure. One organization in the homeland security community decided to pay a visit to discuss the specifics with them. On arriving at the facility, the group found the gates unlocked and unguarded and had to wander through the facility looking for somebody to show them to the main office.

Assessments had to be revised depending on what new security measures were put into place as time went on. Increased security at high-profile targets had consequences beyond the facility, thing, or event in question. Several months into my time in the community, I noticed the topic of conversation turning more and more frequently to hard and soft targets. "Target hardening" is a term used to describe any measures used to make something less vulnerable. So, a hard target is one that has substantial security measures in place. My informants believed hardening of a target to have two benefits. They said it reduces the likelihood that an attack will be successful or, if it is successful, that it will cause substantial harm. They also believed it to be a deterrent. The idea was that terrorists were unlikely to choose a target known to have very good security. However, they acknowledged that an unintended consequence of target hardening was that it might turn attackers' attention to less well-protected facilities, events, or things, referred to as soft targets. Of particular concern

FIGURE 4. Assessing vulnerabilities in the harbor from a Coast Guard vessel. A pleasure craft sails close to the cargo terminal, raising questions about monitoring the approach to the terminal. (Special thanks to Massport Fire Rescue and the fireboat pilot for the smooth ride.) Photo by author.

were buildings or events that, by their nature, required openness. If oil refineries were well secured, might not a terrorist spend his or her efforts trying to attack a shopping mall or a hospital or a school?

Some vulnerability assessments were systematic. Sometimes outside consulting firms were hired to conduct exhaustive surveys, as was the case when the U.S. Coast Guard engaged a major national consulting firm to do a port security study. Sometimes carefully chosen members of the public safety community or people involved in a task force would tour a particular area and produce a report of their observations and analyses. In my notes, I described one such tour with which I was involved when I was working with the Consequence Management Group of the Port Security initiative:

Initially, I wasn't sure what to make of the plans for the trip. There was a great deal of humor associated with planning. "We're bringing our bathing suits for this one, right?" We gathered at the Black Falcon Cruise Ship Terminal to meet the fireboat from Massport Fire Rescue. The boat was a huge, sturdy thing, more like a tug than any boat I had been on in the past. I was not the only first-timer with this type of equipment and we milled around,

looking at the giant water guns and other mysterious bits of apparatus.
We slipped into the harbor with a grace that belied the bulkiness of the
boat. The man guiding it must have a great deal of training in moving it
in delicate situations where precision is necessary. It was a spectacular day.
Warm and still under a perfect blue sky. Not a lot of traffic on the harbor
so we could cruise casually. A fire chief joked that we should have brought
Bloody Mary mix. An emergency management official leaned back in the
sun and said, "Oh, yeah, your tax dollars at work!" It was hard to imagine
that we were about serious business. Then we passed [a facility thought to
be particularly vulnerable and hazardous]. All joking stopped and all eyes
began to scan the area, looking for access points, trying to figure out if there
were places where a shoulder-fired missile could hit it, looking for sur-
rounding facilities that might be in harm's way if it was attacked. Different
fire personnel discussed how they would expect one another to respond and
how that might be vulnerable to disruption. People asked weapons ques-
tions of the National Guard Civil Support Team's commander. We made
plans to discuss the issues further with the Coast Guard in the larger Port
Security meetings. In the distance, I saw one of the giant liquid natural gas
tankers. There was time for a few more jokes and stretches and a bit more
gossip before the Guard commander pointed out another vulnerability and
seriousness descended again. At the start of the trip, I had wondered how
we could systematically go through all the vulnerabilities without making
ourselves crazy. I quickly began to understand that the answer was "one at
a time."

Often assessments were carried out informally as people went about
other duties. People in police and fire services are used to keeping their
eyes open for things that may become part of an incident later on. It was
not a huge leap for some of them to start thinking about terrorism. Shifts
in the state of security at various perceived targets, changes in the physical and political landscape, and the thinking of people in the homeland
security community ensured that assessing hazards, vulnerabilities, and
targets was always an ongoing process rather than something with an end
in sight. It became part of daily practice for many of my informants. With
one particular informant, a fire chief, I would be in midconversation and
his eyes would slide off to something over my shoulder, not a new deli
as I would joke with him later, but some new piece of construction or a
new access ramp in the Big Dig highway project that changed the security
profile of some potential target. He would shake his head and grump a bit,

knowing he would have to make telephone calls and remember to talk to people in meetings about this new piece of the puzzle.

MAKING THINGS SECURE

Perhaps the most difficult task faced by the community was deciding what it meant to make a particular target, or indeed the entire Boston region, "secure." Do emergencies have to be prevented to make something secure? Does security mean that an attack cannot be successful or that a natural disaster can have no effect? Does it mean that a target or community is resilient; that it can bounce back from the damage an attack or natural disaster might cause? If it means resiliency, how many aspects of a community might need to be considered: economic vitality, social and cultural institutions and activities, mental health, perception of the area by outsiders? Does it mean that a target or community is protected from major damage and is resilient enough to cope with smaller problems? Does it mean that responders will be able to handle anything that happens? Does one only secure against likely scenarios?

Answers to these kinds of questions were not developed according to a logical, systematic model, although some tried, and much noise was made about rational planning as time went on. Perceived pressures for endless security had a lot to do with how practitioners thought about their job. One practitioner joked, "When Joe Public sees a team responding to a white-powder call in their moon suits, he's not thinking, 'Gee, isn't it great that they have the right equipment and training to handle this.' He's thinking, 'Where's *my* suit?'" Predictably, different organizations brought their own orientations to understanding and assessing risks, as anthropologists have found in the past (Douglas and Wildavsky 1982, 86, 89). However, by the time I was fully engaged in the field, these attitudes toward risk were already being negotiated, recontextualized, and blended.

The social context in which the homeland security community operated was complex. Nearly every day, local papers would contain an article in which an exercised politician or outraged citizen would point out some flaw in preparedness. Nuclear power plants were unguarded. The water system was unprotected and inadequately monitored. Hospitals did not do anything beyond the most rudimentary syndromic surveillance to catch disease outbreaks. How could people be sure the food in their local supermarket was safe? Illegal aliens were working in security-sensitive jobs at airports. A person with a "dirty bomb" in a suitcase could put it in the middle of the financial district and walk away. No organization in the community wanted to be alone on the podium explaining that it was not possible even to imagine every possible scenario playing out in every possible combination of circumstances, let alone be able to secure the region against them.

During my time in the community, there was a never-ending stream of pronouncements and initiatives designed to bring a sense of order to deciding how to secure things. Generally, the initiators were well intentioned. They realized that decisions were being made in a somewhat haphazard and occasionally unaccountable way. Although there may have been exceptions, my experience with these efforts was that they were much more successful in bringing knowledgeable people together to figure things out than they were in bringing some type of predictable, systematic model to the decision process. I believe that the primary flaw in all these attempts was the inability to recognize the role of social and cultural factors in security decisions. A "rational" model for risk analysis and security configuration can't account for the influence of people who just feel better when they see squad cars. It also can't cope with the vagaries of funding. I have never read an analysis that did not say that the local homeland security community is critically understaffed. Yet much federal funding cannot be spent on staff, only on equipment and training. No formalistic risk-analysis model can intersect with those kinds of realities without coming to bits.

In many cases, the decisions about whether to try to prevent things, make something resilient, and/or focus on effective response came down to discussions among people in the community. People would think out loud about possible scenarios and circumstances. They would weigh those against the resources they had available or thought it was likely they could get and the changes they thought they could effect in the area. The question usually was not whether they were making the best possible risk assessment and allocation of resources but, rather, what could actually get done. They would decide what they should plan for, based on what resources and assistance they had or could expect, and toss up the rest to a combination of personal initiatives to get better resources or simple hope that the feared disaster would not take place.

A lot of things had to go in the too-hard box, filed away under "things we hope the army guys will keep out." This was true of much local-level planning for responding to an attack with a nuclear device. People made jokes about the specific procedures they would follow if such a device was used, chuckling about precision ducking-and-covering or training new hires to "bend over and kiss your butt good-bye." Even among those who knew that an exploded nuclear device would not necessarily mean the end of the entire city, people were not sure if it was worthwhile to try to plan to respond to one. Local public safety leaders questioned whether they could really rely on frontline staff to work under such catastrophic circumstances. How likely was it that bus drivers would show up ready and willing to drive into contaminated areas to carry out the evacuation plans? What was the point of planning with so many unknowns?

Accountability also was a significant problem. There was really no one place for a citizen to go to question why security was (or was not) being handled in a particular way. However, the process of discussing options in a free-form way, rather than as part of a strict algorithm, produced some very creative results. The mudflats around Logan Airport had long been a popular place for clammers (people who dig up clams for personal or commercial use). After 9/11, they were forbidden to use the flats, as officials worried that an attacker might disguise him- or herself as a clammer in order to get close to the airfield. This caused a great deal of upset in local communities, many of which already had strained relations with the Massport. It also caused serious economic hardship for people who worked the flats. Ultimately, a creative thinker in the community realized that the licensed clammers could have background checks, given vests to help identify them from a distance, and allowed back on the flats. Since many of them knew one another and all were aware of the situation, they would be alert to new faces and strange behavior.[3] They ceased to be much of a security risk, if they ever were, and instead were turned into an additional level of surveillance for the airport.

Then there was the question of who gets to decide what security means; what is likely and what is not; what a community needs to recover; and what is beyond the reach of the government's responsibility. In identifying hazards, targets, and vulnerabilities, people in public safety and public health can have some degree of autonomy if they choose to use it. While politics are important in those assessments, it is more important that members of the homeland security community know what they might be up against in a disaster, whether the public and politicians agreed with

3. In fact, several clam diggers were quoted in the *Boston Globe* in support of the measure, suggesting that they would be the best security Logan could have. One assumes this view was not universally held, but certainly some of them saw the reopening of the beds not only as an economic reprieve but also as an affirmation of their role in securing an area about which they already felt protective (Gedan 2002; Medaglia 2002).

them or not. They can consider their own plans, talk to their organizations, mount campaigns to build a more effective response or harden a target, or even support attempts to remove it from an area where its presence threatens too many other things, as many tried to do with the Everett, Massachusetts, Liquefied Natural Gas (LNG) terminal.

Securing something, however, requires a series of decisions that are fundamentally linked to resource allocation, local, state, and national politics, and the ideas or traditions of towns and organizations. Businesses were less interested in paying for security measures than they were in having the government prevent attacks altogether. Communities were sometimes more interested in having a hazard removed than developing the resiliency they would need to bounce back from the potential consequences of the hazard. Of course, the situations were rarely so simple. Shortly after 9/11, there was a brief flurry of discussion about how to protect buildings from planes. Boston's Logan International Airport is very close to the city. When planes take off from certain strips, they come quite close to some of the city's taller buildings before angling up and away. Some citizens hoped that those runways would no longer be used. Their concern might have been commingled with ongoing neighborhood concerns about airport noise, an example of the way people latched their preexisting concerns to discussions of vulnerability and security. In the end, I believe nobody seriously considered abandoning a runway at a busy airport, partly because takeoff is thought to be a very difficult time for a hijacking to occur and partly because the economic costs were felt to outweigh the security risks. The policy community ultimately defaulted to a position that meant security for the downtown buildings would not include removing the hazard of being hit by an outbound airplane, except insomuch as building design could help mitigate the effects of such an event.

The example of the LNG tankers and facility described in earlier chapters also illustrates the complexity. Residents of Everett and the responders who served them wanted to ensure that the tankers and Distrigas facility were secure. However, in the face of calls from many surrounding towns to move the facility to a less congested area, Everett resisted. As one informant put it, "Distrigas has been a very good neighbor to Everett." By that, he meant that the industry brought jobs and taxes to town and that the company had also been very careful to donate generously to civic and public safety projects. In this case, the meaning of "secure" for the tankers and the facility would not include moving it to a location where it could be more easily protected, and the security of Everett and the surrounding communities would not include moving this particular hazard to a location where the consequences of an attack or accident would be lessened.

In some cases, what it meant to secure something was influenced by people's disinclination to comply with laws or recommendations. Even in cases where some security precautions might have seemed to be in the self-interest of a business or other organization, they had to be coaxed. Businesses did not want to spend money on fences and security cameras. Schools did not have the staff to learn about and write security plans. Customs agents had to deal with securing borders while keeping them permeable enough to allow cargo containers and other shipments to enter the country without challenge so that businesses would not complain to Congress. Hospitals had other priorities. Town and state governments could enforce zoning and business laws, and public safety organizations could enforce regulations, but they also had to assign staff to the most critical tasks, and enforcement was not always one of them.

Once again, as these decisions and discussions played themselves out, it was often planners in the homeland security community who were left to act based on the answers to the question mentioned earlier, "What can we actually get done here?" Unfortunately, basing security on that kind of decision process meant that difficult partners sometimes just dropped off the planning map. If a local hospital was mired in discussions about its responsibility as a business versus its public role, eventually the rest of the security planning could not wait for them and decisions were made assuming or hoping things about their role. Schools and other organizations with problems finding staff to do preparedness work might end up being included as a location that could require response during an emergency, but no more. Practitioners had to make decisions in the absence of thorough understanding of how the district or individual schools planned to secure their buildings, their staff, and their students or without knowing whether those districts or schools had even thought about security.

NEGOTIATING ROLES AND RESPONSIBILITIES

All decisions about hazards, targets, vulnerability, and what it meant to be secure were made within the messiness of a community trying to negotiate how roles, responsibilities, and authorities (and the resources associated with those things) were going to be divvied up for an area of practice that nobody had yet defined.

In the broadest sense, it was not clear who was supposed to be setting security goals, defining standards, and determining who should take on what aspects of homeland security. No one agency or government official had the authority to determine what it meant to make something secure. As of this writing, there still is no such entity, although the federal Department of Homeland Security has some initiatives under way (Bush 2003a, 2003b, 2003c). In the year following 9/11, many in the homeland security community were hopeful and fearful that the proposed federal government agency would provide guidance, but most of what was released seemed to confuse more than to guide. When the national color-coded system for alert levels was released, many local actors did not seem to understand what to do with the information. The colors provided no specific information about the threat and no mechanism for sharing such information. People were not sure if they were supposed to wait around for the federal government to tell them what to do, or if they were supposed to develop their own sets of procedures for how their activities would change based on threat level. Some felt that the levels represented another unfunded mandate, with the federal government demanding that local responders and planners provide broad-based security with little guidance on how to accomplish that and with little financial support.

Gradually, Massachusetts and some of the towns, agencies, and businesses within it began to develop their own sets of protocols for what to do at various alert levels. The Office of Commonwealth Security developed basic guidelines for the state and actively encouraged towns and agencies to elaborate those guidelines into specific plans. Many started this process, if only to get a handle on the tremendous expenses that could be incurred through an unplanned deployment of resources when the national alert level was raised. Still, the fact that some towns and agencies had started to think about what they should do in response to this national initiative in no way filled the need for a coherent picture of who would be doing what in homeland security on a day-to-day basis.

This was perhaps the most difficult conceptual work facing members of the community. Determining roles and responsibilities was not just a matter of flow charts. It raised many questions. Who had authority over various types and stages of incidents? Who had access to resources and decision makers? Who got to make decisions? Who would have the benefits and problems associated with being the face of homeland security to the public? Which agencies should be developing which new skill sets and purchasing which kinds of new equipment? Which agencies will adopt which new missions related to homeland security? Who should be involved in which discussions? These were questions of power and resources, but also of pride, tradition, institutional orientations, and cultural capital.

These institutional orientations and models, with their competing and coordinate priorities and assumptions, came into contact during negotiations within the community. Finding mutually acceptable approaches to problems was a significant part of the work that people had to do as they tried to find solutions.

One of the most commonly discussed points of negotiation was between response and investigation. During a response to a suspected terrorist incident, the demands of saving lives and property can be in direct conflict with the demands of criminal investigation. Firefighters and EMTs move through scenes with an eye toward responding to a crisis, sometimes without great concern for the forensic evidence they might be disrupting. Decontamination of people and things may wash away evidence along with the dangerous substance. It may give an attacker time to melt away into the rest of the crowd. This tension between lifesaving and investigation had existed before the focus on terrorism but became highlighted in planning and exercising response to terrorist events. People in the community spent a lot of time educating one another about the importance of their set of priorities and working with one another to find opportunities for the approaches to coexist through simple measures, such as teaching fire and medical personnel to save things that might be needed as evidence, even if they could not preserve something in its original state.

I had to come to understand most areas of negotiation over time, from watching many interactions and gradually seeing the patterns. An example of these less articulated negotiations grew out of increased collaboration among local agencies and the Coast Guard. Local agencies were in the habit of dealing with flexible strategies for preparedness and response. Most had little desire for elaborate and specific protocols for different practices. They were accustomed to relying on generic plans and the tacit knowledge of responders. In contrast, the Coast Guard shared the military tradition of intensive planning and protocol development. They wanted a detailed advance plan for everything. Meetings sometimes consisted of people talking past one another. In one such encounter, a multiagency team of state and local planners spent about an hour describing the flexible mechanism they were developing to respond to a variety of different possible scenarios involving chemical, radiological, or nuclear incidents. Because of the endless variety of possible scenarios, the mechanism focused more on what kinds of questions to ask and how to get help and information than on prescribing specific tactics. The Coast Guard representative listened politely and then asked for the plan that would explain what they could expect Boston Fire to do if a radiological device was set off on a dock. These different approaches were not likely to be reconciled, nor was it possible, given differing jurisdictions, for one approach to "pull rank" on the other and become the dominant position.

In all such negotiations, people involved had to recognize each other's positions over time and figure out ways to accommodate both sets of needs. This took time and patience on all counts. It was influenced by personalities. Some people, recognized as "go-to guys" or good mediators, could make things move along faster. Others, recognized as being stubborn or particularly protective of turf, would cause a collective groan to go up when their names were read on an e-mail invitation to an event. Some actors were particularly good at creating shared discourse about the importance of making concessions and getting the job done, which tended to accelerate negotiations. These efforts were evident in a number of the interagency activities in the harbor, such as planning for cruise ship evacuations, protecting the USS *Constitution,* or escorting the LNG tankers.

Developing new capabilities and skill sets was also often contentious. For Boston, homeland security meant an increased emphasis on certain kinds of response missions, such as hazardous materials, confined space rescue for building collapses, explosive ordinance protocols, and so on. If a police department received approval to develop a special unit for hazardous materials response that could mean that their counterparts in fire would have a difficult time creating such a unit or beefing up an existing one. The number of people sent to various types of terrorism-related training was sometimes watched as an indicator of that agency's intentions with regard to various homeland security missions. Hallways and popular lunch spots were full of sidebar discussions and advocacy about which agencies were best suited to undertake which roles.

Over time I discovered that a great many of these back-channel negotiations were based in an ongoing tension between fire services and other organizations that were perceived to be encroaching on their traditional areas. While I was in the field, a number of firehouses were closed in eastern Massachusetts due to a combination of funding shortages and a perception that the number of fires and other calls had decreased.[4] In 2003, U.S. Representative Edward Markey told a local paper that six hundred firefighters in his district had been laid off due to budget cuts in the preceding two years (Abel 2003). Fire service personnel perceived their role

4. In fact, although the number of fires in the United States has decreased over the last twenty years, the number of firehouse calls has doubled in the same period (Dedman 2005).

to be anything related to immediate incident response and life safety. The existence of Boston EMS as a separate entity rather than a specialty within Boston Fire had been contentious. Members of other fire service organizations expressed concerns about police encroachment into areas, such as hazardous materials, perceived as fire territory. Of course, this was not expressed in the terms of "turf." Rather, these individuals described how their department was already fully competent to handle such incidents and how the police had other missions and no time to train properly. Police services had their own spin on such things, considering it necessary to expand their capacities since they were often the first at the scene.

All discussions, especially in the public view, were couched in terms of where the most competence lay (always with great respect voiced for the unique mission and skills of the opposing agency) and what would be best for the public at large. Actual negotiation rarely took place in public. Instead, there were performances before elected officials and the ever-present back-channel efforts with those who controlled the purse strings ultimately controlling who got what mission. The rare exception to this was when a department or town managed to get a grant to do something on its own. However, these grants more often supported discrete pieces of equipment, an exercise, or a onetime training program than a programmatic change.

Perhaps the most contentious negotiation of role involved who was going to be included in the category of first responder and, later, responder. As described earlier, the use of these terms was dangerous ground in an expanding homeland security policy community. In a field of social action where the location of the front line tended to shift with the location, type, and stage of incident, the categories of actors who could lay claim to being on the front line also changed. Traditionally, the construct of a first responder was limited to police and fire units and, occasionally, emergency medical service personnel, who were among the first on a scene. Over numerous discussions with people in the community, I found the most common factor in people's definition of "first responder" tended to be that the individual (or agency) served in a role that caused him or her to go into harm's way early in an incident. These individuals were the ones assuming the most risk because the nature and scope of an incident is uncertain in its early stages. In the first few minutes, nobody knows exactly what is burning or precisely what weapons an assailant has or what other hazards and vulnerabilities might come into the mix. Many informants qualified their definitions of "first responder" to include those who might show up a bit later but who would also be in harm's way, such as hazardous materials units, bomb squads, or specialized rescue teams. However, these units did not fit inside the existing construct quite so easily.

Whether through a lack of imagination or an attempt to link up with the cultural capital attached to public safety after 9/11, no new term was created to describe the other roles and professions that began to be included in discussions of homeland security. Emergency room personnel who might be dealing with contaminated patients or secondary devices began to be described as first responders, as being on the front lines. Other groups—such as public health officials, the Coast Guard, even postal carriers (after the anthrax attacks in the fall of 2001)—began to be described in similar terms. Many holding traditionally recognized first-response roles felt that this inclusiveness somehow failed to recognize the higher levels of personal risk they faced. While some felt that this attitude was simply turf protection and vanity on the part of the traditional response community, others felt there was value in preserving the distinction. Even if one does not agree that there is a significant social difference between running into a burning building and conducting a controlled epidemiological investigation, there are the political implications of the designation to be considered. Some who wanted the designation simply wanted to take the easiest, if not most accurate, route to recognition for their role in homeland security. Others, who were designated as first responders for the convenience of the press and public, did not want the label. In battles for resources, one of the easiest ways for traditional public safety organizations to gain the upper hand was to accuse their opponents of being "first-responder wannabes." They tried to preserve the authenticity of their distinct category through the usual mechanics of exclusion (Cheng 2004).

An example of this type of exclusion was the National Guard's First Civil Support Team, a follow-on resource that deployed a team of specialists to anywhere in their region in support of the responders already on scene. This deployment could take place only at the request of the governor, something that would not happen in the first few moments of an incident. Unfortunately, the press and some in the policy community lumped them in as first responders. The Civil Support Team's involuntary association with the first-responder label subsequently was used by another public safety agency to try to undermine their importance in homeland security planning and operations. Despite the fact that team members never portrayed themselves as first responders, those who were concerned about turf could point to the team's response time, which could be up to four hours depending on circumstances, and portray them as inadequate for first response. The fact that such actions were never part of their mission did not enter into the calculations of politicians and press, who were trying to absorb a great deal of organizational and procedural detail and may not have been up on the nuances of first responder versus follow-on resource.

Some people in hospitals began to talk about "first receivers," to designate those health professionals who might be the first to see victims of a terrorist attack. However, even that distinction did not work so well, as it had to be expanded from emergency room staff to the primary care physicians who, as in the anthrax cases, might be the first to see signs of a covert biological attack. Even in public safety, the term "first responder" had limited utility for homeland security. It did not recognize the dangers that might be faced by those involved in preventative or protective activities.

However, for representing homeland security activities to the public, the concept of first responders continued to have salience. The ability to control the public face of homeland security was tremendously valuable to traditional public safety organizations, whether they consciously recognized what they were doing or not. A podium backed up with uniformed public safety officials tapped into several wells of cultural capital, even if the practitioners filling those uniforms were likely to be of a high rank that no longer allowed them to participate in frontline response activities.

This type of display connected the public to traditional ideals of trust in public safety: the firefighter rescuing a kitten from a tree or carrying a child out of a burning building or a police officer holding up traffic for baby ducks in the Boston children's book *Make Way for Ducklings* or foiling the robbery of a mom-and-pop store.[5] Linking homeland security to these traditional professions both helped reinforce trust in first responders and also lent some comfort and familiarity to homeland security activities, giving the public a local face to trust. Having first responders represent homeland security to the public also linked the field firmly to the images of the firefighters, police officers, and emergency medical service personnel who died in the World Trade Center attacks and those who worked in the aftermath to try to find their fallen colleagues. It would be a mistake to underestimate the emotional response of large sections of the Boston-area public to these links. At the 2002 St. Patrick's Day Parade in South Boston, I could hear the roar that greeted the marching firefighters from more than a mile away. Two years later, people were still hugging police and firefighters in the street and thanking them for their sacrifice.

5. Robert McCloskey, *Make Way for Ducklings* (New York: Viking Press, 1941).

For a long period of time, this public support made those in or linked to the category "first responder" politically unassailable. No politician wanted to be associated with cutting their budgets, even when funds might have been more effectively used in some other aspect of homeland security. No homeland security event was complete without representation from the organizations associated with first response: police, fire, and EMS. Public and political absorption with first-responder organizations caused mixed feelings in the rest of the homeland security community. While some organizations wanted to see their roles recognized, many also recognized that their best hope for influencing opinions and resources might lie in building alliances with those in uniforms.

Tolerance of public safety dominance in homeland security affairs was more limited within the community. People got tired of having to play second fiddle, even in activities that were outside the purview of normal public safety activities, but did not want to be seen to be disrespectful of the dangers faced by traditionally defined first responders. Practical negotiations concerning who should decide about or do various things became mired in attempts to take authority without appearing to take it. Eventually, I and many others began to talk simply in terms of responders (without marking them as first or follow-on) and planners, in a somewhat hopeless attempt to avoid the controversy. In doing so, we tried to include those on the pre-event side of practice in the responder category under the assumption that they were responding to a perceived threat, if not an actual incident, as well as responders who might not be in the first wave of response but would participate as the incident developed.

It was an extraordinary amount of energy expended on controlling the definition of a category that had no practical weight, only the freight and power associated with it via the post-9/11 boost to the cultural capital of fire and police services. The highly public and political nature of the first-responder category also had implications for how much homeland security was associated with response, as opposed to other aspects of security, a situation described in the next section. Early in my time in the field, I expected that there might be a gradual shift toward an identity category that would encompass responders as well as others involved in the policy community, what Cheng described as a nascent identity (2004, 163). However, this never took shape for reasons linked to the meshing of homeland security practice with other concepts of emergency preparedness, as described later in this chapter.

The ability to negotiate roles and responsibilities and the kinds of things people wanted to negotiate changed a great deal during my time in the field. Many of the changes involved alterations in funding structures. Some of the grants and other funding streams that were stovepiped into specific disciplines, such as fire or hospital programs, began to be consolidated as federal and state governments tried to reorganize their funding around the concept of homeland security. In Massachusetts, the new director of the state's Executive Office of Public Safety announced that homeland security grant funds filtered through the state would be judged in part on evidence of collaboration among agencies. There is nothing like the possibility of thousands or millions in training and equipment funding to help rival agencies work out a truce about their relative responsibilities. Some legacy programs continued to encourage isolationism and turf wars, but Massachusetts and other states made significant changes in the patterns of behavior by dangling attractive carrots.

Other funding changes boosted the influence of organizations that had previously had little negotiating power. The Centers for Disease Control and Prevention and the Health Resources and Services Administration Cooperative Agreement grants for emergency health preparedness and bioterrorism programs provided funds through states to health departments, hospitals, laboratories, and other health organizations. For those organizations that chose to use it, these funds provided potential influence through the ability to include other agencies in training or exercising, as well as providing planning support for health emergencies. The federal mandate that a large percentage of homeland security dollars from the Department of Homeland Security distributed to states should be immediately redistributed to cities and towns gave these lower-level jurisdictions negotiating power with the states and with one another.

Not all the negotiations were associated with trying to gain or maintain power and resources. Some maneuverings focused more on shuffling off or resisting certain responsibilities. The most common type involved negotiations along vertical jurisdictional lines with each level choosing to assume that the other would take care of something and proving curiously resistant to clarifying expectations. The case of mass care clinics served (and continues to serve in many states) as an illustration. In the case of a disease outbreak for which prophylaxis and/or treatment is available, most states developed plans to hold public clinics for pharmaceutical dispensing. From the state point of view, it was up to the town or other substate region to plan the details of these clinics—how parking would be handled, how to find sufficient staff to manage the clinics for the right number of days, how to handle public information, and so forth. Often, however, towns or regions were assuming the same things about states. Faced with the highly complex planning and logistical tasks involved in developing mass clinic capacity, many simply chose to assume that the state would fill in the gaps.

In one community outside the Boston area, I spoke to somebody who would be in charge of operating a clinic for his area. As we discussed staffing shortages for an exercise, he said that in a real event it would be okay because the state would send all the necessary staff to operate the clinic for as long as needed. At first I thought he was joking, then I asked if he thought the state had enough staff to do that for all the clinics that would be running all over the state. He hesitated, then said, "Oh." It was impossible to tell whether he had really never considered this problem before or if his mind had just shuffled it off into the "too-hard box" and focused its attention on solvable problems.

Avoidance of defining certain roles and responsibilities showed up in other areas of homeland security as well. Sometimes the issue was that each level or discipline was choosing to assume that the other would handle something. Sometimes it was a planning gap that occurred between competing interests. I was never able to delve into it too deeply with people. I can only interpret the patterns I saw. Ultimately, some problems in homeland security cannot be solved without a huge increase in staff, a large shift in public behavior, or the emergence of some other unlikely factor. This was the case with airline security. Prior to the fall of 2001, most of the public was focused on convenience, not security. In cases such as these, jurisdictions or disciplines will develop plans that stop just short of one another's borders. Each party can show that they have addressed the problem as required by federal mandate or public opinion. So long as nobody examines the coordination of the plans too closely, the offending problem can be allowed to fall into the gap between them. At least until some anthropologist or journalist wanders in and asks, "What's that thing down there in that crack?"

This kind of pattern is not quite as self-serving as it might initially seem. There is little tolerance among politicians and commissioners for plans that are honest about fissures in the ability to respond or the need to rely on last-minute solutions because of inadequate continuing resources. The fire chief or public health official who turns in that kind of plan will spend most of his or her time trying to answer unanswerable questions to his or her higher-ups rather than working on things that are within the realm of the fixable. Still, this is a significant and dangerous pattern in the work of the community. It was through this kind of gap, one between the competing interests of consumers' wish for speedy airport processing and the need for airline security, that the hijackers of 9/11 were able to move. There is little question in my mind that this was the primary problem in New Orleans when Hurricane Katrina hit in 2005. What politician would have accepted a plan that realistically depicted the city's inability to evacuate its citizens but, rather, included a box showing that this issue still needed work? While planners may have known that there were problems, there was no list of things falling into the category of "We never figured out how to deal with this problem, so if something happens, call for outside help as quickly as you can."[6]

When I left the field, the business of figuring out which agencies would have which missions and skills and which types of roles would have what kinds of influence was still very much an ongoing concern. The absence of a national or even local consensus on what homeland security was going to be meant that the negotiations would be continual. As described above, both new and disappearing funding streams changed what was possible. Every new analysis from a scholar or journalist created new possibilities for how the country's emergency organizations would restructure themselves. Each shift in the structure of the federal government sent ripples through lower levels of jurisdiction and upset working relationship with federal field representatives.

HOMELAND SECURITY AND EXISTING MODELS OF PREPAREDNESS

It was immediately apparent to most locals involved in homeland security (and quickly became apparent to others) that it would be impossible to extricate homeland security fully from other aspects of public safety, emergency management, public health, and national security. As discussed in the previous chapter, the practical effect of this was that certain activities were intensified or given new emphases or new reporting outlets. On a more conceptual level, however, many people holding planning and policy roles in the community struggled to rearrange the blocks in the conceptual Rubik's Cube to show how homeland security was going to make sense with preexisting schemes. This is a rethinking that is still very much in process and will probably result in significant shifts in the

6. In 2005, I spent a good part of my time traveling around one state in New England trying to convince regional planning groups and local politicians not just to accept but to demand that their emergency preparedness and homeland security planners point out gaps in plans. The message was much easier for people to accept after Hurricane Katrina, but I have little sense that the spirit of openness will last.

conceptual apparatus used to understand and discuss all related fields of action.

An article in the *Washington Times* shortly after 9/11 tried to describe the cycle of homeland security: deterrence, prevention, preemption, crisis management, consequence management, attribution, and retaliation (McIntyre 2001). This definition replicates the outward focus of traditional national security frameworks and eliminates all but the most rudimentary references to minimizing or dealing with the consequences of the attack. The popular conception of U.S. national security in the last few decades has tended to focus outward. Until the 2002 implementation of the U.S. Northern Command (NORTHCOM), the U.S. military did not even have a full-force command operation that was specifically directed at defense of the geographic United States. Previous ideas and mechanisms for defense activities within the boundaries of the United States had withered with the decline of civil defense in the post–Cold War era. Even those civil defense concepts that still existed were more geared toward basic survival in a massive nuclear attack rather than the bewildering array of considerations involved in terrorism. Laws such as the Posse Comitatus Act of 1878, as well as practical considerations, made it unlikely that the military would take the lead role in the whole scope of activities involved in coping with terrorism (Drycus et al. 1997, 587; Trebilcock 2000). Ultimately, NORTHCOM and most other military organizations framed their involvement in terms of homeland defense rather than homeland security, although this began to change again after Hurricane Katrina in 2005. This back-and-forth highlights a connotative distinction, discussed in the introductory chapter, between the two terms that may or may not have been intentional on the part of the federal government and policymakers. Whether this distinction was deliberately used, it provided an opportunity for traditional national security organizations to extricate themselves from the messiness of domestic involvement except in a supportive role to civilian authorities.[7]

Historically, U.S. management of emergencies and disasters has been described as cyclical or phasic, such as mitigation, prevention, response, and recovery (Quarantelli 1995; Waugh 1990, 2000). This led some to plan and act as though emergency events will unfold in a tidy and limited manner over a manageable time frame. The ineffectiveness of linear mod-

---

7. The reasons for this are varied but include traditions associated with Posse Comitatus, historical events such as the 1970 shootings at Kent State, and the fact that military personnel were reduced by a third in the decade between 1989 and 1999 (Bruner 2004).

els was quickly apparent in the distinction between crisis management and consequence management. Presidential Decision Directive (PDD) 39 and PDD 62 led to the structural division between crisis management and consequence management (National Security Council 1996b, 1996c). The FBI was designated as the lead agency for crisis management and FEMA as the lead agency for consequence management. Crisis management was intended to address stopping an attack, arresting the terrorists, and gathering evidence for prosecution (Cordesman 2000, 2; National Security Council 1996a; Office of the Press Secretary 1998). Consequence management was meant to encompass all that might follow. This division between crisis and consequence management informed a great deal of subsequent legislation and program development.

Unfortunately, the distinction did not make a great deal of sense in practical operations. Crisis management was described in terms of law enforcement functions, with consequence management encompassing response and recovery operations. In reality, the needs of these two missions overlap in both time and geography. Bleeding patients are not left to wait while evidence is collected, and the local reality is that the organization in charge of rescue operations is likely to be in command of the incident at least until all critical life-safety operations are completed. Shortly after the whole country had the opportunity to watch the operations at the World Trade Center and Pentagon, the crisis management versus consequence management distinction began to disappear from policy.

The phase of trying to define homeland security as something distinct from other kinds of public safety, emergency management, and health activities ended quickly. Not only did people not have the staff to build up totally separate operations for homeland security; there was also simply no need to do so. People began to describe their plans as "all hazards" to indicate that, whenever possible, they would make procedures work for any event regardless of whether it was a natural disaster, an accident, or a deliberate attack. Framing practice in this way had the added benefit of allowing organizations to spend homeland security dollars on planning for events they felt were more likely to affect their communities.

Nowhere was this more apparent than in the public health and medical areas of the homeland security policy community. Public health programming in the United States declined under the application of business models to government programs during the 1980s and 1990s. In part, public health suffered from having an intangible product. On a good day, when everyone worked very hard and luck was with them, nothing happened. Nobody died of diphtheria, and SARS did not enter the country.

Water supplies did not poison users. Absence of harm is a hard product to sell to funding agencies under normal circumstances. Under federal grants for bioterrorism, public health agencies and hospitals have been able to start rebuilding some of the most basic pieces of infrastructure, such as disease surveillance systems, public information campaigns, and outreach programs.[8] They have also been able to start planning for large-scale bioterrorism events involving the need for mass care in ways that can be used just as easily for natural disease outbreaks such as SARS or pandemic influenza.

This "dual use" philosophy toward bioterrorism funding is not without critics. At academic conferences from 2001 to the present, the increase in terrorism funds to public health has been debated. Academics may worry about militarization of public health, drawing on a tradition of scholarship on the interaction of military and civilian aspects of society in the United States and elsewhere (Collier, Lakoff, and Rabinow 2004; Guillemin 2001; McEnaney 2000; McIlroy 1997; Mechling and Mechling 1991; Oakes 1994; Peattie 1984; Schoch-Spana 2004; Zarlengo 1999). Those voicing this concern hypothesize that if public health departments and medical facilities take funding or participate in programs that are framed as being part of national defense, the organizations will absorb more than the funding. They also may integrate models and ethics associated with the military, undermining their own hard-won institutional orientations and feeding into fear-based political manipulations.

The topic was no less controversial among practitioners. They voiced concern about the sustainability of any funding source with the word "terrorism" or "security" in its title. They feared that public interest in the topic would wane and funding pipelines wither as they did with U.S. Civil Defense programs in the past. Their concern was not only for programs specifically related to terror but also those that are carried by the funding. If protective masks were paid for using bioterrorism funds and those funds were cut, would the public understand that masks are also needed for day-to-day protection of health-care workers? If they funded two more public health–outreach workers using security funds, how would they explain their absence to the affected communities when that money goes away? Planners continue to fight their temptation to use bioterrorism preparedness money for broader projects out of concern that the connection to security will mask the more normal needs from the public

8. The previously mentioned Health Resources and Services Administration and CDC Co-operative Agreements with states were the most uniform large source of funds.

eye. Of the health fields, public health in particular has had to struggle for public visibility in the United States and is loathe to do anything that might make each component less individually visible. These dilemmas only add to the problem of trying to mesh homeland security with existing models of organizational practice and broader ideas of emergency management.

Other organizations in the community were interested in the all-hazards model for similar reasons. They remembered waning public interest in and support of civil defense programs and wanted to avoid a repetition with homeland security, especially if they were supporting other programs with the money. To a lesser degree, public safety has the same problem as public health in terms of having to sell absence. The Boston area saw many firehouses close between 2001 and 2003 because the number of fires in the area had dropped or because of town budget shortfalls (Dedman 2005). People voting on taxes and making appropriations were willing to risk a longer response time to fires in certain areas to save money. All practitioners in the homeland security community knew that if the country went for several years without an attack and without public knowledge of thwarted attacks, funding would begin to decline. The social ruptures facilitated by 9/11 and Katrina and sustained by public concerns about overseas wars might heal over without massive shifts in actual practice. The all-hazards approach attached a variety of activities to funding streams and made sustainability of programs and staff seem more realistic, although it is not clear whether that tactic will work, and as in the case of public health, it was sometimes controversial.

The all-hazards model also was attractive as a way to regulate the pace of homeland security practice. Immediately after 9/11, many organizations in the policy community entered crisis mode and were unable to get out of it. Without significant increases in staff, with unpredictable and unclear warnings from the federal government, and with the spotlight of public attention on them, there was tremendous pressure to be working constantly on security and constantly vigilant against possible attack. Some of the pressure also came from inside the organizations themselves. Many practitioners took their responsibility to the community very seriously. They felt that if they didn't do something about homeland security, it wouldn't happen and they would be responsible for the consequences of the next attack. This pressure, coupled with long shifts and frustrating politics, led to exhaustion and burnout. One informant described the need for the community to develop what he called a "battle rhythm," a pace and scope of practice that incorporated homeland security as part of the new normal working day rather than an immediate crisis. The all-hazards model diffused some of the intensity surrounding homeland security, linking it to other issues and practices and making it easier for people in the community to shift back down to a sustainable level of activity.

Many discussions I had about how to categorize homeland security ended up using variations on the basic four-phase theme of preparedness, mitigation, response, and recovery developed by those planning for natural disasters (Waugh 1990). These models, based exclusively on natural disasters, simply reverse the flaws of MacIntyre's externally focused cycle by removing consideration of things related to an attacker. People in the community tried to compensate by adding things about vulnerability assessment and prevention. Organizations within the policy community as well as think tanks are still playing with these conceptual categories, trying to come up with a discursive envelope that has utility for planners.

In the meantime, people in the community tried to figure out sets of concepts that could be used in policy and planning to include homeland security without treating it as an isolated set of practices. This did not happen in any systematic way, but people were forced to reconceptualize their work practices to make room for new homeland security missions and, in doing so, had to rethink their normal categories. My conversations with people in Boston homeland security and elsewhere led me to the conclusion that an attempt to develop firm definitions of any of these usual terms is doomed. At the level of practice, they all blend into one another. The concept of mitigation can serve as an example. Most discussions of emergency management use an operating definition of mitigation that is similar to FEMA's standard definition: "ongoing effort to lessen the impact disasters have on people's lives and property" (Federal Emergency Management Agency 2005). Generally speaking, this means things that can be done before an incident, such as reinforcing flood barriers, providing flood insurance to people at risk, making sure that hospital emergency rooms can be isolated from the rest of the hospital in case of contamination, installing smoke detectors and sprinklers, et cetera. All of these are activities that presume a harmful event might not be prevented and are intended to anticipate the possible consequences and minimize them. However, it is not clear when mitigation stops and response or recovery begins. In an incident where a hazardous materials spill requires decontamination of people, it might be normal practice to hose them down as quickly as possible, causing runoff into a nearby stream. If the town provides berms to contain the runoff, are they responding to the event or are they mitigating the consequences of runoff?[9] If there is runoff and they place absorbent barriers in the stream, are they recovering from the incident or are they mitigating the consequences for those downstream?

These may seem like small questions, but when it comes down to figuring out how you can spend mitigation funds or money for response supplies, they make a difference. Depending on the way homeland security and emergency preparedness is structured in the community, the distinctions may also have implications for who gets to make decisions about what gets done. The other common emergency management terms had similar problems. They were useful only down to a certain level of detail, and then they began to come apart at the seams. The practical reality for the community was that many of their activities could fall into many different categories, such as the physical barriers described in the last chapter, which were a prevention technique but were also felt to have a deterrent effect.

The full homeland security community in the Boston area included those involved in activities that could be categorized as threat/hazard surveillance and detection, deterrence, prevention, preemption, preparedness (including risk assessment), mitigation, response (including law enforcement and investigation), continuity of operations for business and government, and recovery. My key informants tended to be most focused on the preparedness and response categories, so my knowledge of this debate regarding other areas is limited.[10] As of this writing, local people seem to be moving away from trying to revise existing categories around the theme of homeland security. It seems to be losing some of its power as a driving concept to be accommodated. Instead, people seem to be taking one of two approaches. Either they talk about homeland security as a slightly broadened version of normal emergency management, or they associate it almost exclusively with terrorism and describe it as just another mission that flows through the structures they have created, like wildfires, drug-related crime, or disease outbreak investigation. Either way, homeland

9. Berms are the emergency management equivalent of kiddie pools. They are watertight (and often chemical-resistant) sheets with raised sides. A person or thing to be decontaminated is placed inside the berm so that the contamination is contained as it is removed.

10. In particular, I suspect that homeland security activities may form a more distinct set of practices for agencies, such as the FBI, that are heavily involved in trying to prevent attacks and find potential attackers.

security influenced the conceptual and practical structures the community uses but did not subsume them.

This is not necessarily the case at the federal level, where the Department of Homeland Security now encompasses natural and human-made disasters, parts of bioterrorism programs but not the rest of public health, some information analysis and sharing activities, and some but not all federal law enforcement. The Transportation Security Agency, created rapidly after 9/11 to handle airline screening, is now facing the privatization of its screening force. As was the case immediately before and after 9/11, the federal approach to security within the United States is shifting and difficult to predict. Local policy communities continue to try figure things out enough to get on with daily work while keeping an eye on the federal weather.

CREATING AND MAINTAINING A SHARED SENSE OF COMMUNITY

In the face of this conceptual, practical, and political mess, key homeland security practitioners recognized the need for there to be some sense of shared mission, reasonably common terminology, shared understandings of goals and operating parameters, and something approaching consensus on who would be involved in activities. They also had to find ways for organizations in the community to have legitimacy with one another, with politicians, and with the public when working on homeland security issues. The avenues used to create community are described in more detail in the next chapter, which is concerned with how homeland security work gets done. However, it is important to mention that topic here because these activities were one of the most significant and unrecognized ways that homeland security practitioners spent their time.

It is important to recognize that this was essentially an acephalous process and that there was no storybook ending yielding an organized approach to homeland security. While there were several official leaders with positions of authority, no one person or organization emerged with a broad-enough mandate to sway the full community. It was more of an accumulation of ongoing efforts to counteract the centrifugal inertia of organizations with other things to do than a process with a direction and an end goal. As will be described below, there were some official attempts to institutionalize homeland security or at least what was planned for response to terrorism, but none worked during my time in the field. The situation and the combination of possible players were simply too complex and too tense for a standardized, inflexible system to encompass.

My informants did not explicitly describe a need to build and maintain the policy community as a viable and legitimate means of coping with homeland security, but the idea resonated with them. They tended to talk in terms of needing to have everyone "reading off the same page" or "get to the point where we stop fighting with each other and start thinking about the people who want to hurt us" or "think about living up to the public trust." They spent a lot of time discussing the need for relationships that were solid before an event took place. There was also talk about presenting a "unified front," although this always seemed to refer to working with politicians and the public rather than as a way of confronting a feared terrorist. As a result of that type of comment, it is easy to see this cynically, as a way for organizations to avoid criticism, and there is no doubt that some attempts to create a more unified approach to homeland security were supported because it would give organizations some breathing room. However, that interpretation would be no less simplistic than one that attributed only the noblest motivations to community members. Many people involved in homeland security in the Boston area took the public trust placed in them very seriously and felt that it was important to "get it right." They wanted both to be effective in protecting the public and to be reassuring to the public, two things that did not necessarily coincide, as described in the previous chapter.

A big part of building and maintaining the community involved making sure that anyone who might have valuable information, assets, or a role to play felt included in homeland security activities, was able to understand what other organizations were talking about, and was involved in figuring out what should get done. This meant inviting people to meetings, asking their opinions when decisions were made, and ensuring that they got a share of the recognition when things went well. A policy of inclusion rather than exclusiveness was sometimes an uphill battle against old rivalries, perceived slights, and general pigheadedness. In Boston, there were old turf-war scars between the Fire Department and Boston EMS, both of which had roles in providing emergency medical care. Police and fire services in many of the Boston area's communities had long-standing tensions resulting from disputes about who had control of incident scenes. In most cases, these tensions were diffused with jokes and banter, but they were part of the landscape. Because of the acephalous nature of the community, efforts were disjointed and sporadic, but almost all the key players recognized the importance of getting people to the table as part of building a shared concept of homeland security.

A serious example of the problems faced by people trying to get those in the policy community to work actively with one another involved that of health organizations. Health organizations, especially hospitals, had reputations for holding themselves above working with the public safety community, of considering themselves too busy or too important to participate. People on both sides of the divide accused one another of speaking in impenetrable jargon. This tension was compounded by the attitudes of some individuals who "talked down" to members of the public safety community, mistaking a lack of academic degrees for a lack of skills and technical knowledge. One emergency room physician said to me, "Those people have to understand that we can't just drop everything and do exercises. We have stuff going on, work to do," as though public safety and other organizations were just sitting on their hands all day. A public health official in another geographic area complained about attempts to use the standard Incident Command System in an exercise. He said that he wasn't against the system. He just didn't think it would work in public health situations where specialized knowledge and technical skill had to be applied over a wide area. I knew that this individual understood that the Incident Command System had been designed to coordinate the use of highly differentiated fire and logistical technical expertise in wildfires spread over thousands of square miles. I responded, "Good thing those fires out in California can be put out with just a bunch of dumb firefighters randomly spraying water!" before my anthropological censor could step in. I had reached the point where the arrogance was even beyond my patience as a researcher. The fact that Boston public health and hospitals participated in as many initiatives, planning sessions, and exercises as they did during my time in the field is a testament to the perseverance of a few individuals on both sides who were willing to keep pushing the inclusion despite the attitude in both camps.

When community members pushed for inclusion, tried to bring the policy community together, and worked to build local capacity, they had to contend with "experts," often known as "Beltway bandits" in reference to their lobbying for contracts in Washington, D.C. These were individuals who were marketing their knowledge of emergency management or security to the press, businesses, and governments. In some cases, they were motivated by a sincere desire to provide good information. More often the primary motive was profit, sometimes, but not always, coupled with an ethic of doing well by doing good. For specialized technical knowledge, or for events that happened infrequently, such as large exercises, political leaders found it more efficient to bring in outside talent than to spend the time and money developing it at home. This practice not only deprived the policy community of opportunities to come together to develop solutions. It also undermined local capacity. People in the community were very concerned that once the flood of homeland security funding dried up or became more carefully channeled, the experts would go away, leaving the community without the expertise it needed. Use of outsiders also meant that existing structures and mechanisms, as well as new ones, were not always built to operate with only locally available resources and knowledge.

Some preexisting mechanisms, such as mutual aid networks, helped create a sense of community among different organizations. These established channels of information and resource sharing and problem solving served as patterns for cooperative efforts and sources of narratives about successful interagency collaborations in the past. Unfortunately, efforts to get divergent organizations to work together were also occasionally hampered by well-intentioned efforts to institutionalize homeland security by developing new mechanisms. In Massachusetts, one such initiative was called the Statewide Anti-Terrorism Unified Response Network (SATURN), which was intended to foster community-based preparedness by bringing together representatives from key agencies to joint information and training sessions, fostering relationships, and building a common body of knowledge and terminology. At an unspecified future date, the network was supposed to be linked to a notification and information-sharing communication system. Rolled out with great public fanfare, SATURN did seem to be accepted by some smaller communities looking for a way to pull people together. Unfortunately, I found many people in the Boston area either totally unaware that they were supposed to be involved or confused about what the system was supposed to be. Once explained, the idea was a little too "cute" for some in the homeland security policy community. Towns were supposed to develop Red, White, and Blue Teams, with Red representing fire, White representing emergency management, and Blue representing police. As people in the community were quick to point out, the plan did not include the organizations that were proving most difficult in terms of developing working relationships, such as public health and hospitals. There were other omissions in the SATURN model, and its first few months of life were marred by meetings and explanations trying to backfill the network. After the initial rollout, few people heard anything about SATURN, and eventually the state secretary of public safety who had spearheaded it was replaced. The network seemed to disappear, although references to it still exist. Even had the program been more inclusive, it is not clear whether it would have been adopted by the policy community, many of whom seemed to prefer building and maintaining the policy community through the flexible task-based organizations and initiatives described in the next chapter.

In the absence of large-scale homeland security operations, one of the most common ways used to bring the community together and develop a shared social field of action was the meeting. As described in chapter 4, there were meetings about broad homeland security planning, about dealing with specific threats or vulnerabilities, about how the area was going to handle certain federal mandates, and about how to coordinate plans. With Schwartzman (1993) and Zabusky (1995, 2000), I argue that meetings were not simply vehicles for other activities but were, themselves, socially constitutive practices. Although they struggled to articulate it, it was clear that people in the community had some understanding of this as well. Meetings were a confusing issue for many in the community because their community-enhancing and relationship-building aspects were not officially recognized as part of homeland security work. My informants knew that more than the meeting topic got accomplished, but many were also part of organizational cultures that considered meetings to be worse than useless. Perhaps in response to that, people discussed the conversations that took place before and after meetings as the time when things actually "get done." In a sense this was true. These side conversations, without the confusion of many voices, were often where people were able to arrive at concrete proposals or figure out how to work around a particular impasse.

However, the perception that these sidebars were the times when all the work got done and that nothing was accomplished in the official meetings was a superficial assessment. It was a perspective slanted toward an understanding of the "work" of homeland security as operational rather than contextual and social. The operational definition, while valid, is incomplete, and people sensed it, even if they did not articulate it. Building interagency cooperation, coordination, and communication takes more than a set of operational procedures. People who were expected to participate in this new realm needed to know one another face-to-face. They needed to recognize one another, to be familiar with personality quirks, strengths, and weaknesses. This knowledge needed to be part of the background of the response rather than part of the pile of uncertainties. Personal relationships, in combination with official relationships, formed a safety net both for operations and for the preparatory work that lead up to operations.

Beyond what information-sharing and decision-making people managed to accomplish in them, meetings served a critical function in bringing people together outside of exercises or actual responses in order to build relationships and knowledge of one another. They were especially important in building the inclusive approach to homeland security. It was better to have people become acquainted with one another at meetings than to expect them to work well together if they met for the first time during an incident. Building these personal relationships was not acknowledged as part of the work of homeland security in part because traditional personal relationships were taken for granted and in part because they were treated as though they compensated for a dysfunctional official structure or for incompetence that blocked the official structure. This lack of acknowledgment often led to frustration on the part of individuals who felt as though they spent "all my time in meetings and none getting work done." It also generated difficulties in funding. Developing the work context and the personal relationships necessary to that context were not seen as fundable activities. They were treated as things that should happen in the context of normal daily work, as opposed to discrete goals. The funding obstacle should not be underestimated. Staff hours are expensive whether spent in meeting or operations, but it is a lot easier to get budget increases by citing increased numbers of fires extinguished or patients served than with a list of meetings attended. Part of the quasi-applied work I did in the community was to help organizations find ways to articulate interagency network building as a fundable part of capacity building.

Meetings also were one of the key avenues for developing shared understandings and terminology. Building shared understandings was less a conscious effort than an incremental process. At the beginning of my fieldwork, almost every possible concept of the homeland security mission was on the table. Gradually, some ideas—like the possibility of a federal agency that would develop a robust local presence to coordinate local homeland security or the idea of developing a local credentialing system for delivery vehicles—slid off the table. Nobody pushed them off. After a number of meetings at which certain ideas were not discussed, people simply forgot about them and began to take what remained on the table for granted.

Common terminology or at least mutually understood terminology was more actively pursued. People were very conscious of the confusion that could result when an acronym or code word meant different things to different organizations. Sometimes it was not that one term meant different things to different people, but that people were using different terms to refer to roughly the same thing. An example of the latter case is the difficulty in describing what weapons a terrorist might use. Common terms included WMD (weapons of mass destruction), CBW (chemical and biological weapons), NBC (nuclear, biological, and chemical), and CBRNE (chemical, biological, radiological, nuclear, and explosive). All were in use more or less interchangeably when I started in the field, and all are still in use, although CBW is almost gone and CBRNE is becoming common enough that people have begun using it as a word, pronounced "seeburn" or "seeburney." While nobody seemed interested in coming up with a whole new set of terms and acronyms specifically for homeland security, they were very willing to talk about potential problems when they arose.

In a relatively delicate interagency situation, it would have been difficult to ask any organization to give up its own jargon and use somebody else's. In some cases, however, an organization might agree to do so on its own. At least, when issues were discussed, it was possible for everyone to be aware that there might be different terms flying around. Over the time I was with the community, it became common for people to start presentations or discussions with a request that people interrupt if unfamiliar terms started being used. I also noticed that a number of securely placed individuals in the community, those who could afford to look a bit foolish, would take advantage of the offer.[11] In one case, I sent out an e-mail to several people, proud that I had absorbed so much of the local terminology that I could use the acronyms. A few hours later, one of the recipients, the director of Commonwealth Security, called me with a joking reprimand because my e-mail was too full of acronyms for him to understand. These individuals normalized asking for clarification for those in more tenuous positions and made it clear that being ignorant of another agency's terminology was not a reflection of your professional skill. In fact, the shared misery created by different terminology came to be one of the bonding points for the community. Everyone had a silly jargon story to tell. People made jokes about the "alphabet soup" of federal agencies and referred to hazardous materials as "methylethylawfylstuff."

Shared or overlapping stories, jokes, and other narratives became one of the most critical ways that homeland security practitioners could develop a sense of community and legitimacy. Stories of shared experiences, from what a person had done on 9/11 to the shared misery of sitting in a particularly noxious town budget hearing, became things to talk about

11. The role of this type of individual is discussed in chapter 8, in the section on "pathfinders."

over coffee before a meeting. When the national color-coded alert system was unveiled, everyone in the community, from the crustiest fire chief to the most pompous doctor, could find a way to share a joke about it.

Because of the rapid pace of change in community membership, context, and practice, the structure and meaning of these stories were not fixed but, rather, were created in the telling and receiving (Briggs and Bauman 1995). These narratives, or more accurately, the practice of forming and repeating them, were a powerfully constitutive aspect of practice in this community, as has been demonstrated elsewhere (Briggs 2004; Briggs and Bauman 1995). Telling the success stories of other organizations was an important way to demonstrate or enforce inclusiveness. When somebody hesitated at accepting involvement of the National Guard Civil Support Team, somebody from the fire or police services could get up and tell about how they had learned to use important equipment through the free training offered by the team or how team members had responded to an incident and worked for hours without expecting any recognition. Old interagency projects, such as old exercises or special events, were dragged out, dusted off, and displayed to show new community members that it was possible to get things done using an interagency model.

Creating internal and external legitimacy for the policy community was and continues to be somewhat more complex. In contrast to the studies of legitimacy construction in peacekeeping, no shared names, titles, or symbols can be used because there is no official overarching structure to which all members belong and because formal institutionalization of the community was not an overt goal of its members (Rubinstein 1993, 1998b). Inside the community, stories of joint efforts were very important, especially those that described local efforts in contrast to federal bungling or public misunderstanding. Response to the rash of calls that came in about suspected anthrax powder in the wake of the anthrax attacks in 2001 serves as a common theme in many of these stories. People were working long shifts with no days off, trying to figure out the implications of the 9/11 attacks, and, on top of it, they managed to send at least some representative to every citizen call about white powder. The fact that nobody blew up at the woman who called in because she found white powder in her laundry room (or at the people who made many similar calls) was taken as a point of pride and a demonstration of the capacity of responders and planners to handle local affairs effectively.

Every successful operation, exercise, or policy coup created more stories that could be used to bond people and make them feel that they were the right people to be charged with handling local homeland security. On

December 22, 2001, Richard Reid, who became known in the media as "the shoe bomber," tried to light explosive devices on a transatlantic flight from Paris to Miami, Florida. Had he succeeded, he would have almost assuredly caused the crash of the plane, which was carrying 184 passengers and fourteen crew members, including a number of children. He was stopped by a combination of passengers and crew, and the flight was diverted to Logan International Airport in Boston. Although Reid's shoes had been taken away, those charged with removing him from the plane had no way of knowing if he had other explosive devices on himself or elsewhere on the airplane. The interagency effort to remove him and secure the airplane was complex and tense but ultimately successful. People told this story and others of thwarted attacks as part of a chain of narratives used to reinforce an idea of competency that boiled down to "We can do this. It's hard, but we are perfectly competent to work together and figure it out." Similar transformations took place in stories of the response to attacks on 9/11. They became imbued with themes of recovery and improvement rather than loss, a shift that was shared with the larger cultural narratives of 9/11 in the United States (White 2004).

For public appearances of officials, most narratives I heard tended to focus on the premise that homeland security was nothing new, that they had been thinking about this long before 9/11, and that it just meant a little extra effort and a little bit more of everyone pulling together. Many discussions with reporters or presentations to the public started with phrases like "Well, we were a little ahead of the curve on this terrorism stuff," or "Actually, we had been sending our guys to training for dealing with bioterrorism before the anthrax attacks." Most of these narratives of preparedness started with a "well" or an "actually" or some other conversational marker to indicate that the audience should be prepared for things to be a little different from their expectations. This would be followed by one or two concrete examples of something related to terrorism that the organization or town could point to as having been done before the rest of the country got its wake-up call. The stories would go on to provide illustrations of the increased work that was taking place to address homeland security concerns and, sometimes, make mention of the staffing and resource constraints that hindered progress. The braver narrators might go on to talk about how homeland security problems wouldn't be solved overnight and that local people had to be in for the long haul in terms of taking responsibility for their own homes and families and in terms of supporting the organizations involved. Once the all-hazards model became more common, it also became a feature of these narratives as a way of demonstrating how the organization or town was making wise use of available resources rather than simply jumping on the homeland security bandwagon.

Very few people were willing to say publicly that they had never considered terrorism before 2001. Fortunately, the federal programs started in the late 1990s, as well as the personal initiative of many in the community, made it possible to describe some pre-9/11 efforts honestly. These preparedness narratives were not untrue, but they were (and continue to be) incomplete. People presenting one of them to the public rarely go into the larger issues of how difficult it is to fit homeland security into existing work and institutional patterns and how intractable some of the problems have become.

In the first two years after the 9/11 attacks, there was intense public debate about the actions and inactions of the government in the years leading up to the attacks. Either the Clinton administration had failed to take action in time or the Bush administration had failed to heed the warnings of the outgoing Clinton administration. Even as there was concern over increased domestic surveillance, there also was criticism of a lack of sharing between the FBI and the CIA. People argued about intelligence failures. Richard Clark, outspoken critic of pre- and post-9/11 counterterrorism and homeland security policy—known in some federal circles as "hair-on-fire guy"—was quoted in the *New York Times* as saying, "Democracies don't prepare well for things that have never happened before" (Miller, Gerth, and Van Natta 2001).

While a detailed analysis of this period of public discourse is well beyond the scope of this research, it felt, in the field at the time, like most of this critique was directed at traditional national security organizations rather than local organizations. The local "ahead of the curve" narratives served (and continue to serve) one purpose and they do it well, whether it is a good idea or not. They help maintain or restore public trust that local agencies are doing something about homeland security, that they are competent to do so because they were thinking about it long before the rest of us and because they have the best interest of the communities at heart.

This kind of trust helps deflect attention from other issues, both foolish and realistic. It helps minimize the amount of public demand for plans dealing with every conceivable contingency, realistic or not. Unfortunately, it also contributes to public inattention when important gaps exist in plans or capacity. In terms of the overall legitimacy of the homeland security policy community, public performances of preparedness narratives are most effective when delivered from a platform that includes many agencies. For homeland security in the Boston area, as in many other locations around the country, the public was being asked to place its trust in an acephalous network rather than one agency with a concrete building and a spokesperson. The various forms of the preparedness narrative, delivered with multiple agencies present, gave people local faces in which to place their faith.

All of these narratives, whether delivered to one another or to the public, had the effect of creating bonds among community members and reminding them of their shared mission and responsibilities. Like so much in the policy community, they were not so much narratives that described an ideal or a state of affairs. Rather, they concretized the idea of a shared process or struggle to figure out what homeland security was going to mean for Boston and how it was going to get done.

As has been found in analysis of peacekeeping missions, the constitutive power of concepts and narratives often lies not in their individual acceptance and merits (Rubinstein 1993, 552). Rather it is found in the use of the symbols, rituals, practices, and narratives over time in a variety of settings. The daily business of getting homeland security work done was a generative process. In the small negotiations, reassessments, and fostering of relationships, people in the policy community challenged each other's models and began the process of transforming disparate orientations and knowledges into a loosely constructed and flexible hybrid. As described earlier, this hybridity of community practice and its reconstructive nature was similar to what is seen in situations where ideas, practices, and cultures are brought into contact through the processes of globalization (Ferguson and Gupta 2002; Hannerz 1987; Jackson 1995; Nygren 1999). It would be no more realistic to label one account of homeland security practice as authentic than it would be to essentialize any one version of a culture.

Daily practice in the policy community was dynamic, heterogeneous, and contentious. It consisted in something very similar to what Zabusky found in her research on the cooperative venture of the European Space Agency: "the ongoing negotiation of the often irreconcilable differences . . . that proceeds through conflict and ambiguity as much as through solidarity and orderliness" (1995). Or, to put it more plainly, they were figuring it out as they went along, just thinking out loud.

CHAPTER 8 // MAINTAINING FLEXIBILITY: HOW THE WORK GETS DONE

INTRODUCTION

This chapter is about the avenues people in the community use to get work done in a chaotic and confusing environment while maintaining the flexibility of relationships and practice that characterized community action during my time in the field. This introduction outlines the underlying reasons for the community's resistance to institutionalization and its efforts to remain flexible. The next four sections outline patterns I discovered in how the community gets work done. The first addresses the importance of pathfinder individuals who could take the community in new directions despite the confusing and frustrating circumstances. The second section covers the importance of affiliations and channels, both informal and formal, in how the community coordinated and shared. The role of temporary task-based organizations in maintaining flexibility is addressed in the third section. The fourth describes the importance and dangers of tacit knowledge as a community asset.

MAINTAINING FLEXIBILITY

People involved in homeland security immediately following 9/11 faced an unusual set of challenges that one practitioner likened to trying to assemble a 747 in midflight without instructions and with no clear sense of how soon or where the finished product would have to land. Any venture of this sort yields both conflict and cooperation, failures and successes. I have chosen to focus on the cooperative aspects of this community, believing with Ortner that the centrality of domination and conflict in the analysis of practice has led to inadequate attention to patterns of cooperation that are of equal importance in understanding everyday life (1984, 157). Early in my time in the field, I became fascinated with watching people figure out how to work together in circumstances where there were so many tensions and opportunities for misunderstanding and conflict. I do not mean to diminish the importance of these conflicts, but they have been the subject of so much attention that any search of major news sources from 2001 to 2006 will produce plenty of accounts. The same is not true for cooperation.

I also have been influenced in this choice by Zabusky's excellent ethnographic account of cooperation in European space science. As she points out, cooperation "must be understood as something that is actively accomplished in terms of conflict and not despite or without it" (Zabusky 1995). In this chapter I describe some of the cooperative processes people in the community used to get work done while maintaining flexibility in their relationships and practices.

People in the community both hoped and feared that some higher level of government, most likely the federal government, would take the lead in figuring out what needed to get done and how to do it. They hoped for this because the problem was very messy. As described in previous chapters, there was both practical and conceptual work to do, and no one state or local organization had the mandate to make final judgments or push for consensus. Classification rules and a more general federal tradition of withholding detailed intelligence from locals meant that the information needed to arrive at realistic solutions was not available to everyone who would have to be involved in making decisions at the local level. Resources were stretched thin for normal public safety and health work, and some hoped that if homeland security was driven by the federal government that new federal dollars would be provided to cover costs. On the response side, where I spent most of my time, homeland security was primarily an analytic and planning task. For many in training and operations-focused organizations, such as fire services, another desk job was not particularly welcome, especially when it seemed impossible to understand the larger context of homeland security in which they were supposed to be planning.

However, most of my informants simultaneously feared federal involvement. They wanted to know what the larger national picture would be, but they did not want the federal government to dictate what homeland security would mean for the area. No one solution could possibly work for all geographic locations. Any federal mandate would have to interface with the specific physical, historical, and social characteristics of the area, accounting for the complex configurations these characteristics imposed on all homeland security activities from prevention to response and recovery. During 2002 and 2003, while the federal government reorganized itself, the practitioners in the Boston area perceived increasing pressure to codify their practices into written plans and to institutionalize their relationships. It is difficult to distinguish among the specific pressures coming from state and federal agencies, state and local politicians, the press, and the general public, and those pressures that were perceived in a more general way as a result of the sociocultural shifts taking place across the country. It is not my purpose to do so here. Regardless of the source or validity, people felt the pressure and reacted to it both consciously and unconsciously.

Codification of practice and institutionalization of relationships were problematic for the community for several reasons. As has been found in other cooperative projects, resistance to formalization of structure and practice arose in part from people's attempts to keep themselves free (Zabusky 1995). However, this desire for freedom was not necessarily based in a need to preserve professional autonomy. In the homeland security community, the concern was much more pragmatic. All organizations had general emergency operations plans and sets of procedures for various tasks but not detailed narratives of actual practice at specific incidents or operations.

Codification of practice would have meant putting a tremendous amount of labor into writing down expected responses to every imaginable type of incident, at every possible location, involving every possible combination of circumstances. This was not practical for reasons that are discussed in more detail below, in the section titled "Tacit Knowledge." Community members were also concerned about the security risks of written plans. You don't necessarily want to have fully articulated accounts of your response written down where they could fall into the hands of somebody who will use them to find gaps and vulnerabilities. It seemed safer to have the broad outlines in the written plan with the details trained into the minds of the people who would be carrying them out. However, reluctance to create detailed plans was also influenced by concerns about accountability. If you know that your resources are inadequate to handle a particular situation, you don't necessarily want to publicize the fact by

FIGURE 5. A rainy, low-visibility morning spent guarding a normally stationary land-mark, the USS *Constitution*, as it makes one of its infrequent "turnarounds" in the busy port at the same time that a large cruise ship puts into the Black Falcon Cruise Terminal and the landing path of a plane headed for Logan Airport takes it across the harbor. (Special thanks to the master and crew of the Coast Guard vessel *Flying Fish* for allowing me along.) Photo by author.

writing a detailed plan describing what you should be able to do. If you are not able to manage your relationships with other agencies well enough to coordinate plans with them, you don't necessarily want those short-comings highlighted in your operating procedures.

Institutionalization of relationships raised similar concerns. Docu-menting and formalizing expectations of relationships would have meant accounting for the same bewildering sets of possible circumstances as codification of plans. It also would have meant having to end old rivalries in an official and organizationally broad-based way, something that was not likely when competition for resources was still keen. It was much simpler to ease around old tensions in an unofficial and personal way, as described in the following sections.

However, the most significant reason for community resistance to the institutionalization of practice and relationships was pragmatic. There was no way to tell what the big picture of homeland security would be. Nobody knew if there would be a federal organization specifically geared toward homeland security. Nobody knew what the goals of homeland security would be. Nobody knew if homeland security would become permanently separated in policy and funding from traditional public safety, public health, and emergency management practice. Nobody knew how much authority the federal and state governments would ultimately receive or how much responsibility (practical and financial) they would take for day-to-day activities. Nobody knew whether there might be whole new agencies created at the state and local levels to take some of homeland security off the hands of existing organizations.

One of most persistent demands on the community was that homeland security activities be coordinated among agencies across disciplines, across horizontal and vertical jurisdictions, but it was impossible to predict what shapes and directions those other organizations, disciplines, and jurisdictions might take. Rumors circulated constantly about what might be happening next in homeland security policy and organization. They ranged from ideas that homeland security would become the new unifying vision for government agencies to the belief that this would all blow over when there were no subsequent attacks and everything would go back to "normal." Nobody wanted to be in the position of having solidified all their plans and relationships only to find out that policy had changed overnight and they now had to reorganize themselves completely. It is also important to recognize that everyone in the homeland security policy community had other things to do than follow and react to every flutter in the national policy landscape.

With staff shortages and competing demands on time and resources, it seemed essential to keep plans, practices, and relationships as flexible as possible. This allowed the community to shift around obstacles and stretch itself to meet changing demands on its time and resources. However, it also was necessary for organizations and individuals within the community to be able to get homeland security work done and to demonstrate that work to politicians and the public. There were varied strategies for accomplishing this, but significant successful patterns emerged that may be transferable to other policy communities operating in times of change. The homeland security policy community in the Boston area got work done through the initiative of people who were able to step outside the normal bounds of expected behavior or opinion by exploiting informal channels and nontraditional relationships, by focusing efforts on temporary task-based organization, and by relying on tacit knowledge and personal relationships.

A caveat is necessary before discussing each of these largely unofficial strategies for getting things done. It is important to keep in mind the distinction between planning or workaday attitudes toward how things should be done and the attitudes during response activities. Most of my experience was in activities of the former sort. In my conversations about response activities and in the few limited observations I was able to conduct, I could see that there was more overt respect for official channels and processes during response. Personal relationships and tacit knowledge still play critical roles during responses, but they are managed through more official structures. Throughout this section, I will note when I am referring to response activities. All other references are to planning and other nonresponse practices.

THINKING OUT LOUD

As in any community, the Boston area's homeland security policy community had exceptional individuals who shaped practice and ideas, who were popular representatives of the group, were valued for their political savvy, and/or were seen as "go-to guys" for getting information or assistance.[1] These individuals were important to the daily work and maintenance of the policy community, but in the work of figuring out what homeland security was going to mean for the Boston area, they were joined by others of equal or possibly greater importance. Lacking a better term, I will refer to these individuals as the pathfinders of the policy community. For one of several reasons discussed below, those acting as pathfinders were less constrained by convention and were more willing to take chances in looking foolish or raising the ire of other community members for suggesting unpopular things. These are the people who were "just thinking out loud here" in the most effective ways. They did the conceptual heavy lifting for the community by being willing to try out new ideas, to fall on their faces and get back up, and by example making it easier for others to speak up. They also were the people who could call out the emperor's new clothes, pointing out gaps, poorly designed plans, and logical impossibilities of funding, and raising other topics necessary for the community to remain accountable to itself and the public.

A good example is interoperability of communications. This was a very

---

1. Interestingly, I found that the term "go-to guy" seemed to be applied equally to males or females, although I was not able to do a systematic survey of usage. Sometimes it was applied to females with a touch of awkwardness, as though the speaker wasn't sure it was appropriate, while at other times it was applied without any apparent hesitation or notice.

hot topic while I was in the field, but most of the discussion centered on the technological reasons that people were not able to communicate—incompatible radios and so on. Pathfinders did most of the work of getting the policy community to recognize that there were also behavioral and procedural reasons for such problems. Even though the radios of two organizations may allow communication, if one person does not know to pass information along to the other or uses unfamiliar jargon, communication will not occur. After 9/11, many in the response community bemoaned the fact that interoperability issues prevented the police helicopters from notifying firefighters when it looked as though one of the World Trade Center Towers was going to come down. Later accounts indicated that although fire services did not have access to the live video feeds from the helicopters, police did pass along some warnings and could have shared additional information. However, there were not procedures in place to remind them to do so, and the mechanisms to get that information back to fire command were not clear. In part, this was because neither police nor fire followed their official procedures, which would have put a fire representative in a helicopter during such an event. It took a brave and politically protected person to point out the error, as it was much easier for everyone to think that it had been impossible, not just an oversight.

I do not wish to suggest that the community was systemically averse to new ideas, challenges, or debate, but it was subject to the normal afflictions of American groups. People did not want to suggest things that might upset their bosses or mark them as troublemakers the next time they were up for promotion. Some people did not want to say or hear new ideas because they were somehow hoping that the whole thing would blow over and they could go back to their normal jobs. The concern I heard most often was "I don't want to sound like an idiot." In a social arena of great change, nobody could reasonably assume that he or she was up-to-date on all the most recent rumors, news reports, and policy changes. There was so much change, so many new possibilities, that it was overwhelming for a great many people in the community. Opening your mouth on any topic made you vulnerable to appearing ill-informed, something no more popular in the homeland security policy community than in any other group. Under such circumstances it was quite possible for people to miss important information-sharing and idea-generating opportunities. One pathfinder standing up and asking the right question could open the discussion and make everyone a little more comfortable in the imperfection of their information.

Pathfinders tended to fall into one of four categories: marginal, liminal, old-timers, and untouchables.[2] These categories are described below, but it is very difficult to provide examples or stories without compromising confidentiality. Pathfinders were not exactly rare, but they were noticeable and any illustration of a specific activity would be instantly identifiable. The temptation is great to illustrate for the simple reason that many of them have put themselves at far more risk than I could manage with a few ethnographic examples, but I believe that choice should remain theirs, not mine.

Some pathfinders held marginal positions in the community. In some cases, this was because the community did not fully accept them.[3] In others, it was because they had no designs on being fully integrated. Either they had very little status to protect or their views were not seen as threatening. In one case, a person was detailed from a political office to work in the community. He was something of an idealist and often pushed the limits of what could be expected of people in the course of an already long workday. His connection to the politician (in contrast to his colleagues' own allegiance to their organizations) allowed others to disassociate him and disregard what he said if it did not suit them. Rather than allowing this to silence him, this individual made use of it. Since his ideas could be disregarded, he felt free to suggest just about anything that came to mind. Consequently, many ideas that might not otherwise have been expressed were floated at least once. If they were thought to be valuable, others could pick them up and champion them.

Other marginal pathfinders came from professions that were not likely to ever have a seat at the policy community table, such as academics. Researchers were assumed to be a little flaky, a bit idealistic, and ignorant of the realities of what it took to get practical work done. I fell into this category, although in a very limited way, along with the few other academics

2. I distinguish here between marginal and liminal for practical, not theoretical, purposes. Marginal pathfinders were those who had roles wholly outside preparedness and intersected with the policy community only in one aspect of their work lives. These people also shared a characteristic of not being fully accepted as complete community members. Liminal pathfinders were those who were in transition (or close to transition) between two roles associated with preparedness or preparedness organizations.

3. I have some limited indications that sex and gender sometimes marginalized community members and led to the same opportunities for being outspoken. Unfortunately, the majority of people involved in homeland security planning in the organizations in which I spent most of my time were white, male, and apparently heterosexual. There were simply not enough data to tell whether what I was seeing was based on personality, sex, gender, or some other factor.

who ventured into the community during this time period. While some people intentionally sought out my opinion so they could get an outsider's perspective, most assumed my ideas would be "ivory tower" impractical. People assumed I would ask strange questions and they were free to ignore anything I said. Consequently, nobody ever made much of a fuss if I brought up controversial topics. By the end of my fieldwork, I used to jokingly refer to myself as "the anthropology channel" in reference to the fact certain community members would use me as a way to test the waters with a new idea they preferred not to voice themselves.

There also were pathfinders who were liminal in some way. Either they were part of an organization that crossed the traditional lines of organizational affiliation described below or they were on their way out of their current jobs. Those from cross-affiliation organizations were expected to have a perspective that spanned disciplinary or jurisdictional lines. Therefore, they were expected to voice ideas or make suggestions that sounded a little different or were based on unexpected arrangement of priorities. Some of these liminal pathfinders were the greatest advocates of the Incident Command System described in the next section. They were able to be strong advocates for coordination and resource sharing without appearing to be less than loyal to their own organization.

Liminal pathfinders also included those who were about to retire and/or move into the increasingly lucrative private sector of security, but especially those near retirement. These pathfinders had "lame duck" freedom. They had no more worries about promotions and few about the consequences of appearing foolish in front of other community members. I found people near retirement to be some of the most outspoken in the policy community. Sometimes this was the result of no longer caring what happened, but more often they drew their motivations from caring very greatly what happened and wanting to take advantage of their protected positions. One of the most persistent advocates for a coordinated approach to dealing with port security in the face of turf wars and public/private issues was less than a year from retirement when we met. At the state level, the director of Commonwealth Security, brought in shortly after 9/11 by then-governor Jane Swift, was a retired FBI agent who was heading for rest and recreation on Cape Cod when he got the call. He was somebody who had nothing to gain from the position he accepted except the delay of a well-earned retirement, and the people in the policy community knew it. He was respectful of the confidence placed in him by the governor, but he also wasted no time on foolish ideas and very little on unnecessary political games. Had he been given resources and authority to use in his office, he would have been a powerful force for any agenda he advocated. As it was, he was able to "think out loud" a great deal more than others in state government.

Some pathfinders were able to voice opinions and take chances with looking foolish because of their existing reputations as honest brokers or their personal experiences related to homeland security. Pathfinders in this category were often "old-timers" who had "been there and done that" enough that people listened to what they had to say on any topic simply because of the body of experience that would inform their musings. They had a type of cultural capital highly valued in organizations with a tradition of valorizing practical experience. Some also had long reputations as network and agreement builders, people who would help solve problems without giving into the temptation to be self-serving.

They were the individuals who could pull together the people necessary to run a multiagency exercise or get people to start talking about thorny issues such as interoperability of equipment. They might be hard to pick out at a meeting because they did not engage in a great deal of personal display, but you could tell who they were because of how people behaved when they spoke and how they were discussed by others in the community. People listened, even when they did not agree. People described them as resources in the community. The confusion surrounding homeland security in 2002 and 2003 placed these pathfinders in very powerful positions. Their value increased with every new complexity thrown into the homeland security puzzle. Although they often did not fully grasp how much people relied on them to break new ground, the weight of the responsibility did take its toll. There were too few such shoulders for the load, and burnout became a problem, as described in the section "Tacit Knowledge" below.

A final category of pathfinder also made use of cultural capital, but of a slightly different kind. These were people who had some direct connection to the events of 9/11 or, to a lesser degree, the anthrax attacks that took place later that autumn. Even several years later, it was common to introduce speakers by way of describing what they did on 9/11 or how they handled an anthrax incident. Many people in the Boston area's public safety community lost friends and colleagues in the collapse of the World Trade Center buildings in New York City, but few discussed it to any degree. Others in the community had gone down to work on "the pile," as the rubble was called. They could produce strangely distanced, almost "canned" descriptions, recited in tones that made them sound as though they were describing something that somebody else had done.

A few community members had lost somebody close, and a fewer still had lost somebody close who was a responder. Those in this last category were nearly unassailable. They could stand at any meeting and speak for as long as they wanted on any idea they might have for improving things. Even on the most unpopular topics, nobody wanted to be seen undermining them or detracting from their loss and their right to speak in any way. One of the most powerful examples of the use of this cultural capital was the medical director for public safety in Boston who lost a son, one of the firefighters who was killed in New York City. His death, along with those of many other responders, may have been attributable to a lack of interoperable communications equipment and protocols among police and fire at the scene. The director rarely mentioned it. When he did, it was in a very quiet way, described in terms of honoring his son by trying to fix the coordination problems that had contributed to his death. His story was well known in the community, and newcomers were often told in whispers when he appeared at meetings. His advocacy was one of the reasons that the debate over serious solutions for interoperability and coordination stayed alive when it would have been easy to bury these intractable problems under the mass of other work that needed to get done.

These individuals were critical in helping the community wade through the constant barrage of rumor, news, policy, and research that flowed through this area of practice in the first few years after 9/11. Even when their efforts did not solve a problem, they kept debates alive, kept issues visible, and helped create an atmosphere in which the absolute necessity of thinking out loud was recognized. They were a key resource for being able to figure out what to do and how to do it without waiting for formal guidance.

AFFILIATIONS AND CHANNELS

As described in the chapters on the work of homeland security, a great deal of people's time was consumed with finding ways to learn about one another, to understand and mesh perspectives, to learn how to coordinate plans and activities, and to share (and sometimes withhold) information and resources. The community coordinated and shared through sets of affiliations and relationships and the formal and informal channels among them.[4] Some of these were long-standing; some were being developed

4. The community was certainly a social network. Under other circumstances, I could have systematically examined it as such. Given the community's chaotic reality while

while I was in the field. This section describes the way people used affiliations, relationships, and channels in the community, with particular focus on problems and tactics of information sharing.

AFFILIATION. As in any community, the relationships that form the network of the homeland security community are not static or unidimensional.[5] People who might be expected to work well together because of shared backgrounds or interests may have personality conflicts that prevent this or their bosses might. Unlikely partnerships are formed on the basis of things having little to do with homeland security, such as a favorite lunch spot or shared hobbies. Shared backgrounds sometimes yield similar perspectives on priorities or interpretations of events. These bits of common ground make it a little faster to explain things, a little easier to work through differences of opinion. However, nobody I knew felt especially constrained by these expectations and sometimes deliberately sought out people with only marginal common ground as a way of broadening their understanding of and capability within the network.

I refer to the "normal" patterns as the expected axes of affiliation: discipline, jurisdiction, public/private/voluntary, and civil/uniformed illustrated in table 2. People reach along one or more of these lines of affiliation to find common ground and common understanding of problems and appropriate solutions. I use these axes as a framework to help understand an idealized version of relationships in the community rather than to reify existing organizational and institutional models. The axes serve to illuminate some of the more common ways people might be expected to build and use relationships and to provide a background against which unusual relationships can be more clearly identified. Interesting things happen when people step outside those expectations.

Disciplinary affiliation refers to relationships based on a common professional category, such as law enforcement or public health or fire service or medicine. In this type of affiliation, a local police officer may feel that she has more in common with a state police detective than she does with

---

I was there, I felt constrained from asking people to give me time for lengthy network analysis interviews. Also, the idea of network analysis seems to set up expectations of regularity that would obscure rather than illuminate in this case. For these reasons, I have chosen to focus on the affiliational and relational aspects of the network, rather than trying to describe the network itself.

5. I use "affiliation" in the sense of a voluntary association in contrast to relationships that are officially designated.

TABLE 2: Expected Axes of Affiliation

Axis	Sample Categories
Discipline	Fire service, law enforcement, medicine, public health, planning, administration, government, military
Jurisdiction	Local, substate regional, state, suprastate regional, federal (regional or field office), federal (national headquarters)
Public, private, voluntary	Government, private business, contractor or consultant for preparedness activity, utility, church organization, charitable organization, school
Civil—uniformed	Uniformed public safety, active military, national guard, civilian public safety, government, administration, business

a firefighter. Jurisdictional affiliations are based in geography or level of government. The same police officer making use of jurisdictional affiliation may feel more at ease with a firefighter from her own town than she does with an FBI agent, even though that agent shares a law enforcement background. Alternatively, she may be able to build a relationship based on geography with the firefighter from her town that she is not able to create with a police officer from another town.

Affiliations based on public/private/voluntary divisions revolve around the similarities and differences among agencies that are public, such as public safety or health; those that are voluntary, such as the Salvation Army; and those that are private, such as businesses, some hospitals and ambulance services, and consultants. This type of affiliation is complex, involving not only the ownership of the organization but also the motivation behind it. For example, a private ambulance service and a large chemical facility that needs to be secured would not be thought of in the same way, but in both cases, those from public institutions would articulate a difference based on the idea of "business." To return to the example of the police officer, she might find it simpler to develop working relationships with another person in public service than with security personnel from a private facility.

The civil/uniform axis also is complex and should not be misconstrued as a civil-military divide. Although of course there is militarism at the root of it, it has more to do with the symbols of uniform and the idea of a disciplined, ranked organization than whether somebody is in the military. In this case, the police officer might work more easily with a member of the National Guard than a city planner or somebody in public health. The uniformed service category served an important purpose with the public as well. People associated it with ideas of public safety, and no politician wanted to speak on homeland security without uniforms by his or her side. An example of the importance of the civil/uniform distinction is Boston's Emergency Management Agency (BEMA), which combined civilian and uniformed fire officials. Initially, the uniformed side of the house was given more publicity and prestige. The civilian employees were gently, and sometimes not so gently, teased about their status, even though their work in bringing together nonpublic safety members of the community was recognized. They were discouraged from officially representing the agency. Then suddenly, for reasons that nobody would ever explain completely, the Fire Department decided that its BEMA employees should work in civilian clothes but continue to use the rank titles of chief and so on. My interpretation was that the Boston fire commissioner had decided to position BEMA as an emergency management asset that should have a leading role in the area's homeland security activity and minimize the impression that it was simply another arm of the Fire Department. Certainly, it brought them more into line with the appearance of emergency management agencies in other cities. Regardless of the specific reasons behind the shift, the change illustrates the importance of the idea of "uniformed service" in contrast to civilian service.

In practice, relationships rarely fall neatly along only one of these axes of affiliation. They are simply a conceptual tool to help tease out some of the ways people in the community find common ground. As in any social situation, people create their segments of the network along multiple axes, according to individual needs, opportunities, and preferences. I saw more than one unlikely affiliation formed over things like an interest in overseas travel, a shared taste for a sub shop nobody else liked, or similar senses of humor. In the Boston area, many individuals were very adept at maintaining complex networks of affiliation that, with only one or two phone calls, could put them in the loop on almost anything going on in the area. I later found that this ability was mirrored in other urban areas and magnified greatly in rural areas where few towns had all the resources they needed to respond to any significant event on their own.

CROSS-AFFILIATION ORGANIZATIONS. It would be a mistake to think that all the interagency focus came about after 9/11. Interagency cooperation was both an official stance and an unofficial practice in public safety and public health long before concerns about domestic preparedness began to increase. Officially, many cities and states have had programs that required cooperation between law enforcement and social workers, between law enforcement and fire services, between emergency medical professionals and public health workers. Unofficially, people have used their professional networks to cut across organizational boundaries to share information, develop programs, or simply maintain awareness of what other agencies were doing.

However, homeland security work, especially just after 9/11, did require an increased focus on relationships and operations that spanned organizational boundaries. The atmosphere required a strange balance between the need for increased interagency cooperation and the need to keep relationships flexible. The press and government officials were calling for increased interagency cooperation, but there was little guidance on what relationships would be made official or on what operations were supposed to have the "co-" attached to them. Consequently, it seemed necessary for organizations to be more visibly involved with other organizations— through meetings, trainings, and actual operations—while simultaneously maintaining the ability to change relationships in response to new pressures or policies.

One of the easiest ways to do interagency work while preserving flexibility turned out to be making use of organizations that naturally spanned lines of affiliation. These agencies not only held common ground for more than one discipline or jurisdiction; they also could provide a temporary (or permanent) social network spanner between two nodes that had previously been only indirectly or loosely connected. Emergency Medical Service (EMS) organizations were one type of bridging organization. Emergency medical services, also known as prehospital emergency health care services, generally have two components. The first is rapid assessment and treatment of medical problems with the goal of stabilizing the patient for long enough that they can be moved to a treatment center or, in less serious cases, seek treatment on their own. In some cases, patients are well enough that they are treated by EMS providers and released on scene. The other component of EMS is transport, both transport of medical supplies, equipment, and skills to the scene of an incident and transport of patients to treatment facilities. Sometimes the transport is by ground ambulance; sometimes it is by air, by water, or on foot.

People in this discipline tend to be credentialed as emergency medical technicians or paramedics with various levels and certifications possible. Their knowledge base can range from basic lifesaving to highly specialized incident-specific lifesaving and emergency treatment. They are familiar with the routines of incident scenes and of emergency rooms. Consequently, people in EMS organizations are sometimes able to understand the priorities of both public safety organizations and medical ones and to translate between them. Emergency medical services also span a divide between public and private preparedness and response organizations, depending on how they are configured. Some EMS organizations are privately owned and operated. The most common examples of this are private ambulance services. However, even when the service is a public agency, as was the case in Boston, they must still regularly interface with hospitals that are frequently private institutions.

RELATIONSHIPS. People in the community were quite explicit about the importance of relationships for both planning and response. These relationships were often friendly, involving lunches or beers after work. Sometimes they were purely professional but contained a deep trust and confidence in one another. The saying that people used to crystallize their perspective was "You don't want to be exchanging business cards at the incident." In using this statement, they highlighted the critical role of personal relationships in supporting official structures and procedures.

As described in the section on pathfinders, homeland security was a messy and constantly shifting area of knowledge. It was difficult for people to feel confident that they were on top of the latest developments in every aspect, and nobody wanted to look foolish. A firefighter and a member of the police department's hazardous materials response unit who could call each other up and share information were both more likely to be well informed than either operating in isolation. An exercise planner who had enough contacts to pick up the phone and get people's unofficial reactions to an idea for a large-scale exercise was more likely to come out with a proposal that would actually be accepted by the community.

The role of relationships in responses was much more dramatic, sounding very much like tales of military units that form very strong bonds of trust on which they rely in operations. On a simple level, frontline firefighters have to trust one another to do the job right and not endanger the rest of the group. An incident commander has to believe that his section chiefs can be trusted to do their jobs effectively. However, there is also an element of familiarity involved. If the incident commander knows that a particular individual is very good at beefing up morale, she or he may choose to hold that person back until well into the incident when frontline staff are beginning to get tired or frustrated. Similarly, she or he may know that a responding unit from another town has a particularly difficult individual in command or that a frontline responder is worried about his wife who is about to give birth or that another responder has a special rapport with older victims on scene.

Sometimes the role of relationships is starker. In the case of "shoe bomber" Richard Reid (described in chapters 6 and 7), press attention focused on the actions of the flight attendants and passengers who were able to subdue Reid, preventing him from setting off the explosives in his shoe (Kurkjian and Tench 2001; Martinez and Crittenden 2001). However, when the flight landed at Logan International Airport in Boston, there was more to be done than simply allowing passengers to walk off the airplane. Once passengers and crew had been evacuated, there was still the not inconsequential matter of getting Reid out. He had been tied up by crew and passengers and sedated by two doctors among the passengers. Nobody among those who had been on the airplane or those on the ground could be sure of the situation. It was possible that Reid still had explosives on or near him. He might have a mechanism for setting them off. He could have been infected with a biological agent to spread disease if his initial mission failed. There could have been radiation involved in the explosive devices. The scales of the incident were tipped toward uncertainty.

The State Police Explosive Ordinance Disposal Unit had to send some-body into the aircraft to assess the situation and bring Reid out. The officer could not bring a radio or cell phone with him, as both have the capacity to trigger certain types of explosive devices. In order to communicate what he was seeing to the responders outside and receive guidance, he had to have somebody stand in the door of the aircraft, relaying information back and forth. A fire chief who had known and worked with the officer for years took on that role. The officer had to trust that the chief would relay information quickly and accurately and that he would be knowledgeable enough not to interrupt if he saw the officer doing something delicate. The chief, standing in the door of an aircraft known to have contained at least one device capable of destroying it, had to trust that the officer could do his work safely for both of them and that he would both send and receive the information necessary for a good end result. If either of them did not have sufficient trust in the other, operating procedures alone would not have been enough. Their relationship and knowledge of how each other operated allowed them to focus exclusively on the task at hand. At the end of that afternoon, the only person who didn't go home to his family was Richard Reid. No news stories featured the two other people I just described.

That kind of trust and the level of operational confidence it provides is not something that can be mandated by job description or procedure. It has to be built and maintained over time through planning and operating together in a range of circumstances. The relationships that support that trust sometimes reinforce and sometimes span expected affiliations. These relationships are one of the key elements that undermine any attempt to codify how the community gets things done or to institutionalize arrangements. They also are the basis for many of the channels that people in the community create and use to get homeland security done.

CHANNELS. People in the Boston homeland security policy community shared information and resources through both formal and informal channels. These ranged from highly codified chains of command to the kind of personal relationships formed over long careers. A full description of the informal network channels would undermine informant confidentiality. The channels are, after all, ways of getting around the sanctioned processes. However, it is possible to illustrate some of the ways people used channels in homeland security activities, the problems and solutions they presented, and attempts to impose order on them, such as the Incident Command System.

At the time I was in the field, the homeland security community had a set of partially formed official relationships among organizations and thriving informal channels used to supplement and circumvent the officially sanctioned arrangements. People used all available channels to mobilize assistance; pass and receive information about work, technology, or just what other organizations and people in the community were doing; and sometimes to get access to resources.

Some of the official channels in the community were based in preexisting relationships formed as a result of prescribed or openly sanctioned patterns of cooperation in response, planning, and information or resource sharing. Police and fire departments had officially described cooperative systems for responding to and investigating incidents. The U.S. Coast Guard and the Boston Harbor Patrol were able to coordinate their operations in the port. The FBI's Joint Terrorism Task Force (JTTF) brought members of many local, state, and federal agencies together to collaborate on preventing terrorism in the area. State-level agencies, such as the Massachusetts Emergency Management Agency, ostensibly served as hubs for coordination across different local jurisdictions. Communities had mutual aid agreements with one another that allowed them to share personnel and resources in crises without having a legal and financial mess to clean up later.

Informal channels were composed of professional and personal relationships that developed over time. They grew in importance during the post-9/11 uncertainty about how governments at all levels would reorganize themselves. New tasks, new partners, and a new pace of activity challenged both the official channels and the informal aspects of it that people had used to smooth over any bumps. Changing the official structure to meet every new twist would have been impossible, even if it had been desirable. It was much easier for the unofficial channels to bend and stretch and broaden to incorporate new needs. Using unofficial channels to handle new homeland security ideas and work maintained a certain degree of flexibility for the community. As described above, so long as relationships, communication channels, and job descriptions were not formalized, they could shift with the winds of policy or public opinion. At the same time that people tried to maintain this flexibility in some areas, they worked to create structure in others. Flexibility to cope with a changing policy or response environment was desirable, but so was having enough scaffolding to hold on to so that certain things could become routine. This was especially true during a response when an incident commander needed to be able to let some things happen automatically, so that she or he could focus on those aspects that could not be predicted. These two goals, flexibility and predictability, were always in tension in every effort made by the community.

A lot of the time I spent with committees and work groups was spent trying to formalize the mobilization of the community and information flow during a response. These issues can serve as a means of illustrating the uses and problems associated with both formal and informal channels in the community. Willingness to respond was a favorite theme in how people described the community. Everybody "knew" that turf wars stopped when the response began and that everyone would show up and do the right thing. In practice, it was necessary for an incident commander to know that an asset existed in the community before they could call it up. She or he also needed to know the official procedures for getting the resource. Notification during a response also was a difficult issue. Anyone who might have a jurisdictional or other interest in the incident or who might be asked to respond at some point was supposed to be notified early in a response. People in the community reported that much of this had taken place less formally in the past, with less-than-thorough procedures in place. They also made it clear that it had not always worked to everyone's satisfaction. People felt that their jurisdictions or operational turf were stepped on; sometimes relationships became strained. Long hours were spent creating notification trees, assembling correct telephone numbers, and sorting out people's assumptions about who called whom. "But I thought *you guys* called the Coast Guard!"

The most comprehensive effort to impose temporary order on these channels during responses is the Incident Command System (ICS), now also known as the National Incident Management System. This system, developed by fire services and modified for other types of events, imposes an organizational structure on one or more responding organizations. In its most basic form, it consists of an incident commander supported by four section chiefs, one each for operations, logistics, planning, and finance/administration, and officers to handle liaison with other organizations and public information. The incident commander is responsible for oversight of the entire incident. The operations section chief is responsible for all the different operations—several different firefighting fronts at a forest fire, for example. The logistics section chief handles the resource management and dispatch. The chief of the planning section looks at the incident over the long term, figuring out the best approach and considering what assets should be mobilized in the future. The finance and administration section handles general administrative responsibilities and tracks resource use and purchases, ensuring that vendors are paid and that the paperwork trail exists for future reimbursement. Each section may be elaborated into branches and units or may hold only one person, depending on the size of the incident.

Regardless of their normal rank or job title, people working within ICS are supposed to perform the roles assigned to them under the system. Roles are supposed to be clearly described on what are called Job Action Sheets, so that anyone with basic knowledge of the type of response should be able to fill the role. All roles under ICS have command or managerial functions rather than frontline response functions, so the system would not put a firefighter in a law enforcement function. In large-scale incidents, one or more emergency operations centers may be activated to support the forward incident command post. In these centers, representatives from many agencies can coordinate how assets are gathered and deployed when requested, as well as helping get decisions from higher-ups in the community.

The Incident Command System is designed to make interactions predictable both for those in the response and for those who have to integrate themselves later. Given the differences among procedures in response organizations and the variability of local homeland security networks, some type of standardization is necessary if multiple resources are to be integrated in a fast-paced response. An incident commander is not supposed to have to pause to tell a truck driver where to offload his delivery of widgets. The driver is immediately directed to somebody in a staging area. A specialized team arriving to help with operations should be able to integrate through the operations section without disrupting the rest of the response. Communication likewise is supposed to flow in predictable patterns. If somebody running part of the operation wants a widget, she or he is not supposed to order it. The request must go through the operations section chief to logistics, which will make sure that administration/finance gets the paperwork it needs. This flow is supposed to keep operational people free from logistical and financial concerns, ensure that resources are obtained in an orderly manner, and preserve the financial viability of the response.

If all the rules and documentation processes of ICS are followed, the system provides predictability and a series of checks to make sure that information and resources flow where they are needed rather than just where they would normally flow in the network. In practice, some organizations and locations have an easier time with ICS than others. People with well-developed personal relationships would much rather pick up the phone and get what they need than go through an ICS channel that might take longer. While this may be more efficient in the short term, it can cause mixed or contradictory messages and duplicate orders. Some disciplines, such as public health and medicine, have technical specialists who are not comfortable with the idea that decisions might be taken out of their hands.[6] The idea of having somebody with the wrong credentials making the final decisions about health matters is of great concern to them. It made many health professionals reluctant to admit that ICS could have any place in their responses, although this situation is improving rapidly now.[7]

The broad use of ICS for many types of responses is something that is going to take time and effort at the local and federal levels. One of

6. This is not to suggest that the other disciplines do not have technical specialists. They are just more comfortable with command-and-control systems than those in the health fields seem to be. A great deal of my later applied work involved balancing the concerns of health and medical experts against the need for a predictable incident management structure in large-scale or long-duration incidents.

7. Unfortunately, these concerns were sometimes used to mask a general unwillingness of some medical professionals to work with other responders and concede certain types of expertise. This tension appears to run along lines of class and begs further field research and analysis.

the problems has been the "command" aspect. The system was designed for fire operations, which are carried out by organizations accustomed to working within a rank system. The idea of carrying out a superior's decision, even when you don't agree with it, is not foreign, even though it is still unpleasant to comply. New revisions of ICS tend to refer to it as an Incident Management System (IMS), with the incident commander transformed into an incident manager. This shifts the emphasis away from decision making and focuses attention on how the system can be used to support operations, taking logistical and administrative detail off the plates of those who have to operate. While this shift may alleviate some specialist's fears of being overly controlled, it does little to confront the issue of people who would prefer to use their own connections within the network.

Another aspect of ICS that comes from its roots in the fire service is that it is designed to handle incidents that are geographically focused. Even in a wildland fire with several different fronts, each operation is taking place in a distinct location. As ICS/IMS comes to be used in public health settings, there are some questions about how it will work to support something like an epidemiological investigation, where there may be several operations, all taking place within the same broad geographic space. The problems with using ICS in a health response were just beginning to bubble up while I was in the field. Health organizations were making their initial steps into using ICS. Incident Command System or IMS seemed like a promising tool to allow local variability in the way homeland security was structured while still providing some predictability and accountability in responses.

Regardless of these efforts, the official channels could not necessarily handle all the kinds of traffic that needed to move in the community, especially those that took place in nonresponse daily activities and planning. New ideas were sometimes more easily worked out in an informal lunch than an official meeting with bosses watching. Getting to try out a new piece of equipment was easier to accomplish by "dropping by" during a training session a colleague mentioned to you rather than placing an official request for cross-training. Sometimes the official channels were too slow to handle an urgent request for assistance during a response. For example, a request from a local incident commander to activate the National Guard's First Civil Support Team must go through the Massachusetts Emergency Management Agency, who arranges for the governor to tell the National Guard's adjutant general to activate the team. These additional steps take time, and it is a constant temptation for incident commanders to circumvent them.

Mobilization of assistance can also be hindered if the official channels do not ensure that the asset can arrive and be properly integrated. In a dirty bomb exercise I attended, a state police officer was dispatched to stop traffic on a road leading to the incident site. During the exercise debriefing, he brought up an important concern about his work. He explained that, in an actual event, the Department of Health's radiological specialists would have had to travel on the road. He had no orders to allow them to pass and would have turned them back. The official channels did not work in the heightened activity of a response. Passing information to site-access control points about needed responders and others who should be allowed access needed to take place much more quickly than was possible using normal procedures for communicating to officers on traffic control.

However, the official channels serve a purpose in pinpointing accountability and financial responsibility for response assets that are deployed. The accountability (and attendant paperwork trail) provided by using official channels is critical in recouping response costs from the federal government after a disaster declaration or from a private company after a hazardous material spill. Use of these channels also is intended to remove responsibility from the shoulders of those who have not voluntarily assumed it. A local police officer who happens to be first on the scene of an accident should not have to be responsible for calling out an expensive response unit, such as a hazardous materials team.

In the example of the Civil Support Team mentioned above, in order for the costs of team activities to be supported, the state must approve the deployment. While I was in the community, the Civil Support Team used informal channels to let local people know that an incident commander could call both the state and the Civil Support Team. They mentioned this casually in trainings, exercises, and side conversations. They explained that the advance warning allowed the team to be preparing for deployment while it waited for approval from the state, saving precious time in response. This is an example of using the informal channels to supplement, rather than circumvent, the official process. Nothing that the team suggested went against the official plan. It minimized the harm that could be caused by a strict interpretation of procedure, without undermining accountability.

In the case of the police officer stopping the radiological specialist, his reliance on information from official channels should have ensured that he was not placed in a position of having to make critical judgment calls with insufficient information. Unfortunately, the official channels moved too slowly to provide him with needed information, forcing him to act in ways that could have been harmful to thousands had the event been real. The situation was not so much that the information had to go through many channels before reaching him. Instead, it seemed that other activities took precedence over giving information to site-access control personnel. Too much other activity was clogging up the channels. In this case, there was little that the officer could do through informal channels to fix the situation other than making individual calls each time somebody requested access. On a busy road, this would not have been practical.

Most of the problems my informants described with the official channels were related to information flow. I believe this is in part because information is the most important thing that moves through the community without constant monitoring. The movement of resources and mutual assistance are much more carefully described, as they are associated with legal and financial obligations. However, the emphasis on information sharing also reflects a general unease expressed by many community members about their access to information. The organizational and operational landscapes were changing; new players and new threat possibilities had to be considered. Although vague, this sense of not quite knowing what was going on, either with other organizations or with a particular incident, led to an increased emphasis on information flow.

Concerns about information flow in the community can be categorized as (1) general awareness of other organizations' activities and programs, (2) structural barriers or impediments to sharing the sort of information generally referred to as "intelligence" about specific events, situations, or persons that could bear on prevention or response activities, and (3) procedural.

The first type of problem was frustrating, but not crippling, for community members. It meant that you might try to develop something useful to the community, such as a calendar of training events, and then find out that your counterpart in another agency had been working on the same project for several months. You might spend months creating a proposal to develop a new special operations unit, only to find out that the next town over was in competition for the funds. This also led to lack of knowledge of who had what types of assets available. I spent a great deal of time after meetings and exercises listening to people talk about how much fire-suppression foam of various types they kept on hand (or did not keep). There was always a surprise or two. There were no effective official channels in place to help organizations be aware of the capacities, assets, skill bases, programs, and initiatives of one another. People used informal channels to share information about what they were doing.

The fire services in Massachusetts had a tremendous professional gossip grapevine. I rarely participated in or overheard a conversation among fire service workers that did not include a comment on some company's new piece of equipment, a captain's grant proposal, or a specialist's intent to retire. Other segments of the community used the network in similar ways. There was enough overlap in relationships to allow this type of information to flow across disciplinary lines. There was simply too much information for anyone to pass along or absorb without something more systematic in place.

Structural impediments to intelligence sharing were of greatest concern to the people with whom I worked. Pre-event intelligence can be anything from specific information about a group targeting something in your town to simply knowing about a pattern of events taking place in the region, such as a series of chemical thefts or a missing fertilizer truck. Intelligence sharing during an event is mostly concerned with the operational situation as the incident unfolds. A commonly discussed example of this took place during the attacks on the World Trade Center in 2001. As described earlier in this chapter, people in police helicopters had information to suggest that one of the towers was about to collapse, but for technological and procedural reasons this information did not make it to the firefighters in the tower.

Some structural impediments to intelligence sharing were purely technological, not based in the formal or informal procedures of the community. The flow of information can be limited by the ability of technology to perform. Fire services sometimes have difficulty in large structures where radio signals can be blocked unless repeaters have been installed. Cellular telephones are often the first service to be overwhelmed in a large event. This was the case in New York on 9/11. As thousands picked up their phones to tell friends and families what they were seeing, they blocked responders trying to use the same circuits. The situation was repeated in Boston a few months later when the Patriots football team won the Super Bowl, and Boston's public safety organizations were faced with communicating in a parade of 1.25 million people, many of whom picked up their phones to tell friends where they were. One emergency management official was almost crushed as he tried to maintain a crowd barrier, unable to call for police support. However, most of the technological problems had to do with interoperability. Communications interoperability refers to the ability of people using one communications system to hear and speak to people using another system. Police, fire, and marine assets all use different radio frequencies. This separation helps filter the content that responders need to process but also inhibits the ability of one discipline to know what the others are doing.

Procedural impediments were generally based either in a desire to minimize the spread of sensitive information through the network or in simple ignorance of another organization's need to know something. All the technical interoperability in the world won't help if people don't realize they should share a particular type of information. A common procedural impediment to sharing was intentional—the classification of information. In the example described in chapter 6, a local police official complained that he sent an officer off to bring his local expertise to the JTTF. The subordinate could not share what he had learned due to issues of classification. The information flowed in only one direction. So the officially designated lines of cooperation in this area of activity did not form a reliable channel from the local perspective.

However, there were broader structural impediments as well. As with information flow about organizational capacities and activities, there was no intelligence-sharing system in place that was acceptable to all, or even a majority, of the stakeholders in the community. Classification of information or reluctance to pass along sensitive information was part of the problem but not the whole of it. One person's intelligence can be another person's trivia. A public safety planner gave me the example of dumpster fires. Like an epidemiological investigation, a single dumpster fire in a community was not significant. Three such events in three separate towns was a pattern, yet there was no official way to share that type of information. Every town had too many of these incidents to share each one with surrounding jurisdictions. Each only rose to significance as part of a pattern. In the first two years after 9/11, Massachusetts tried to develop a computer system that would facilitate this type of pattern recognition. Unfortunately, the initiative collapsed under the weight of financial and political problems, as well as the fact that the system relied on entry of data and reading of data by already overworked police officers. As I left the field, there were intelligence-sharing initiatives at all levels of government but nothing that systematically addressed the whole of the community.

The same concerns hold for sharing information during a response. It is not always clear which of the thousands of pieces of information that bubble up during an incident are relevant to anyone else. Every discarded paper bag might hold an explosive device designed to kill first responders, but most don't and people can hardly be expected to broadcast a warning every time they see one. It also is not always clear who needs to know what pieces of information, even when they are relevant. Developing an information-sharing structure that would help responders manage that information deluge has proven to be a daunting task. Despite all the attempts described above to formalize notification and information-sharing processes, it is often still up to the judgment of responders and incident commanders, using their community-based knowledge of what other organizations might need, to decide how to process the flow.

People in the policy community used relationships and both official and unofficial channels to move information and share resources but also to make decisions and build consensus. The situation when I left the field was still very messy, and I have reason to think it remains so. However, the labyrinth of affiliations and channels in the community serves its purpose as a flexible means of coordinating and sharing during daily practice without every connection having to become permanent.

TEMPORARY TASK-BASED ORGANIZATION

One of the most significant ways people managed to get things done without institutionalizing roles or assuming official responsibility for new tasks was through organizing themselves around temporary task-based activities. I noticed this pattern fairly early on in fieldwork, as I was discovering the policy community. Interagency work, including the conceptual business of figuring out how the community would coordinate its activities both formally and informally, often took place under much humbler auspices. The places where homeland security practice became most visible were meetings of groups that shared certain characteristics: a designation apart from any permanent organization, at least the appearance of temporariness, and a focus on a specific task, threat, or area.

Coming together under a designation such as "initiative" or "work group" or "task force" allowed some degree of organization without the permanence or the fixity of membership that a formal organization would involve. Although one group often spearheaded the organization, a great deal of discursive effort was put into emphasizing the interagency nature of the work. Sometimes meetings were even rotated so that no one agency appeared to be in full control. The group's work might be temporally bounded in a clearly defined manner, as with a temporary organization convened to develop, run, and review an exercise. Alternatively, the "temporariness" might be implied rather than spelled out, as with an initiative to secure a particular feature of the area, such as "the port" or "schools." Either way, the arrangements were always discussed as having a limited existence, both in terms of time and scope of activity.

Creating such a group to plan an exercise, to develop strategies for port security, or to consider technology options was much simpler than trying to reorganize into a formal structure that could encompass these activities. Organizing around a particular project allowed community members to address a need without necessarily assuming permanent official responsibility for any particular activity. It also allowed organizations to work together without formalizing relationships beyond the scope of a bounded project while creating opportunities for building and maintaining informal channels and personal relationships. Some of these projects also provided the chance for people in the homeland security community to display their interagency efforts. They could get press coverage or political attention to focus on their ability to work together to solve problems and improve security, again without having to formalize relationships or responsibilities.

I observed at meetings of many temporary task-based organizations but was routinely involved in two that I can describe. One was the Port Security Initiative, a large effort spearheaded by the Coast Guard. Its purpose and title and the major players changed over time, but when I became involved the intent was to involve all major private and public port stakeholders in a major effort to capture security issues in the port and begin developing solutions for them.

The Port of Boston is a complex environment. It spans multiple jurisdictions, different towns, different disciplines of authority, and different levels of governments. Private businesses see it variously as scenery, a transportation venue, a resource, or an obstacle. The challenges it poses for security preparation, safety planning, and response vary depending on the tides, the season, the flux of commerce, special events in towns, environmental concerns, and a host of other factors. The concerns addressed by members of the initiative are far too numerous to list, but a few examples include balancing the security of hazardous cargos with the desire of business vessels, pleasure craft, and transit and other government vessels to move freely in the port; wrangling the legal issues surrounding the ability of responders to make use of private berths or other waterside property to handle emergencies; identifying facilities around the port that might become targets or simply contained hazardous materials; addressing issues of intelligence sharing among public and private organizations; and so on.

The initiative was also designed to bring stakeholders together for the explicit purpose of building good working relationships. Many people who had an interest in the port knew each other from past initiatives or simply from moving in the same circles in the same area. The Coast Guard hoped to build a spirit of partnership and involvement in port security rather than having some organizations heavily involved in security planning and others willingly or unwillingly being excluded from the process. It was important that people from different jurisdictions and different disciplines or industries at least have the opportunity to develop some shared ideas about what it would mean to make the port safer and more secure.

The initial large group was subdivided, after a great deal of negotiation, into a number of smaller working groups to handle certain issues. There was a group assessing the state of intelligence gathering and sharing. Another looked at transportation issues. I spent time with a group that was supposed to work on protocols for handling the consequences of a CBRNE incident in the port. The Coast Guard occasional sponsored large meetings at which people reported their work group's progress and others spoke about policy or gave speeches to recognize everyone's efforts, but the bulk of the activity was in the work groups. The initiative gradually shifted into something that was much more focused on the Coast Guard, who hired an outside contractor to come in and do a security assessment of the harbor. This decision, made without significant discussion with other response organizations in the port, decreased people's enthusiasm for devoting time to the initiative. However, I have no doubt that the initiative fostered interagency relationships and helped build knowledge of the various plans and operating procedures that would need to be coordinated in an incident, as well as the hazards and resources in the area. The initiative also gave the community a venue to dig more deeply into the security issues of the port, which continue to be some of the most complex facing the policy community.

Another temporary task-based organization in which I was involved was set up to develop and run a multiagency exercise of response to the explosion of a dirty bomb at Logan International Airport. Dirty bombs are conventional explosives combined with relatively small amounts of radiological material. The damage they cause is from (1) the blast from the explosives, (2) contamination of people and areas with the radiological material, and (3) immediate and future disruption caused by misunderstandings of radiological materials and their misassociation with nuclear bombs. Although there are real concerns about contaminated air traveling away from the site of such an explosion and about the training of response personnel to notice the radiation and protect themselves, dirty bombs are considered to be primarily a weapon of terror and disruption rather than destruction. People in the homeland security community believed that the public lacked essential information about radiation that would allow them to act "rationally" in an event. There was concern that people might panic and try to evacuate rather than staying indoors and away from the contaminated particles. Practitioners also were very concerned about the long-term economic and social viability of any place known to have been the site of a dirty bomb attack. Although a site might be successfully decontaminated, it is difficult to prove a negative, as was seen with lingering concerns and mistrust about the cleanup of anthrax-contaminated postal facilities. Planners were concerned that the public would hesitate to begin using an area or a building again, leading to significant economic and social damage to the area.

Massport Fire Rescue Department, responsible for Logan Airport and other Massport facilities, wanted to conduct an exercise that would fulfill certain regulatory requirements for the airport but also saw the opportunity to spearhead a highly visible example of coordinated preparedness and interagency cooperation. Boston Emergency Management and Boston Emergency Medical Services became heavily involved in planning the simulated events and response that would take place on the runway at the airport. Other local public safety and public health organizations became involved, as did FEMA and several other federal organizations, such as the ATTF and the FBI. Eventually, the exercise was expanded to include another day of "play" when area hospitals could test their plans to handle large numbers of potentially contaminated patients arriving at already-crowded emergency rooms.

Planning the exercise took several months, which were spent in meetings and more meetings, sending e-mails, making telephone calls, doing document reviews, and attending yet more meetings. Exercises are costly affairs. Even setting aside the hours of planning, what happens on the day of the event is not free. Equipment requires gas and maintenance. Those involved in the exercise often have to have their shifts filled by somebody else. Facilities have to be rented, and food has to be bought. Supplies that are used up in "play" have to be replaced and restocked. Every organization involved has to be sure that it is getting its money's worth in terms of improving performance, getting positive attention for the agency, and building relationships in the policy community. This means that exercise planning meetings are often delicate negotiations. In simplistic terms, the negotiations boil down to making sure that everyone has chances to try out equipment and procedures either that they want to practice or that they want to show off, that everyone receives ample credit and attention for participating in the exercise, and that things are designed to minimize the potential embarrassment to participants in the event that their plans do not work out quite as well as they had hoped. People also have to feel comfortable about who will see any reports that are generated as a result of the exercise, and it must be decided if the press will or will not be given access to various stages of exercise play.

Exercise planning also serves the purpose of allowing people in the community to come together, learn about one another's operations and capacities, and build relationships. However, more critically for the work of figuring out what homeland security was going to mean in the Boston area, exercises also are places where people have to talk over their plans in great detail. The planners have a very thorough understanding of what each organization can be expected to do in response to various stimuli in order to develop a good scenario for an exercise and a timeline that can be controlled to move events along or slow them down depending on how things are going. There is an aphorism in the community (and in other homeland security policy communities in the country) that in exercises about 90 percent of the learning takes place before the day of the exercise, as planners learn what to expect from one another.

In the case of the dirty bomb exercise, this learning served a double purpose. Not only did people learn about one another's plans and procedures for dealing with a radiological incident or an incident on an airfield or an incident involving a large number of casualties. They also talked to one another about how those plans and procedures might need to be refined to handle the new or enhanced concerns inherent in the homeland security mission. For example, newly heightened security for incidents at the airport meant that responders from outside the public safety community might have trouble getting access. So the group had to start talking about how credentialing would be handled. New standards for responder protection meant that personnel and vehicles not currently in use had to be farther back. So planners had to rethink their designated staging areas. If the Civil Support Team had different contamination plume–modeling software than another organization, somebody had to start thinking about who would be in charge of deciding between the systems if they gave a different answer in terms of how to operate or what advice to give the public.

Many exercise planning meetings turned into sessions where people worked together to identify areas where plans needed to be more carefully coordinated or retooled. I later came to understand that this is a very common occurrence now, as organizations struggle to make sense of what their plans should allow them to do. In fact, in one subsequent exercise design process, the plan revision overtook the exercise development process to such a degree that the design leader had to step in after four months and tell them to stop tinkering with their plans so that they could have something to exercise.

Getting this broader work done in meetings that were supposed to focus on exercise planning served several purposes. It gave a concrete, immediate focus for planning questions. (Will the plan drive responders to do X? Does it account for Y? How does it handle the fact that another agency plans to do Z?) It gave planners a common goal on which to focus, as opposed to focusing on preserving their own agency's particular way of doing things. It involved people who were knowledgeable about actual operations, who could not have been spared to a permanent planning detail. It also was temporary. Nobody in any meeting was faced with doing this work or working with these people forever. Finally, it had the flexibility of all temporary task-based organizations. It was able to accommodate hospitals when they wanted to play and was able to handle the fact that on the day of the exercise, the airport was unable to provide the expected runway location for play. People could come and go in the organization as their participation was necessary or as they felt there was value in it for their organization. These are all elements that would have been difficult to achieve in a permanent organization with paid employees and a defined planning mandate.

Unfortunately, exercise planning processes have the weaknesses of temporary task-based organizations as well as their strengths. With no permanent mandate, limited funding, and dispersed accountability, many exercises lead nowhere. Scenarios become contrived, evaluation becomes weak, and reports thin or nonexistent. Even when reports are created, without the authority to implement changes, even the most well-intentioned exercise planner may not be able to use what is learned to improve preparedness. This is characteristic of many of the solutions I saw in the community. They circumvent poor structures or structural voids in order to get things done but, simultaneously, rely on the ability of relatively few people to implement the solutions thoroughly and to hold the community accountable for its actions.

Although I had only a few opportunities for participant observation in it, one of the most publicly visible examples of a temporary task-based organization was the escort of liquefied natural gas (LNG) tankers through Boston Harbor. Such tankers move into Boston Harbor from a number of international ports, including some, such as Algeria, that were considered to be particularly vulnerable to terrorist activity. After 9/11, there were intensified concerns about the safety of all cargo vessels in the port, but the LNG tankers came under particular scrutiny for several reasons.[8] An attack on an LNG vessel could cause fires in pooled material on the surface of water or land. It could cause the explosion of a vapor cloud or a rapid-phase transition incident.[9] The consequence most feared among my informants was vapor cloud. While the other possible consequences of an attack would have been devastating to the area directly around the tanker, vapor clouds could flow anywhere. They could extend far inland before a chance encounter with a flame source caused them to ignite, spreading the range of danger from an attack on an LNG tanker far into the communities around the harbor. This consequence, nearly impossible to contain, was a nightmare for planners and responders alike.

Initially, efforts to get the situation under control were hampered by tensions among those agencies with some responsibility for the safety of the port, political officials, and the company. A passage from my field notes captures the atmosphere of the time period.

The tensions among public and private as well as federal, state, and local participants in the area's homeland defense have already been demonstrated. After September 11, there was much public debate over who was accountable for lapses in security at Logan International Airport. The Boston police commissioner has refused to join the governor's special terrorism task force, saying it duplicates and may hamper federal efforts. There are rumors that Attorney General Reilly may do the same. At this writing, the mayor of Boston is in conflict with the Coast Guard over whether natural gas tankers should be allowed into port. Acting Massachusetts Governor Jane Swift has said she is satisfied with existing security. The Coast Guard says it now has a plan to protect the tankers from perceived risks of terrorism but is refusing to share the plan with local authorities. The mayor is asking the newly appointed federal director of Homeland Security [Tom Ridge] to intervene on behalf of the city.

8. The fluid mechanics and fire physics of LNG incidents are debated. Here I draw on sources that were relatively well accepted in the community at the end of my fieldwork (Fay 2003; Havens 2003; Maritime Incident Resource and Training Partnership 2003).

9. Rapid-phase transition can happen when large amounts of LNG come into contact with water rapidly. The heat transfer from the water can cause the LNG to change instantly to its gaseous state. The transition can cause a noncombustive but powerful explosion. This concern has recently been popularized by Stephen Flynn in his book on building resilience (Flynn and Council on Foreign Relations. 2007).

For some time, the mayor refused to allow the tanker to enter the harbor. Ultimately, this was not a position he could maintain unless he was willing to stop the flow of LNG in the Northeast. Everett, the town in which the gas terminal is housed, was not interested in seeing the terminal relocate, given that it would mean the loss of an important economic asset. Tom Ridge, busy trying to ramp up his new office in the White House, was unlikely to set a precedent by intervening in one city's dispute. The situation had to be resolved locally. No official organization was created. No one official was put in charge of developing a solution and then dictating it to the rest of the community. In fact, given that the problem crossed so many vertical and horizontal jurisdictional lines, it might have been impossible for anyone to impose a solution. Instead, people met and made telephone calls. Officials and trusted community members worked hard to get buy-ins from stakeholders, both public and private, and to build a common sense of purpose in finding a balance between the importance of bringing the tankers into the harbor and the need to ensure the safety of the communities around the port.

Gradually, stakeholders negotiated a plan that everyone could at least tolerate, if not fully support. Among the other precautions taken, tankers were brought in with a significant escort, in a sort of security bubble that controlled the ability of other port traffic to come near the tanker or to cross its path, with patrols on land and in the air watching any location that might be used to stage an attack. The tug company that was contracted to move the vessel through the tighter parts of the harbor had employee security checks performed, and the tugs were inspected inside and out prior to each escort. I traveled on a police boat for one "transit," as the passages of the tankers were called. All the organizations having even the slightest jurisdiction or interest were in evidence. From local fire departments to the Massachusetts Environmental Police, people were either out as part of the escort or they were in communication with some organization that was.

I wish to stress that there is no reason that this problem had to be worked out in this particular way. Other solutions were possible. As has happened with many other problems, such as the need for ongoing exercise design and evaluation, the group might have given up on a full-blown interagency approach, resorting to private contractors under the control of one agency. While I know of no private contractor who possessed the resources for such an operation at the time, I have no doubt that firms such as Blackwater or DynCorp could have developed a solution if the price was right.

Although it might have been simpler to assign escort duty to one organization or to hire contractors, the interagency effort resulted in several important things. It would have been difficult for any organization or town to say that they did not have at least some opportunity to be involved in the operation, meaning they also shared responsibility. Using multiple agencies decreased the expense for any one jurisdiction or organization. The inclusiveness ensured that each organization had a continuing eye in the transits, watching for things that were of particular interest to them, making sure that their concerns continued to be addressed in each operation. It had the effect of spreading both praise and blame throughout the policy community.

It also gave the policy community a very powerful and visible symbol of their efforts to work on security issues using a coordinated interagency approach. The LNG tankers are very large and, once you know what is inside them, very impressive. They are visible from almost anywhere in the port, and the slight disruptions that their transit causes on land and water serve as reminders to the public, officials, and the policy community as a whole that it is possible for local practitioners to solve complex and delicate problems without a great deal of federal guidance or assistance. Again, the loose network that formed to solve this problem was flexible enough to add and subtract members as stakeholder interest waxed and to accommodate potential changes in state and federal policies.

Indirectly, these same state and federal policies supported reliance on temporary task-based organization. Funding streams and policy initiatives favored hierarchical organizations where authority and accountability could be firmly fixed, rather than lateral or network-based organizations, where it was more difficult to monitor and assess performance, so permanent network-based organizations would have been hard to create. Unfortunately, it was the latter sort of organization that fostered the coordination among equals and collaboration in capacity building that was necessary for homeland security to be anything other than isolated sets of activities and stovepiped ideas in disconnected agencies.

Although towns and the state added positions and offices that were specifically charged with working on homeland security issues, during my time in the community, most of the ground-level work seemed to get done through these temporary task-based organizations. They provided just enough structure to allow a group of practitioners to focus, but not so much that they had to worry too much about the long-term implications of who was sitting around the table. They allowed the community to pull in the shreds and patches of tasks and concepts that related to a particular homeland security task, to make use of knowledgeable experts without reassigning them permanently, and to experiment with relationships and plans.

TACIT KNOWLEDGE

One of the quietest ways that the work of homeland security gets done is through the reliance of organizations in the policy community on the tacit knowledge of experienced members. These are the crusty old dogs, go-to guys, the veterans of both planning and operations. Much of the knowledge needed to mount a geographically and situationally appropriate response to an emergency has never been codified for reasons discussed in more detail below. The same is true of planning tasks, although the ability of a knowledgeable planner to convene an effective meeting to coordinate triage protocols is somewhat less dramatic than an incident commander who can size up the resources needed to control an emergency with a quick glance. Homeland security as a field of practice had many shifting variables and so many unknowns that it was essential that the community be able to work without finalized written policies and plans. Tacit knowledge became both an absolute necessity and a great weakness for the policy community.

The term "tacit knowledge" has been used to describe a variety of human skills, knowledge bases, and behaviors. While in the field, I used the term as shorthand for experience-based, often unarticulated knowledge that allows a person to sort through a range of contextual and situational variables unconsciously or semiconsciously. Tacit knowledge is sometimes used synonymously with embodied knowledge and situated knowledge, but the following distinctions can be drawn. Embodied knowledge is generally used in reference to activities in which physicality is perceived to play an important role, such as dance or craftsmanship (Rapport 2001). Situated knowledge as described by Haraway is close to tacit knowledge, focusing on experiential acquisition (1991). However, I wish to focus attention on the difficulties of codifying experiential knowledge. Therefore, I use an operating definition of tacit knowledge as "knowledge that has not been (and perhaps cannot be) formulated explicitly and, therefore, cannot be effectively stored or transferred entirely by impersonal means" (MacKenzie and Spinardi 1995, 45).

Tacit knowledge in public safety and health may be associated with embodied knowledge in the form of operational skills. Minds and muscles together become familiar with dragging fire hose, stitching wounds, firing a gun accurately, or guiding a boat through a crowded port. However, for long-term members of the community, these skills are informed and refined by tacit knowledge. A police officer with a sense of his or her community can make better choices about whether to aim that accurate shot at a leg or a heart or the ground in front of a running suspect. A fireboat captain with long experience of Boston tides can control the boat in such a way that the tides have minimal impact on operations.[10]

A critical aspect of this knowledge for understanding the response community is that it tends not to be articulated. In some cases, the matrix of variables under consideration is too complex to be articulated in any meaningful way. Clearly, this is important for frontline operations, training, and command, but it also has political implications. The speed with which this knowledge allows decisions to be made can be crucial in saving lives and minimizing consequences, sometimes even in preventing an incident. Unfortunately, it also means that the knowledge cannot be easily transferred to others in long-term events when outsiders have to be brought into the operation or if a responder is removed from action due to injury or death.

Training programs for responders must contend with the importance of tacit knowledge both in practical and psychological ways. The practical is perhaps more easily understood. You can train somebody in the area's critical incident exodus plan, the design for getting people out of metropolitan area in an event. You cannot provide classroom training that will give them an intuitive sense of the way tides, seasonal and daily traffic patterns, weather, and local events will affect this plan. Those factors are simply too many and too variable to be written into a manual and consciously memorized.

Psychologically, there are three obstacles related to tacit knowledge. The first is that trainees know the value of experience-based knowledge, even if they are not sure in what that knowledge will consist. This can lead them to dismiss classroom learning as useless or simply as a way of racking up overtime hours. As one trainer put it when preparing for a hazardous materials refresher training program for firefighters: "Nap time!" Trainees may feel that they will learn what they need to know "in the field." The

10. There are now a number of popular treatments of tacit knowledge that may be of interest to some readers. In particular, recent works by Klein and Gladwell present scenario-based discussions of the concept (Gladwell 2007; Klein and NetLibrary Inc. 1999; Klein and U.S. Army Research Institute for the Behavioral and Social Sciences, Research and Advanced Concepts Office 1997).

second psychological obstacle is closely linked to the first. Responders recognize the importance of experience, but some fail to see that experience comes in many forms. Training, exercises, and drills may serve to provide the experiences required to build needed tacit knowledge, but from my discussions in the community, I gather that this is rarely communicated to trainees. Trainers have simply not thought out the process well enough to be able to convey the importance of that aspect of formal training.

The third psychological aspect of training that bears on discussion of tacit knowledge, the distinction between competence and confidence, affects even those trainees who take training a little more seriously. The push for greater security has led to increased skill demands on responders. They are expected to know about more types of threats, more types of response equipment, and more types of operating environments than has been the case in the past. However, the time and resources available for training have not increased in proportion. Responders may be familiarized with a particular piece of equipment but have little opportunity to use it. Their regular duties preclude additional training and drill. Budget shortfalls may cause the agency to restrict the use of certain pieces of equipment for training. In one exercise, I overheard representatives from a federal agency criticizing firefighters for not wearing radiation monitors. In fact, that department does have a few such monitors but cannot afford to have them depleted or damaged in exercises. One fire chief explained the result of these problems as responders who felt "competent, but not confident." It is also described by some in the community as the lack of "automatic" behavior with regard to a particular threat or piece of behavior. The inability to accrue sufficient experience to make the knowledge tacit results in responders who are uncertain and may result in operational delays or errors.

All of these obstacles can lead to significant gaps in continuity of knowledge in the community. Every time a practitioner retires or switches positions, there is a potential for years of knowledge to be lost. Some organizational leaders try to pair up senior practitioners with juniors in something like an informal apprenticeship, but there is no guarantee that the junior practitioner will stay with the job long enough to pass the knowledge on to others. This is especially problematic in federal agencies, many of which require that their employees take tours in different locations if they are to advance in their careers. This policy also is held up as a way to inhibit staff from developing personal relationships with locals that could lead to corruption or less than equal application of policies. Unfortunately, it also means that people are often expected to move just when they have acquired enough information about their location to start building a useful base of tacit knowledge about the area. Without explicit institutional support for ensuring that such knowledge is passed on, all attempts are fragmentary.

For the purposes of understanding how the policy community uses this asset in responses, the most important arena of tacit knowledge is in command and planning. In an actual event, most agencies will use some form of the Incident Command System, guidelines for breaking down necessary tasks and delegating authority for different aspects of the incident such as operations, logistics, and communications. The incident commander will be in charge of the command post, where he or she can manage operations and communicate needs and incident information to the outside world. The person in this position often has very little information with which to start operations and the questions multiply. There has been an explosion; people are lying on the ground. Is it a bomb? An accident? Is there radiation or another dangerous substance involved? Are the people injured as a result of the explosion, or have they collapsed because of a chemical agent? Is there a secondary device? Are people trapped in the rubble?

The energies of the incident commander have to be spent on figuring out the event, not the context in which it is happening. This is where tacit knowledge plays its most critical role for public safety. Contextual issues that may flit through the incident commander's mind should only flit, not linger, before an answer appears. What way is the wind blowing and is it likely to change soon? Is the incident close enough to the water that tides are a factor? What time of day is it? Will ambulances have any difficulty making it in this direction through traffic? Are there large non-English-speaking populations in the area? Which hospitals are most likely to be able to take additional emergency patients? What staff members are working today who have skills I need right now? Are schools about to let out? What other organizations have resources that I need now or may need shortly? Where is the best place to put incoming resources to strike the right balance between having them remain safe and having them readily available? What do I need to do now so that this can be most fruitfully investigated as a crime scene later when life-safety operations are complete? The answers to these questions must be part of the background of decision making, not part of the pile of unknowns. They are all questions that are answered rapidly, using knowledge that is gained through experience with local people and patterns. An incident commander distracted too much by these questions of operational context cannot focus on resolving the incident.

FIGURE 6. A customs agent stands in a little-known but complex area of the port region. Photo by author.

These same issues arise in emergency preparedness planning. I had been working for several months on port security issues when I spent a day with a customs agent in the Port of Boston. Toward the end of the day, as the sun was setting behind the skyscrapers, he decided to take me to see if we could get me on board one of the tankers or cargo ships. We headed for Chelsea Creek, an inlet from Boston Harbor that is home to petroleum tank farms and several other shipping operations that had always been mysterious to me. Traffic on my drives through the area was never quite slow enough or close enough to see what some of the enormous vessels were loading or unloading. We arrived moments too late to board an oil tanker, which had left early, so he took me to a spot where we could view a ship with a crew that was making local officials slightly suspicious (whether due to drugs, immigration, or terrorism fears, I never learned). As we stood in the one spot where the fading light still permitted a view of the vessel, I realized the amount of knowledge this man carried and used without thought. He knew local patterns of vessel traffic, weather, tides, traffic, and light. The little spot in which we stood gives a view of tank farms, several vessel berths, a pipeline, housing, airport parking, air traffic lanes, private yachts, and even an archaeological site if the tide is right. I realized that this man and many others like him in the response community must know thousands of such spots, all different in their resources and vulnerabilities, all different in how the changing daily and seasonal patterns of the region affect those resources and vulnerabilities. How would it ever be possible to write all those variables down in a response plan? It wouldn't.[11]

The perception in the response community is that it is not only impossible to codify that knowledge and institutionalize responses but also undesirable. I am in agreement. Codified knowledge has the value of being more widely transferable, but it is also more stagnant than tacit knowledge. There are fewer opportunities to incorporate new data or refine connections among bits of information. A change in traffic patterns due to construction is easily added to tacit knowledge, but by the time it made it into the official version, the new building might be an archaeological site. Homeland security at the ground level is still a social sphere where computers are not yet imbricated with daily life and paper copies are the norm. There are no mechanisms for tracking who has copies of what information and getting updates to them. Knowledge written down is knowledge used as a doorstop.

Similarly, institutionalized responses have limited utility when linked to highly variable information. Some responses must be institutionalized and practiced so that responders are confident and can focus on other aspects of the incident. Others require judgment calls. For example, the exact combination of assets an incident commander requests is linked to many variables and requires rapid decision making about not only what is best for the incident at hand but also how resource call-up may affect capacity in other places. In many cases, it is not the exact action plans that need to be worked out in advance but, rather, the decision points and the types of information a responder will need to make the best possible choices.

The preceding leads into the political aspects of tacit knowledge in homeland security. The homeland security policy community at the state and local levels in the Boston area found itself in a nearly impossible tangle of perceived demands. Federal agencies seemed to expect local people to be their eyes, ears, hands, and feet, with minimal information about what to pay attention to or what to do, although this has improved since

11. Similar concerns about knowledge continuity and transmission have been observed in other settings associated with security. See McNamara and Schoch-Spana's excellent ethnographies (McNamara 2001; Schoch-Spana 1998a, 1998b).

2001. The public expected that attacks would be thwarted before they were manifested or that competent officials would immediately know what was happening and communicate a clear message on the best course of action. Everyone seemed to expect a coherent set of plans that addressed every potential threat in every possible set of circumstances, leaving them with a feeling of security in every situation. The suspicion among practitioners was that the public expected all this to be accomplished with no inconvenience to them and certainly with no infringement on their civil liberties and at little personal financial cost. Businesses expected to be able to carry on, unimpeded by searches, inspections, and new security measures. They were similarly reluctant to bear the cost of new measures, expecting the public sector to take the lead.

This kind of dilemma was most obvious in the case of hazardous materials. The private liquid natural gas (LNG) tankers described above were escorted into Boston Harbor by a sizable public-sector interagency protection force. Similarly, nuclear power plants resisted hiring and adequately training private security forces to handle potential terrorist attacks. Cyber security issues got occasional press, but few businesses or private users started taking even basic security measures. In the absence of a clear message from the public or significant guidelines from the federal government and without sufficient funds for even normal operations, the response community found itself in a position of having all of the perceived responsibility without adequate authority or resources. They could have represented their flexible mechanisms as an alternative to codification, but they did not. The possibility of flexible response inherent in their tacit knowledge base went unarticulated and therefore unappreciated.

For some reason, the response community failed to make use of existing categories of prestige to articulate and make acceptable the role of tacit knowledge. Many public safety organizations appealed to tradition and revered the "crusty old dogs" in their stations as the keepers of that tradition. However, few actually made effective political use out of the tacit knowledge present in their organizations. They did not articulate the role of this knowledge in their plans, grants, and reports. This gave the appearance of gaps where there was actually simply flexibility. For example, a plan for dealing with a crashed aircraft may not specify a particular triage area. To a novice reader, this may look like an omission, when it actually just indicates an area of discretion for the incident commander. He or she will choose the site based on knowledge of the kinds of local patterns described above. After 2001, these kinds of documents came under much closer scrutiny than in the past. Previously, plans tended to be roughly updated only when required by law, by grant, or as a result of a tragedy that brought the plan temporarily into the spotlight. New social and political pressure to secure everything for every possible threat ensured that there were suddenly plenty of novice readers to make such incomplete interpretations.

Public safety planners seemed to assume that elected officials, the press, and the public would make the link between conceptions of honor and tradition and the "slushy" areas of plans. They did not connect the dots. To follow the example above, they neither listed possible staging areas and indicated that the incident commander would choose one nor did they simply explain that the choice of staging was at the incident commander's discretion. The plan readers saw only holes, and recriminations followed. Morale was lowered, frustration increased, and little improved.

This failure to articulate a valuable asset was frustrating to watch. From the perspective of a citizen who hoped for saner policies, it was a missed opportunity to point out the absurdity of striving for complete security. From the perspective of the responders, the resulting confusion seemed like an attack. They talked about the press playing "gotcha" by looking for holes in their plans and spoke with bitterness about politicians or citizens who did nothing but "throw darts" at any attempt they made to think through the issues at hand. Neither group has had the time or opportunity to think through the issue enough to see the pattern in the problem. When I discussed my analysis with people from various groups, my explanation resonated, but moving the kind of flexibility that can make use of tacit knowledge into a visible part of the plan is still difficult.

One of the reasons for this difficulty involves accountability. Responders and often planners are held accountable for their work. When a response goes wrong, people get hurt or die. Even if nobody is hurt, if the public finds out that something went amiss, people might lose promotions, raises, jobs, and even entire careers. Part of the process for judging the response is the plan itself. If a plan clearly states that a certain action should be taken and it was not, investigators can point a finger. Plans also can be guidelines for how much training of a certain type is needed for a particular agency to be sure it can carry out required tasks. When only decision points, rather than specific actions, are articulated in a plan, it leaves outside readers with the feeling that responders could be negligent and that there would be no standard against which they could be judged. There is good reason for such fears. In more dysfunctional organizations, vague and/or discretionary areas are used not as a place to employ tacit knowledge but as a way to wiggle out of responsibility.

Also at stake with reliance on tacit knowledge, as alluded in the discussion of training above, is continuity. This applies both to continuity in an operation and to overall organizational continuity or institutional knowledge. If relatively few people in an organization have any particular knowledge, tacit or otherwise, the organization is vulnerable. It lacks what is known as "depth," sufficient numbers of skilled people to maintain a response over time. An incident commander, no matter how dedicated, must sleep if he or she is to make sound choices and maximize the safety of everyone involved. The incident will not wait, and the transfer of command is always a ticklish situation until the new person is established and demonstrates the necessary knowledge and skills.

In organizational terms, knowledge densely packed into a few individuals may be effective for day-to-day operations. Every area has its go-to guys, the people who know everything and everyone and are ready to help. Unfortunately, these individuals are compact repositories of institutional memory, and the loss of them can be very difficult. The loss comes not only through death or injury. Increasingly it comes from individuals voluntarily leaving their organizations. Once an audience member at a conference asked me what all the organizations I visited had in common. I joked in response that all the best practitioners knew how many shifts they had left before they retired. The increased responsibilities in terms both of the numbers of things a responder is expected to know about and of the threats against which he or she is expected to defend can be exhausting. When that increased pace is coupled with the low morale resulting from budget cuts and public scrutiny, early retirement can look very attractive. As more and more consulting firms spring up around homeland security, there also are new opportunities for responders to move into the private sector. The high pay and prestige offered by "Beltway bandits" to responders willing to cross the line are big incentives to leave the frustration behind and make institutional memory another casualty of the failure to acknowledge the importance of tacit knowledge.

This lack of acknowledgment is reflective of the larger problem of how all practice is viewed among practitioners. While the assets and processes described in this chapter are all valued by practitioners, their unwillingness or inability to articulate that value at the levels of politics and policy has led to some significant problems, discussed in the next chapter. At the same time, the power of practice also has led to a system that is not in permanent thrall to any particular national vision of homeland security. It can bend and move in response to changing assessments of need, whether that need is based on risk assessment or political expediency. Practitioners can make use of the resources designated for homeland security to build the basic infrastructure needed to support all of the regular public safety, public health, and emergency preparedness activities that have become imbricated in popular and policy versions of homeland security. They can interpret and manipulate policy to meet local needs. The results of these manipulations serve as the interactive faces of this aspect of national security, ensuring that at least some of what the public comes to believe about homeland security will be driven by practitioners. However problematic those abilities are, the role of practitioner agency is significant and worthy of continued attention.

PART 3 Conclusion

CHAPTER 9 // OPPORTUNITIES AND PROBLEMS: FINAL COMMENTS

In all respects unready for a fall
They fell, our first progenitors, and these
Two traumas still disturb us most of all:
High places and our own unreadiness.
Towers or wells unfoot us in our dreams
Repeatedly. Old-fashioned people still
Believe that nothing saves them but their screams
And that an unawakened fall would kill.
Anticipation cannot really ease
The other trouble; waiting for the day
When such and such will happen or will pass,
It is not hard to wish your life away.
Apart from angels, wingèd and prevised,
Nobody likes to fall or be surprised.

—WILLIAM MEREDITH[1]

On the evening of September 12, 2001, I needed something to remind me of my family. I had brought with me a book of poetry by a family friend

---

for a bit of escape and illumination. I turned to it. It fell open to the poem above, written many decades before 2001. That day, and in the years that followed, it seemed to capture something of the uncertainty and anxiety, our own unreadiness. Practitioners and the public alike were unable to imagine clearly what might be next and what we should do. We were unsteady on our feet. In the preceding chapters, I have tried to capture some of that feeling as it manifested itself for me in terms of authorial identity, methods, and ethnography, as well as how it was for homeland security practitioners. Things in all of those realms are still up in the air.

In this chapter, I comment on the implications of homeland security practice and provide some concluding thoughts about the study. These comments and thoughts are drawn from my fieldwork in the Boston area but also from my later work as an academic/practitioner in other states. In the first section, I highlight the concrete policy opportunities available to anthropologists who chose to engage with this aspect of national security. The second section describes some of the "ugly secrets" of subfederal homeland security with special attention to how the processes described in the preceding chapters have led to these problems, even as they tried to solve others. The third section contains conclusions about the significance of practice and the challenges of engagement for the discipline.

POLICY OPPORTUNITIES

People in the homeland security community work within and through tensions. They work to create a sense of shared mission and community among homeland security practitioners, while simultaneously trying to maintain the traditions of their organizations. They look for guidance from the federal government, yet resist attempts to formalize their affiliations, relationships, and channels. They openly acknowledge that building and maintaining relationships is critical to the field but are hesitant to acknowledge the importance of meetings and other socializing in providing opportunities for this aspect of their work. They rely heavily on tacit knowledge, yet fail to address it in official documents or funding requests. The idea of social networks resonates with them, but most plans and policies are still written to support hierarchical organizations. They describe homeland security as important but are upset at how it detracts from other work in their fields. These tensions affect how policy is formed and implemented. They also provide the kinds of openings that can be used to engage with practitioners and policymakers to become part of the debate.

No doubt there are some big hills to climb. There is the larger scholarly project of helping homeland security policymakers and practitioners, as well as the public, to understand the global implications of our security institutions, how they are formed, and what connections and assumptions the country should examine. However, that should not lead us to ignore smaller ways that anthropology can contribute to this area of the policy process.

CONCEPTUALIZING. The most common way I made anthropology of use to practitioners while in the field was by helping people conceptualize homeland security and make effective use of language to support their goals. Anthropology is very good at taking a black box of discourse or behavior, unpacking and disassembling it, and enumerating its contents and parts. As an outsider, I was able to do this with concepts that were so naturalized that people couldn't understand that they had become obstacles. One example of this was the use of the word "capacity." In common usage, this term was associated with the materials and supplies needed for response—sometimes, but not always, including trained personnel. Even when organizations knew that they needed people to take time to become knowledgeable about homeland security topics, to build interagency relationships, and to spend time doing vulnerability assessments, they became trapped in the old definition of "capacity" when they were requesting staff or funds. I developed a brief that gave them language they could use to include new things in their discussions of capacity building.

NETWORKS AND HIERARCHY. Although most of homeland security gets done through acephalous or multicephalous cooperative networks of organizations and individuals, most policy is still written for hierarchical structures. Federal agencies channel funds through the state to towns, often without any attempt at regionalization. They write about the need for interagency efforts in their guidance, but funds are sent to individual organizations and individual organizations are held accountable. There are few provisions for regions to have their policy communities supported in official policy or funding. Federal agencies can use anthropological assistance in several ways. First, anthropologists can help policymakers understand the functional differences between network-based organization and hierarchy. Second, they can help officials find and use the policy communities or networks locals have already created, often without being able to clearly articulate their existence. Third, they can work with policymakers to develop creative ways to write policy that supports, rather than undermines, the strength of network-based organization.

LOCAL AGENCY. The tension between the desire for local autonomy and the need for accountability and thoroughness will not go away. People at all levels of government need help articulating the need for flexibility, as well as the limitations on it. At the federal level, people need to learn how to write policy that can make use of flexibility rather than trying to chase it down and fix it into a rigid set of protocols. At the state and local levels, people need to learn how to explain the need for flexibility and propose accountability measures that do not require rigid codification and formalization of relationships. Practitioners at all levels also need help identifying and supporting tacit knowledge through apprenticeships and other creative initiatives. Anthropology provides tools for understanding how agency and structure can interact. It also can help policymakers assess the degree to which community skill and information is maintained in the tacit knowledge of individuals and find ways to ensure that these assets are not lost in a system that relies too heavily on formal training.

LOCAL EXPERIENCE, LOCAL KNOWLEDGE. The broadest way in which anthropology can contribute to the homeland security policy process is through applied ethnography. Studies of the impact of homeland security policy and practice can be presented in ways that help policymakers, policy implementers, and the public understand the variable implications of security policies across different communities, classes, races, genders, and ethnicities. Studies of what locals are doing that works (or doesn't work) can inform the next generation of federal mandates. Such studies also can be used to share information horizontally, among local planners and responders who sometimes work in geographic isolation from one another. Research in the latter category is one of few ways anthropologists are likely to have access to the machinery of homeland security, informing the process and, one hopes, making it a little less damaging in the process.

COMMENTARY, UGLY SECRETS

The opportunities described above are practical in nature, but anthropology also can influence the public discussion about macrolevel questions of the legitimacy of homeland security and midlevel concerns about how we go about preparing to deal with emergencies, regardless of source. Fieldwork-based analyses of any security topic have some of the "been there, done that" credibility that practitioners use to their advantage when trying to influence the public or politicians. Prior to Hurricane Katrina in 2005, I resisted the idea of speaking or writing publicly about the systemic problems I saw with homeland security and emergency preparedness. I preferred to work within the system, trying to empower people within it to make better choices, think about more factors, resist implementing policies with which they did not agree. After Hurricane Katrina devastated the Gulf Coast, I came to see this stance as incomplete. It was based on my misunderstanding of the degree of unawareness among the public and politicians about what homeland security and emergency preparedness actually is, beyond the level of federal policies and political discourse. Broader understanding of practice and its implications is necessary if we are to minimize repetitions of the problems with preparedness and response that the 2004 and 2005 hurricane seasons demonstrated.

Although most of the public discourse about failures in the Katrina response centered on federal-level problems, I suspect that was because those were the agencies and issues people could see. The Bush administration, FEMA, the Department of Homeland Security, NORTHCOM—these were easy targets. They also were politically expedient. Few politicians or members of the press were willing to be seen criticizing local responders. They did not know how to criticize the circumstances and processes in which local practitioners were enmeshed without appearing to criticize individual performance. The reality of the responses to Hurricane Katrina is that federal assets are supposed to supplement and integrate with state and local mechanisms. If those response systems are flawed, if plans have glossed-over gaps, or if the system is critically understaffed, outside assistance has no way to engage. This is not a critique of any one group in particular unless it is a critique of everyone living in the United States during this time period. As described below, the problems stem equally from problems at all levels of government but also from lack of public engagement with the topic of homeland security and emergency preparedness in more than a superficial way.

After Katrina, I tried to use my relatively protected position as an academic to help people understand why it is so hard to get homeland security/emergency preparedness done. I spoke openly and often about what I viewed as the five ugly secrets of preparedness, described below. Each of these problems is enmeshed in a reciprocal relationship with the increased use of security or military models and language to understand homeland security, emergency preparedness, public safety, and public health. As Schoch-Spana suggests, there is evidence of deliberate efforts to subsume different types of preparedness into the security metaphors already set out (Schoch-Spana 2006a). This may be being done as part of a larger vision of a militarized preparedness linked to a specific political agenda, or it simply may represent ad hoc attempts to justify past actions and link preparedness with other political goals. Regardless of intent, it has the same potential impacts, some of which are discussed in chapter 7 and about which there is an ample literature (Collier, Lakoff, and Rabinow 2004; Guillemin 2001; Helmreich 2005; McEnaney 2000; McIlroy 1997; Mechling and Mechling 1991; Oakes 1994; Peattie 1984; Schoch-Spana 2004; Selmeski 2006; Zarlengo 1999). While these trends are important, what is of more interest to me in this particular research has been what the analysis of practice exposes about the intersection of public and political assumptions with the realities of these activities below the federal level.

The commentary below is based on observations made during my field research but also on subsequent applied work. Each has its roots in the tasks, processes, and dilemmas described in the preceding chapters. These are not secrets in the sense that anyone is deliberately trying to hide them. They are secrets only in the sense that they go largely unacknowledged, unexamined, and unrepaired, even though most practitioners are painfully aware of them.

ROMANCE WITH RESPONSE. As a country, we have a romance with emergency response that leaches attention away from the critical preparedness tasks, such as planning, mitigation, public education, and system building, each of which is necessary for response activities to be successful. This preoccupation also has the effect of playing into past assumptions about the military that make it easier to comply with a militarized vision of preparedness. As described in the preceding chapters, responders have a special place among practitioners, as well as in the hearts of much of the American public. Responders are valorized in the media as authorities on all aspects of security and preparedness. This often leads them to be put in jobs where they are expected to craft plans or systems or to write policy, something for which many have no training. However valiant a responder is, however much she knows about the physics of fire, it will not help her develop a sustainable, interagency system for ongoing planning. This romanticizing further leads to an emphasis on response in funding, even at the national level, when what is needed is infrastructure—plans, systems, mechanisms, training, and development of tacit knowledge. Some of what happened during the response to Katrina was the result of this focus.

While sometimes the valorization extends to doctors, it is less common. The symbolic embodiments of 9/11 are firefighters and policemen. New York City firefighter calendars are a booming business. Nobody is selling calendars of scantily clad emergency managers or public health officials. Further, the romanticizing seems to be associated with what informants have called the "I love a man in uniform" syndrome, where the public is more comfortable hearing about their security from a uniformed member of public safety or a military figure. This trust feeds into an assumption I have heard many times from members of the public (and sometimes from civilian practitioners). They assume that when things go really wrong, the military will be able to step in and clean it up. The response to Hurricane Katrina fueled that assumption. In one sense, this is not incorrect. In many states, civilian versions of public safety, public health, and emergency management are not funded even at the level necessary to do their regular work, let alone handle a significant emergency. The only organizations that *might* have the staff, equipment, supplies, and training to respond to a large-scale or long-duration event are the National Guard, Reserve, and active duty elements of the military that happen to be in the region.

The public, as well as state and local officials, are understandably reluctant to pay for staff and resources that may never be used, especially when we have a collective delusion that there are military facilities full of equipment, supplies, and personnel just waiting to be used. This perception is a relic of the Cold War, civil defense era. It reflects neither the reduction in military personnel over the last several decades nor the impact of current deployments in some states. It also does not account for differences in training and legal issues that make it impossible for the military to serve as "backfill" when civilian response systems fail. The military is no longer the emergency backup plan for our emergency backup plan. There is a social feedback cycle to this error even among practitioners. Lack of funding for basic public health, public safety, and emergency management leads those organizations to look for funding wherever they can find it, often in security programs that are associated with responders, with uniforms, and, consciously or not, with the military.

LACK OF PUBLIC DISCUSSION OF LIMITS AND ROLES. The second "secret" is that there is no true public discussion happening about how we want to do homeland security. How far do we want to take homeland security and what risks we are willing to assume? What are the limits of the federal and state roles in security and preparedness under a federal system and how should we cope with that? Few politicians are willing to stand up in public and suggest that there are some things for which we cannot realistically prepare or that some preparations are so expensive that we need to take the risk. For example, preparations for pandemic influenza have made headlines and absorbed the time and effort of countless state and local practitioners. Even in places with some of the best preparations, the real assessments of practitioners do not make it into plans. During the first part of a pandemic, the plans for "surge capacity" beds, mass vaccination clinics, and public outreach would have some effect. However, if the outbreak became truly pandemic and the disease was significantly incapacitating or deadly, the picture changes. No plan, no effort, can change the fact that responders would become ill and community ability to staff the systems would fail. If the outbreak was national or global, from where would "outside" help come? These concerns are present even in smaller-scale incidents. My public talks often left me with the uneasy feeling that the American public expects local responders and/or the Department of Homeland Security to keep everything completely normal and convenient during an emergency. Fortunately, recent research shows that the vision of a disengaged, panicky public may be unfounded. The public is willing to engage in these discussions, participating at every level of analysis if policymakers and practitioners provide the opportunities (Schoch-Spana 2006b; Schoch-Spana et al. 2006; Simpson 2002; Working Group on Governance Dilemmas in Bioterrorism Response 2004).

With regard to the federal role, there is a critical distinction between a national approach and an approach based on federal support for local solutions that remains confusing to many in the public. For preparedness and planning, the federal system makes funding available for certain types of programs and provides guidelines on some areas of security and preparedness that must be followed if a state or town wishes to receive funds. Federal power encourages, channels, and restrains but does not dictate the shape of homeland security at the local level. In countries with a national system, programs can be implemented in a more uniform way, for better or for worse.

During incidents, the vast majority of the federal emergency response structure is set up as described above, to supplement and integrate with local response, not to replace it. Assets are limited because the burden of responsibility falls on state and local structures. What assets exist take time to arrive and, in a large-scale event, may not be available to all areas. Most practitioners now expect to be on their own for long periods of time. Immediately following hurricanes Katrina and Rita in 2005, there was some discussion about revised roles for the military, some discussion about renaming or shifting the bureaucratic position of FEMA, but little substantive analysis made it into public debates. The discussions that need to happen are those that involve how much the public wants to invest in security and, among practitioners, how to educate the public about the limits of response.

MORE DOCUMENTS WON'T HELP. Third, more guidance and templates won't solve the problems. Another exposé or commission report will go largely unnoticed. Nobody at the local level has time to read them. Few have broad-enough backgrounds to assess critically the content or local utility of existing documents even when they get a moment to look at them. This is tied into problems described earlier about the romance with response. At the moment, vendors and consultants play a large role in interpreting guidance and literature for practitioners under the rubric of "technical assistance," a situation that is problematic at best. The field is too diverse to expect that a process of professional peer review will emerge. Engaged academics can play a balancing role in sifting through the deluge of information and guidance that has been produced since 2001, but that seems a shaky system to institutionalize. Without more staff, trained in the critical and analytic skills needed, and without starting to articulate time to read as part of necessary capacity, policy communities will continue to have a difficult time assessing available information and incorporating it into their practice and processes.

REALISTIC PLANS ARE NOT WELCOME. Fourth, there is little political or public support for writing realistic plans and truly identifying gaps. No local fire chief or emergency manager wants to be the first to turn in a plan that has sections saying "we haven't figured out how to handle this yet." Unfortunately, such honesty is the only way for local, state, and federal officials to know where aid will be most needed during a disaster. If plans gloss over gaps, the next time those gaps will be noticed is when somebody falls through them. The example given above of pandemic planning continues to serve as a case for this problem. Most pandemic plans I read, from 2001 on, present a tidy description of legal authorities, notification protocols, bed surge capacity, and mass vaccination facilities, and a few mention mass fatality management. There are many informal, worried conversations about how to cope when surge-capacity beds run out or when there are too few people to staff the tidy models, but nobody is willing to put these concerns in official plans. What state would be willing to write legislation that truly captures the way patient care standards would have to be altered in such a situation? There are too many unknowns, too many horrific Hollywood visions of plague hospitals full of the infected, the dying, and the dead, lying unattended. We move directly from "difficult, but manageable" to "the apocalypse," with very little planning in between.

However, sometimes this glossing over of gaps is not the result of this sort of overwhelming problem. More often the problems that are hidden in this way are simply things that have not been worked out yet. They require a rearrangement of resources or confrontations with higher-ups or public discussions that are difficult but not impossible. In some cases, the solutions are already under way, just incomplete. There are ample personal accounts to suggest that practitioners in New Orleans knew they still had work to do on their evacuation plan. How might things have been different if they had felt comfortable turning in a plan that accurately reflected their concerns?

Other times, the plans are what is known as "a six-story firefighting plan in a seven-story town." In other words, the plan is adequate for what it describes, but it fails to acknowledge the presence of other hazards or vulnerabilities. It covers only those aspects of response it has the resources to address. The process of normalizing gap acknowledgment is long and difficult. It makes sense to people on a surface level, but what politician wants to be the first to announce that his jurisdiction's plan is full of holes? The only solution for this problem is for the public and the press to raise questions. Even these must be carefully couched, if they are to produce a climate in which gap acknowledgment becomes not only accepted but actually demanded. There is a big difference in the way a practitioner can be expected to react to a question that implies that a practitioner is not living up to his or her role as a protector—"How will you protect my children during the fifth week of an outbreak?"—versus a question that engages the questioner as a partner in the process: "What are the problems you still have to solve and what kind of resources would you need to solve them?"

HIDDEN SOLUTIONS. The fifth and final "ugly secret" arises directly from the importance of subfederal practice. Much of homeland security and emergency preparedness takes place outside official structures and policies. As described earlier, reliance on unacknowledged assets and structures—pathfinders, unofficial channels, temporary task-based organization, and tacit knowledge—means that much of what is especially good and bad is hidden in plain sight. This is compounded by the romance-with-response factor that leads to there being more documentation and discussion of how a jurisdiction plans to respond than how they are organized to conduct any of the rest of the work of homeland security described earlier. It also is complicated by the unacknowledged gaps described above. A concerned member of the public can request official information about organization and response, but what will they get?

There are broader issues. The hidden-in-plain-sight nature of some elements of homeland security places them outside normal channels of accountability. It places them outside normal funding channels as well, making the good aspects especially vulnerable to financial catastrophe. Ultimately, although this is generally not the intention of the practitioners to whom I spoke, the fact that critical processes of homeland security are hidden may feed into climates of hypersecrecy and the disengagement of the public from substantive discussions about how homeland security gets done.

These observations may seem simple, and there are clearly no easy solutions to them. However, they are the kind of things that government employees cannot say without risking their careers. It has been my experience that practitioners at the subfederal level want to see these problems fixed. They simply do not have the job security, the venues, or the time to make the sustained effort it would take. The basic acts of standing up, pointing out the emperor's new clothes, and refusing to be quiet are things that are much easier for anthropologists and other academics.

CLOSING THOUGHTS

Indeed, they would have had such a list had the FAA simply compiled and sent, as they now had done on September 12th, the separate lists that the FBI and the CIA had been sending the FAA for at least the prior six months, naming people who were flight risks. . . . But according to an FAA official and a Justice Department official, two of the hijackers were on those September 10 lists . . . "We just never got around to setting up a protocol for who would control the list and how we would get the airlines to implement it," says the FAA person (Brill 2003, 30).

THE IMPACT OF PRACTICE. The passage above from Steven Brill's *After* illustrates the ramifications of seemingly small decisions or inactions, of organizational priorities and orientations. The policies and technology necessary to stop the attacks of 9/11 were already in place that September. However, practice does not always follow policy in lockstep, especially when the policy and the degree of urgency behind it are unclear. A great deal of homeland security consists in people figuring out what they should be doing and then "getting around to it." Practice matters.

The preceding chapters have explored homeland security as practice— specifically, practice that played a role in shaping homeland security as it is experienced by many others in the United States. Chapter 4 described the policy community formed by those in the Boston area who were drawn into homeland security–related activities by the direct or indirect dictates of evolving federal, state, and local policies. Chapters 5–7 presented the ground-level practice of homeland security: the things people went to work to do, the things they worried about, the problems they tried to solve, and the conceptual constructions with which they struggled. Chapter 8 explained the desire of homeland security practitioners to maintain enough local autonomy of action and structure to respond to changing policies and operational needs and the means they used to get things done while preserving that flexibility. The preceding sections in this chapter illustrate policy opportunities and problems that become apparent as the result of research at this level.

Although national policies and debates are powerful shapers of homeland security, they are not the only ones. The preceding chapters have shown that much of what homeland security came to mean in the Boston area was the result of people in the policy community "just thinking out loud," trying to manage the unwieldy construction project as best they could. As practitioners wove their developing ideas and activities into a coherent pattern of policy and practice, they made systems, relationships, plans, and organizations through which national policy would be manifested. They created the homeland security with which the majority of Boston area's residents and visitors interacted.

As I write this, it is not at all clear to me whether homeland security will continue to be developed as a distinct area of practice or whether it will be subsumed in existing categories and discourses of emergency management and national security. I have little doubt that it will remain a significant area of national policy, if only because the reorganization of so many agencies into the Department of Homeland Security lends it greater bureaucratic momentum than civil defense programs ever enjoyed. However, at the local level, after filtering through local concepts and practices, it probably will look more like a modification of existing patterns of law enforcement, public safety and health, emergency management, and local governance. This in no way detracts from the significance of how people in the community interacted with, fed into, and transformed national policy and sociocultural changes. In fact, since it is largely their ideas and practices that will drive such changes, it simply strengthens the argument for their importance in shaping this aspect of U.S. culture.

My focus on practice is less a political stance than an anthropological and personal one, although I agree with Deborah Cameron that there is no neutral way of speaking about anything. As she puts it, "It is impossible to come up with a description which could not be interpreted as in some way taking sides" (Cameron 1995, 74). In favoring practice over critique, I may in some way contribute to the acceptance of policies I find personally objectionable. Despite these concerns, following the disruptions of 2001, members of the Boston-area policy community opened their doors to me. I had an opportunity to study security practice with a level and breadth of access that are unlikely to be duplicated. I took it.

I set out to make anthropological contributions to the study of security by investigating some of the groups that maintained and transformed our ideas and structures related to security. I also wanted to contribute an ethnographic study of practice, producing a work that would illustrate and support practice as an organizing concept in anthropology. Although I feel I have accomplished these goals, others have emerged, the seeds of which were only partially formed in 1999 when I first crafted the project. These involve the methodological challenges and the issues of disciplinary politics and authorial identity described in the first half of the book. There are two sets of ideas that I especially want to highlight in conclusion.

The first set of ideas is methodological. Chapter 3 describes some of the methodological challenges I faced in this process. Many of them can be resolved to some degree by refinements in the human-subjects review process and by approaching the study of security organizations from the standpoint of action anthropology. However, neither of these solutions resolves the issue of writing up. As a discipline, we can no longer rely on the same standards of informant confidentiality that worked during the last century. As many anthropologists are finding, geographic and economic distances no longer serve to cloak our informants, while we relate anecdotes that would easily identify them in their own communities. My informants will read parts of this book. In fact, some of them have been part of the process of writing it, helping me check and recheck to make sure I was not exposing security flaws or identifying individuals.

There was no possibility that I could use normal anthropological conventions for ethnographic writing. I have had to abstract both people and settings to a degree that was very uncomfortable for one who has enjoyed the lushness of much anthropological writing. As more anthropologists conduct heavily engaged studies among the powerful and as more communities gain the means to access our work, the discipline will have to engage more energetically in discussions about informant confidentiality and writing conventions. The only alternative is to restrict our research to only those communities and informants who have no vulnerabilities, if we could find them.

These concerns are highlighted in communities, such as those involved in national security, where access is very hard to obtain and participant observation may be conducted in unusual contexts, perhaps even through applied work or employment. While such problematic contexts and relationships can constrain what can be shared or critiqued, they also provide a means of obtaining data and research ideas that can be used by others in the discipline. In this case, one anthropologist may simultaneously be researcher, employee, and informant. Yet more reason to add a sense of greater urgency to our conversations.

The second set of ideas is, I believe, more important from a disciplinary standpoint. Since choosing anthropology as a field, I have been troubled by the tendency of many of my colleagues to reify institutions or trends that they oppose on political and/or moral grounds. The "security apparatus" and the "military-industrial complex" and the "federal government" are discussed as through they were formed of some superorganic Kroeberian ether. Objections to the actions of people within these institutions are framed in polemical terms rather than the careful nuance, which was one of the reasons I chose the field. While this reification makes it easier to discuss institutions, it also makes it easier to dismiss them. If national policies and organizations related to security appear monolithic and impenetrable, it absolves us of responsibility for doing anything other than railing against them. This disengagement does little other than deprive anthropology of any opportunity to influence large social institutions, such as those involved with defense and security.

However, if one conceives of national security as consisting in the ideas, assumptions, and practices of people, options open. Recognizing that no anthropological subject can be understood thoroughly at a distance, some of us will be impelled to engage, to understand, and, perhaps, to contribute to those ideas, assumptions, and practices, to become part of the next round of construction. The full range of studies and critiques is necessary, but some of them must be conducted in close and problematic relationships with practitioners. This will mean that anthropology must answer some fundamental questions about its willingness to work within flawed systems and must tease apart issues of disciplinary ethics from political, historical, and emotional reactions, developing grounded, useful guidelines for researchers and applied anthropologists. Engagement, carefully monitored by the discipline, will be key to our ability to understand institutions of national security and how they operate in the world.

APPENDIX //
SAMPLE ORGANIZATIONS IN THE BOSTON AREA'S HOMELAND SECURITY POLICY COMMUNITY

FEDERAL

U.S. Department of Justice
  U.S. Attorney's Office, District of Massachusetts—including the Anti-Terrorism Task Force
  Federal Bureau of Investigation—who play the lead in the Boston-area Joint Terrorism Task Force, as well as holding several specialized units/offices dealing with terrorism locally and nationally
  Office of Domestic Preparedness
  U.S. Marshals Service
  Immigration and Naturalization Service
  Federal Emergency Management Agency
U.S. Department of Health and Human Services, including the Centers for Disease Control and Prevention and the National Pharmaceutical Stockpile Program
Environmental Protection Agency
U.S. Department of Treasury—including the Bureau of Alcohol, Tobacco, and Firearms, Customs, and the Secret Service
U.S. Postal Service Inspection Services
U.S. Department of Transportation—including the Federal Aviation Administration, the Federal Railroad Administration, the Transportation Security Administration, the Hazmat Safety Office, and the Coast Guard
U.S. Department of Defense—including the Soldier Biological and Chemical Command National Protection Center just outside Boston, the 401 Chemical Company in the Boston area, and other active and reserve components in Massachusetts

U.S. Department of Agriculture
U.S. Nuclear Regulatory Commission
U.S. Department of Energy

STATE AND REGIONAL

Office of Commonwealth Security

Massachusetts Water Resources Authority—including the management of the waste treatment plant that was also considered to be a potential target due to the presence of explosive gases

Executive Office of Public Safety—including the Office of the Chief Medical Examiner, the Department of Public Safety (which includes with State Police), Department of Corrections, Department of Fire Services (which includes regional hazardous materials teams), and the Massachusetts Emergency Management Agency

Executive Office of Health and Human Services

Massachusetts Department of Health—including the Radiation Control Program, Office of Emergency Medical Services, Food Protection Program, Division of Research and Epidemiology, Public Health Council, and the public health laboratory resources

Massachusetts Department of Mental Health

Executive Office of Transportation and Construction—including the Massachusetts Bay Transportation Authority (subway, buses, ferries, etc.), the Port Authority commonly known as Massport (the water and airports), which incorporates Massport Fire Rescue Department, the Turnpike Authority (which was in charge of the Big Dig), the Highway Department

Office of the Massachusetts Attorney General

Massachusetts National Guard—including the Joint Forces Headquarters, Air National Guard, Army National Guard, and the First Civil Support Team—Weapons of Mass Destruction

American Red Cross of Massachusetts Bay

Salvation Army of Massachusetts

BOSTON

Boston Fire—including Boston Emergency Management, as well as hazardous materials response teams and other special operations units

Boston Police—including a bomb squad, harbor patrol, hazardous materials response team, other special operations units, and intelligence units

Boston Emergency Medical Services

Boston Public Health Commission

Boston Inspectional Services Department

Boston Public Works

SAMPLE REGIONAL TEAMS, ASSOCIATIONS, AND INITIATIVES

National Disaster Medical System Teams

FEMA Urban Search and Rescue Teams

Joint Terrorism Task Force

Metropolitan Medical Response Systems—Boston, Springfield, and Worcester

Local Area Planning Committees (established throughout the United States
    after 1989 to help communities become more aware of the chemical haz-
    ards in their communities and work with industry to mitigate them)

New England Disaster Recovery Information Exchange

Maritime Incident Resource and Training Partnership

Metrofire (a mutual aid system of area fire departments)

Operation Safe Commerce

REFERENCES

Abel, David. 2003. "Senators Rap State Security Readiness Hearings Set to Address Terror-Response Strategy." *Boston Globe,* September 2.

Abrams, Herbert L. 1983. "Civilian-Military Contingency Hospital System: Preparing for 'The Highest Rate of Casualties in History.'" *Bulletin of the Atomic Scientists.* Suppl. 39:S11–S16.

Abu-Lughod, Lila. 2000. "Locating Ethnography." *Ethnography* 1 (2): 261–67.

———. 1991. "Writing against Culture." In *Recapturing Anthropology: Working in the Present,* ed. R. Fox, 137–62. Santa Fe, NM: School of American Research.

Adams, Richard N. 1970. *Crucifixion by Power: Essays on Guatemalan National Social Structure, 1944–1966.* Austin: University of Texas Press.

Advisory Panel to Assess Domestic Response Capabilities for Terrorism involving Weapons of Mass Destruction. 2000. *Toward a National Strategy for Combating Terrorism: Second Annual Report to the President and the Congress of the Advisory Panel to Assess Domestic Response Capabilities for Terrorism involving Weapons of Mass Destruction.* Washington, DC: Advisory Panel to Assess Domestic Response Capabilities for Terrorism involving Weapons of Mass Destruction.

———. 2001. *For Ray Downey: Third Annual Report to the President and the Congress of the Advisory Panel to Assess Domestic Response Capabilities for Terrorism Involving Weapons of Mass Destruction.* Alexandria, VA: RAND.

Agar, Michael. 1986. Speaking of ethnography. Beverly Hills, CA: Sage Publications.

Alibek, Ken, and Stephen Handelman. 1999. *Biohazard: The Chilling True Story of the Largest Covert Biological Weapons Program in the World—Told from Inside by the Man Who Ran It.* New York: Dell Publishing.

American Anthropological Society. 1998. *Code of Ethics of the American Anthropological Association.* American Anthropological Society. http://aaanet.org/.

———. 2004. American Anthropological Association Statement on Ethnography and Institutional Review Boards. American Anthropological Society. http://aaanet.org/.

American Society of Newspaper Editors. 2002. The Kansas City Star Code of Ethics. American Society of Newspaper Editors. http://asne.org/.

Appadurai, Arjun. 1990. "Disjuncture and Difference in the Global Cultural Economy." *Public Culture* 2 (2): 1–24.

Associated Press. 1977a. "Picariello Defense Rests: Defendant Not on Stand." *Kennebec Journal,* February 3.

———. 1977b. "Gullion Jury Starts Deliberating." *Kennebec Journal,* March 17.

Bakalaki, Alexandra. 1997. "Students, Natives, Colleagues: Encounters in Academia and in the Field." *Cultural Anthropology* 12 (4): 502–26.

Banks, William C. 1999. "The Devil and the Demon: The Threat of Bioterrorism in the U.S." National Security Studies Case Series. Maxwell School of Citizenship and Public Affairs of Syracuse University and Paul H. Nitze School of Advanced International Studies of Johns Hopkins University.

———. 2003. "And the Wall Came Tumbling Down: Secret Surveillance after the Terror." *University of Miami Law Review* 57 (4):1147–94.

———. 2004. "The Normalization of Homeland Security after September 11: The Role of the Military in Counterterrorism Preparedness and Response." *Louisiana Law Review* 64:735–78.

Bartlett, James A. 2001. "Homeland: Behind the Buzzword." *Ethical Spectacle* 7 (12). http://www.spectacle.org/.

Bauman, Zygmunt. 1992. *Intimations of Postmodernity.* London: Routledge. Cited in Ulf Hannerz, *Transnational Connections* (London: Routledge, 1996), 22.

Bennett, John W. 1996. "Applied and Action Anthropology: Ideological and Conceptual Assets." In "Anthropology in Public," Special Issue of *Current Anthropology* 37 (1):S23–S53.

Bernard, H. Russell. 1994. *Research Methods in Anthropology: Qualitative and Quantitative Approaches.* Thousand Oaks, CA: Sage Publications.

———. 1998. *Handbook of Methods in Cultural Anthropology.* Walnut Creek, CA: AltaMira Press.

Blanchard, Boyce Wayne. 1980. "American Civil Defense, 1945–1975: The Evolution of Programs and Policies." Ph.D. diss., University of Virginia.

Blim, Michael L. 1992. "Introduction: The Emerging Global Factory and Anthropology." In *Anthropology and the Global Factory,* ed. F. A. Rothstein and M. Blim, 1–30. New York: Bergin & Garvey.

Bogdan, Robert. 1980. "Policy Data as a Social Process: A Qualitative Approach to Quantitative Data." *Human Organization* 39 (4): 302–9.

Bornstein, Avram. 2005. "Antiterrorist Policing in New York City after 9/11: Comparing Perspectives on a Complex Process." *Human Organization* 64 (1): 52–61.

Boston Metropolitan Area Planning Council. 2004. Metro Area. http://www .mapc.org/.

Bott, Elizabeth. 1971. *Family and Social Network: Roles, Norms, and External Relationships in Ordinary Urban Families.* New York: Free Press.

Bourdieu, Pierre. [1972] 1999. *Outline of a Theory of Practice.* Translated by R. Nice. Cambridge: Cambridge University Press.

Branum, Tara L. 2002. "Screeners Fail Public with Politically Correct Searches." *USA Today,* April 11.

Brennis, Don. 2004. "A Partial View of Contemporary Anthropology." *American Anthropologist* 106 (3): 580–88.

Briggs, Charles L. 2004. "Theorizing Modernity Conspiratorially: Science, Scale, and the Political Economy of Public Discourse in Explanations of a Cholera Epidemic." *American Ethnologist* 31 (2): 164–87.

Briggs, Charles L., and Richard Bauman. 1995. "Genre, Intertextuality, and Social Power." In *Language, Culture, and Society,* ed. B. G. Blount, 567–608. Prospect Heights, IL: Waveland Press.

Brill, Steven. 2003. *After: How America Confronted the September 12 Era.* New York: Simon & Schuster.

Brosius, Peter, Judith Goode, and Kendall Thu. 2002. "Policy and Public Engagement: Recent Developments." Anthropology News 43 (2): 27–28.

Brown, JoAnne. 1988. "'*A* Is for Atom, *B* Is for Bomb': Civil Defense in American Public Education, 1948–1963." *Journal of American History* 75 (1): 68–90.

Bruner, Edward F. 2004. "Military Forces: What Is the Appropriate Size for the United States?" *CRS Report for Congress.* http://www.fas.org/.

Buchalter, Alice R., John N. Gibbs, and Marieke Lewis. 2004. *Laws and Regulations Governing the Protection of Sensitive but Unclassified Information: A Report.* Washington, DC: Federal Research Division, Library of Congress.

Bush, George W. 2003a. *Homeland Security Presidential Directive/HSPD-5: Management of Domestic Incidents.* Washington, DC: White House Office of the Press Secretary.

———. 2003b. *December 17, 2003 Homeland Security Presidential Directive/ Hspd-7: Critical Infrastructure Identification, Prioritization, and Protection. Washington, DC: White House Office of the Press Secretary.*

———. 2003c. *December 17, 2003 Homeland Security Presidential Directive/ Hspd-8: National Preparedness.* Washington, DC: White HouseOffice of the Press Secretary.

Cameron, Deborah. 1995. *Verbal Hygiene.* New York: Routledge.

Carter, Ashton, John Deutch, and Phillip Zelikow. 1998. "Catastrophic Terrorism: Elements of a National Policy." A Report of Visions of Governance for the Twenty-First Century. John F. Kennedy School of Government, Harvard University, Cambridge, MA.

Chambers, Erve. 1989. *Applied Anthropology: A Practical Guide.* Prospect Heights, IL: Waveland Press, Inc.

Cheng, Vincent J. 2004. *Inauthentic: The Anxiety over Culture and Identity.* New Brunswick, NJ: Rutgers University Press.

Cohn, Carol. 1987. "Sex and Death in the Rational World of Defense Intellectuals." *Signs* 12 (4): 687–718.

Collier, Stephen J., Andrew Lakoff, and Paul Rabinow. 2004. "Biosecurity: Towards an Anthropology of the Contemporary." *Anthropology Today* 20 (5): 3–7.

Collins, Samuel Gerald. 2006. Review of *Analytic Culture in the U.S. Intelligence Community: An Ethnographic Study,* by Rob Johnston. *Anthropology of Work Review* 27 (1): 25–26.

Comaroff, Jean. 1985. *Body of Power, Spirit of Resistance: The Culture and History of a South African People.* Chicago: University of Chicago Press.

Comaroff, John L., and Jean Comaroff. 1992. *Ethnography and the Historical Imagination.* Boulder, CO: Westview Press.

Cordesman, Anthony H. 2000. "Defending America: Redefining the Conceptual Borders of Homeland Defense." Rough draft, Center for Strategic and International Studies, Washington, DC.

D'Andrade, Roy G. 1992. "Schemas and Cultural Models." In *Human Motives and Cultural Models,* ed. R. G. D'Andrade and C. Strauss, 23–44. New York: Cambridge University Press.

Dedman, Bill. 2005. "Slower Arrival at Fires in US Is Costing Lives." *Boston Globe,* January 30. (Multiple Published Corrections—Date: February 8, 2005.)

Denicola, Lane. 2006. "The Bundling of Geospatial Information with Everyday Experience." In *Surveillance and Security: Technological Politics and Power in Everyday Life,* ed. T. Monahan, 243–64. New York: Routledge.

de Rugy, Veronique. 2005. "What Does Homeland Security Spending Buy?" Working Paper no. 107. American Enterprise Institute, Washington, DC. http://www.aei.org/.

Department of Homeland Security. 2004a. "History: Who Became Part of the Department?" http://www.dhs.gov/.

———. 2004b. "National Incident Management System." http://www.dhs.gov/.

———. 2004c. "National Response Plan." http://www.dhs.gov/.

———. 2005. "READY AMERICA: Overview." http://www.dhs.gov/.

Dewalt, Kathleen M., Billie R. Dewalt, and Coral B. Wayland. 1998. "Participant Observation." In Handbook of Methods in Cultural Anthropology, ed. H. R. Bernard, 259–300. Walnut Creek, CA: AltaMira Press.

Douglas, Mary, and Aaron Wildavsky. 1982. *Risk and Culture.* Berkeley: University of California Press.

Drehle, David Von. 2001. "Bush Pledges Victory; Reagan National Closed Indefinitely." *Washington Post,* September 14.

Drycus, Stephen, Arthur L. Berney, William C. Banks, and Peter Raven-Hansen. 1997. *National Security Law.* Boston: Little, Brown, & Co.

Dunlap, David W. 2006. "Civil Defense Logo Dies at 67, and Some Mourn Its Passing." *New York Times,* December 1.

Editor. 1962. "The Medical Consequences of Thermonuclear War: Editor's Note." *New England Journal of Medicine* 266 (22): 1126–27.

Eisgruber, Christopher L., and Lawrence G. Sager. 2003. "Civil Liberties in the Dragon's Domain: Negotiating the Blurred Boundary between Domestic Law and Foreign Affairs after 9/11." In September 11 in History: A Watershed Moment? ed. M. L. Dudziak, 163–79. Durham, NC: Duke University Press.

Epstein, A. L. 1961. "The Network and Urban Social Organization." *Rhodes-Livingston Institute Journal* 29:29–62.

Falkenrath, Richard A., Robert D. Newman, and Bradley A. Thayer. 1998. *America's Achilles Heel: Nuclear, Biological, and Chemical Terrorism and Covert Attack.* Cambridge, MA: MIT Press.

Farmer, Paul. 1996. "Social Inequalities and Emerging Infectious Diseases." *Emerging Infectious Diseases* 2 (4): 259–69.

Fay, J. A. 2003. "Model of Spills and Fires from LNG and Oil Tankers." *Journal of Hazardous Materials* 96 (2): 171–88.

Federal Emergency Management Agency. 2001. "Records of the Federal Emergency Management Agency [FEMA] (Record Group 311), 1955–89: 311.1, Administrative History." National Archives and Records Administration. http://www.archives.gov.

———. 2005. "Mitigation." http://www.fema.gov/.

Ferguson, James, and Akhil Gupta. 2002. "Spatializing States: Toward and Ethnography of Neoliberal Governmentality." *American Ethnologist* 29 (4): 981–1002.

Fidler, David P. 1996. "Globalization, International Law, and Emerging Infectious Diseases." *Emerging Infectious Diseases,* vol. 2, no. 2. http://www.cdc.gov.

Fluehr-Lobban, Carolyn. 1998. "Ethics." In *Handbook of Methods in Cultural Anthropology,* ed. H. R. Bernard, 173–202. Walnut Creek, CA: AltaMira Press.

———. 2006. "Ethical Challenges, New and Old: In National Security and the Global War on Terror." *Anthropology News* 47 (3): 5.

Flynn, Stephen E. 2007. *The Edge of Disaster: Rebuilding a Resilient Nation.* New York: Random House, in cooperation with the Council on Foreign Relations.

Foucault, Michel. 1982. "The Subject and Power." *Critical Inquiry* 8 (4): 777–96.

Funigiello, Philip J. 1990. "Managing Armageddon: The Truman Administration, Atomic War, and the National Security Resources Board." *Journal of Policy History* 2 (4): 403–24.

Gao, Helen. 2001. "Should City Prepare for Terror? City Considers Large-Scale Emergency Plan." *Daily News of Los Angeles,* September 11.

Gedan, Benjamin. 2002. "Clam Diggers Get a Reprieve, Security Zone OK'd at Logan." *Boston Globe,* August 11.

Geertz, Clifford. 1973. *The Interpretation of Cultures.* New York: Basic Books.

———. 2002. "An Inconstant Profession: The Anthropological Life in Interesting Times." *Annual Review of Anthropology* 31:1–19.

Gellman, Barton. 2002. "In U.S., Terrorism's Peril Undiminished, Nation Struggles on Offense and Defense, and Officials Still Expect New Attacks." *Washington Post,* December 24.

Giddens, Anthony. 1991. *Modernity and Self-Identity: Self and Society in the Late Modern Age.* Stanford, CA: Stanford University Press.

Gladwell, Malcolm. 2007. *Blink: The Power of Thinking without Thinking.* New York: Back Bay Books.

Gordon, Colin. 1991. "Governmental Rationality: An Introduction." In *The Foucault Effect: Studies in Governmentality,* ed. G. Burchell, C. Gordon, and P. Miller, 1–51. Chicago: University of Chicago Press.

Greenspan, Jeff. 2001. "What Is Homeland Security? Info from Government Websites." http://www.lewrockwell.com/.

Guillemin, Jeanne. 1999. *Anthrax: The Investigation of a Deadly Outbreak.* Berkeley: University of California Press.

———. 2001. Anthropology in the U.S. Military: Insightful Interpretive Tool, Valued Policy Contributor, or Disdained Discipline? Discussion presented at the hundredth annual meeting of the American Anthropological Association, Washington, DC.

Gupta, Akhil, and James Ferguson. 1992. "Beyond 'Culture': Space, Identity, and the Politics of Difference." *Cultural Anthropology* 7 (1): 6–23.

Gusterson, Hugh. 1996. *Nuclear Rites.* Berkeley: University of California Press.

———. 2003. "Anthropology and the Military—1968, 2003, and Beyond." *Anthropology Today* 19 (3): 25–26.

———. 2005. "Spies in Our Midst." *Anthropology News* 46 (6): 39–40.

Hannerz, Ulf. 1987. "The World in Creolization." *Africa* 57:546–59.

———. 1996. *Transnational Connections.* New York: Routledge.

Haraway, Donna. 1991. *Simians, Cyborgs, and Women.* New York: Routledge.

Hart, Gary, and Warren B. Rudman. 2002. *America Still Unprepared— America Still in Danger: Report of an Independent Task Force Sponsored by the Council on Foreign Relations.* Washington, DC: Council on Foreign Relations.

Harvey, David. 1996. "The Social Construction of Space and Time." In

Justice, Nature and the Geography of Difference, 210–47. Cambridge, MA: Blackwell.

Havens, Jerry. 2003. "Terrorism: Ready to Blow?" *Bulletin of the Atomic Scientists* 59 (4): 16–18.

Helmreich, Stephan. 2005. "Biosecurity: A Response to Collier, Lakoff, and Rabinow." *Anthropology Today* 21 (2): 21.

Henretig, Fred. 2001. "Biological and Chemical Terrorism Defense: A View from the 'Front Lines' of Public Health." *American Journal of Public Health* 91 (5): 718–20.

Howe, Peter. 1989. "'76 courthouse blast victim feels 'forgotten' after mistrial." *Boston Globe*, December 3.

Hunt, Jennifer. 1984. "The Development of Rapport through the Negotiation of Gender in Field Work among Police." *Human Organization* 43 (4): 283–96.

Jackson, Jean E. 1995. "Culture, Genuine and Spurious: The Politics of Indianness in the Vaupes, Columbia." *American Ethnologist* 22 (1): 3–27.

Jaschik, Scott. 2006. "Torture and Social Scientists." *Inside Higher Ed,* November 22. http://www.insidehighered.com.

Johnson, Jeffrey C. 1998. "Research Design and Research Strategies." In *Handbook of Methods in Cultural Anthropology*, ed. H. R. Bernard, 131–71. Walnut Creek, CA: AltaMira Press.

Kaplan, Amy. 2003. "Homeland Insecurities: Transformations of Language and Space." In *September 11 in History: A Watershed Moment?* ed. M. L. Dudziak, 55–69. Durham, NC: Duke University Press.

Keane, Webb. 2003. "Self-Interpretation, Agency, and the Objects of Anthropology: Reflections on a Genealogy." *Comparative Studies in Society and History* 45 (2): 222–48.

Kerr, James W. 1968. "Organization for Civil Defense." *Military Review* 48 (3): 75–82.

Klein, Gary A. 1999. *Sources of Power: How People Make Decisions.* Cambridge, MA: MIT Press.

———. 1997. Making decisions in natural environments. [Alexandria, VA]: U.S. Army Research Institute for the Behavioral and Social Sciences, Research and Advanced Concepts Office.

Kurkjian, Stephen, and Megan Tench. 2001. "Airliner Bomb Threat Foiled, Struggle Forces Plane to Logan." *Boston Globe*, December 23.

Lamperti, John. 1983. Crisis Relocation Planning: "What Harm Can It Do?" *Bulletin of the Atomic Scientists.* Suppl. 39:S7–S10.

Lasker, Roz D. 2004. *Redefining Readiness: Terrorism Planning through the Eyes of the Public.* New York: New York Academy of Medicine, Center for the Advancement of Collaborative Strategies in Health.

League of Women Voters. 2005. "Massachusetts Government: County Government." http://lwvma.org.

Leaning, Jennifer. 1987. "Star Wars Revives Civil Defense." *Bulletin of the Atomic Scientists* 42 (4): 42–46.

Leaning, Jennifer, and Matthew Leighton. 1983. "Federal Emergency Management Agency: The World according to FEMA." *Bulletin of the Atomic Scientists.* Suppl. 39:S2–S7.

LeCompte, Margaret D., and Jean J. Schensul. 1999. *Ethnographer's Toolkit, 1: Designing and Conducting Ethnographic Research.* Walnut Creek, CA: AltaMira Press.

Low, Setha M. 2002. "Lessons from Imagining the World Trade Center Site: An Examination of Public Space and Culture." *Anthropology and Education Quarterly* 33 (3): 395–405.

———. 2006. "The Erosion of Public Space and the Public Realm: Paranoia, Surveillance and Privatization in New York City." *City and Society* 18 (1): 43–49.

Macero, Cosmo, Jr., and Jonathan Wells. 2001. "Attack on America; Mass. Eyed as Key Nest for Osama's Thugs." *Boston Herald,* September 16.

MacKenzie, Donald, and Graham Spinardi. 1995. "Tacit Knowledge, Weapons Design, and the Univention of Nuclear Weapons." *American Journal of Sociology* 101 (1): 44–99.

Marcus, George E. 1998. *Ethnography through Thick and Thin.* Princeton, NJ: Princeton University Press.

———. 1999. *Critical Anthropology Now: Unexpected Contexts, Shifting Constituencies, Changing Agendas.* School of American Research Advanced Seminar Series. Santa Fe, NM: School of American Research Press.

Maritime Incident Resource and Training Partnership. 2003. "Interoperability and WMD Vulnerability Study: Port of Boston." Maritime Incident Resource and Training Partnership, Boston, MA. (Restricted document.)

Martinez, Jose, and Jules Crittenden. 2001. Air heroics—Passengers, Crew Subdue Bomb-Threat Suspect. *Boston Herald,* December 23.

Masco, Joseph. 2002. "Lie Detectors: On Secrets and Hypersecurity in Los Alamos." *Public Culture* 14 (3): 411–67.

Massachusetts Department of Housing and Community Development. 2004. "Community Profiles." http://www.mass.gov.

Maxwell, Bruce. 2004. *Homeland Security: A Documentary History.* Washington, DC: CQ Press.

McEnaney, Laura. 2000. "Civil Defense Begins at Home: Militarization Meets Everyday Life in the Fifties." Princeton, NJ: Princeton University Press.

McGrory, Brian. 2005. "A Second Chance to Do It Right." *Boston Globe,* January 4.

McIlroy, Andrew. 1997. "No Interest, No Time, No Money: Civil Defense in Cleveland in the Cold War." *Ohio History* 106:59–86.

McIntyre, Dave. 2001. "Winning This One—the Logic of Homeland Security." *Washington Times,* September 16.

McNamara, Laura A. 2001. "Ways of Knowing about Weapons: The Cold War's End at the Los Alamos National Laboratory." Ph.D. diss., University of New Mexico.

———. 2006. "Where Are the Anthropologists?" *Anthropology News* 47 (7): 13–14.

Mechling, Elizabeth Walker, and Jay Mechling. 1991. "The Campaign for Civil Defense and the Struggle to Naturalize the Bomb." *Western Journal of Speech Communication* 55 (Spring): 105–33.

Medaglia, Angelica. 2002. "Steamed over Clams, Shell Fisherman Object to Limits." *Boston Globe,* May 23.

Miller, Judith, Jeff Gerth, and Don Van Natta Jr. 2001. "Planning for Terror but Failing to Act." *New York Times,* December 30.

Miller, Susan L. 1999. *Gender and Community Policing: Walking the Talk.* Boston: Northeastern University Press.

Mitchell, J. Clyde. 1969. *Social Networks in Urban Situations: Analyses of Personal Relationships in Central African Towns.* Manchester: Manchester University Press for the Institute for Social Research University of Zambia.

Miyazaki, Hirokazu. 2000. "Faith and Fulfillment: Agency, Exchange, and the Fijian Aesthetics of Completion." *American Ethnologist* 27 (1): 31–51.

James Martin Center for Nonproliferation Studies. 2001. "Federal Funding to Combat Terrorism, including Defense against Weapons of Mass Destruction FY 1998–2001." Chemical and Biological Weapons Resource Page. James Martin Center for Nonproliferation Studies, Monterey Institute of International Studies, Monterey, CA. http://cns.miis.edu/.

Moos, Felix. 2005. "Some Thoughts on Anthropological Ethics and Today's Conflicts." *Anthropology News* 46 (6): 40–42.

Mullian, John. 2001. "Homeland: Protection Racket." *Guardian* (London), October 24.

Nader, Laura. [1969] 1974. "Up the Anthropologist—Perspectives Gained from Studying Up." In *Reinventing Anthropology,* ed. D. Hymes, 284–311. New York: Random House.

National Science Board. 1999. "Statement by the National Science Board on the Sharing of Research Data." Document no. nsb9930. National Science Foundation. http://nsf.gov/publications/.

National Security Council. 1996a. Presidential Decision Directive 39 [unclassified synopsis]. Vol. 2000: National Security Council, for Office for State and Local Domestic Preparedness Support, U.S. Department of Justice.

———. 1996b. Presidential Decision Directive 62 [unclassified synopsis]. Vol. 2000: National Security Council, for Office for State and Local Domestic Preparedness Support, U.S. Department of Justice.

———. 1996c. Presidential Decision Directive 63 [unclassified synopsis]. Vol. 2000: National Security Council, for Office for State and Local Domestic Preparedness Support, U.S. Department of Justice.

Nelson, Nancy L. 2005. "Ideologies of Aid, Practices of Power: Lessons for Medicaid Managed Care." *Medical Anthropology Quarterly* 19 (1): 103–22.

Northcutt, Susan Stoudinger. 1999. "Women and the Bomb: Domestication of the Atomic Bomb in the United States." *International Science Review* 73 (3–4): 129–39.

Nygren, Anja. 1999. "Local Knowledge in the Environment-Development Discourse." *Critique of Anthropology* 19 (3): 267–88.

Oakes, Guy. 1994. *The Imaginary War: Civil Defense and American Cold War Culture.* New York: Oxford University Press.

Office of the Press Secretary, White House. 1998. "Fact Sheet: Protecting America's Critical Infrastructures: Presidential Decision Directive 62." Office of the Press Secretary, White House, Washington, DC.

Ortner, Sherry B. 1984. "Theory in Anthropology since the Sixties." *Comparative Studies in Society and History* 26 (1): 126–66.

———. 1997. "Thick Resistance: Death and the Cultural Construction of Agency in Himalayan Mountaineering." *Representations* 59:135–62.

———. 2005. "Subjectivity and Cultural Critique." *Anthropological Theory* 5 (1): 31–52.

Peacock, James, Robert Albro, Carolyn Fluehr-Lobban, Kerry Fosher, Laura McNamara, Monica Heller, George Marcus, David Price, and Alan Goodman. 2007. "AAA Commission on the Engagement of Anthropology with the US Security and Intelligence Communities Final Report." American Anthropological Association. http://www.aaanet.org/.

Peattie, Lisa. 1984. "Normalizing the Unthinkable." *Bulletin of the Atomic Scientists* 40 (3): 32–36.

Pellow, Deborah. 2001. "Cultural Differences and Urban Spatial Forms." *American Anthropologist* 103 (1): 59–75.

———. 2002. *Landlords and Lodgers: Socio-Spatial Organization in an Accra Community.* Westport, CT: Praeger.

———. 2003. "The Architecture of Female Seclusion in West Africa." In *The Anthropology of Space and Place: Locating Culture,* ed. S. M. Low and D. Lawrence-Zuniga, 160–83. Malden, MA: Blackwell.

Peterson, Wolfgang. 1995. *Outbreak.* Warner Studios.

Pogrebin, Mark R., and Eric D. Poole. 1988. "Humor in the Briefing Room: A Study of the Strategic Uses of Humor among Police." *Journal of Contemporary Ethnography* 17 (2): 183–210.

Powdermaker, Hortense. 1966. *Stranger and Friend: The Way of an Anthropologist.* New York: W. W. Norton.

Preston, Richard. 1995. *The Hot Zone.* New York: Anchor Books.

———. 1997. *The Cobra Event.* New York: Ballantine Books.

Price, David H. 1997. "Anthropological Research and the Freedom of Information Act." *Cultural Anthropology Methods* 9 (1): 12–15.

———. 2006. "American Anthropologists Stand up against Torture and the Occupation of Iraq." *Counterpunch,* November 20. http://www .counterpunch.org.

Quarantelli, E. L. 1995. "Disaster Planning, Emergency Management and Civil Protection: The Historical Development of Organized Efforts to Plan for and Respond to Disasters." Preliminary Paper no. 227. University of Delaware, Disaster Research Center, Newark, DE.

Rapoport, Amos. 1982. *The Meaning of the Built Environment: A Nonverbal Communication Approach.* Beverly Hills, CA: Sage Publications.

Rapport, Nigel. 2001. "Towards a Post-Cultural Anthropology of Personally Embodied Knowledge." *Social Anthropology* 9 (1): 95–102.

Regan, Keith. 1993. "Local Awareness of Terror Threat Heightened: Explosion in New York." *Boston Globe,* February 28.

Reporters Committee for Freedom of the Press. 2001. "Appellate Panel Finds No Reporter's Privilege Exists before Grand Juries." Reporters Committee for Freedom Press release, August 18. http://www.rcfp.org/.

Robert T. Stafford Disaster Relief and Emergency Assistance Act. 1988. Public Law 93-288, codified at U.S. Code 42, secs. 5121–5207.

Rosaldo, Renato. 1993. *Culture and Truth: The Remaking of Social Analysis.* Boston: Beacon Press.

Rubinstein, Robert A. 1984. *Science as Cognitive Process: Toward an Empirical Philosophy of Science.* Philadelphia: University of Pennsylvania Press.

———. 1986. "Reflections on Action Anthropology: Some Developmental Dynamics of an Anthropological Tradition." *Human Organization* 45 (3): 270–79.

———. 1989. "Culture, International Affairs and Peacekeeping: Confusing Process and Pattern." *Cultural Dynamics* 2 (1): 41–61.

———. 1993. "Cultural Aspects of Peacekeeping: Notes on the Substance of Symbols." *Millennium* 22 (3): 547–62.

———. 1998a. "Methodological Challenges in the Ethnographic Study of Multilateral Peacekeeping." *Political and Legal Anthropology Review* 21 (1): 138–49.

———. 1998b. "Peacekeeping under Fire: Understanding the Social Construction of the Legitimacy of Multilateral Intervention." *Human Peace* 11 (4): 22–29.

———. 2000. "Notes on the Ethnographic Study of Peacekeeping." *IUS Newsletter* (Winter), 9–10.

———. 2001. "Cross-Cultural Considerations in Harmonizing Military and Civilian Action in Complex Peace Operations." Maxwell School of Syracuse University, Syracuse, NY.

Rubinstein, Robert A., Susan C. Scrimshaw, and Suzanne E. Morrissey. 2000. "Classification and Process in Sociomedical Understanding: Towards a

Multilevel View of Sociomedical Methodology." In *The Handbook of Social Studies in Health and Medicine,* ed. G. L. Albrecht, R. Fitzpatrick, and S. C. Scrimshaw, 36–49. London: Sage Publications.

Safire, William. 2002. "On Language: Homeland." *New York Times,* January 20.

Sahlins, Marshall. 1985. *Islands of History.* Chicago: University of Chicago Press.

———. 1999. "Two or Three Things That I Know about Culture." *Journal of the Royal Anthropological Institute* 5:399–422.

Sassen, Saskia. 1996. *Losing Control? Sovereignty in an Age of Globalization.* New York: Columbia University Press.

Scheper-Hughes, Nancy. 1992. *Death without Weeping.* Berkeley: University of California Press.

Schoch-Spana, Monica. 1998a. "National Security and Radiological Control: Worker Discipline in the Nuclear Weapons Complex." In *More Than Class: Studying Power in U.S. Workplaces,* ed. Ann E. Kingsolver, 21–52. Albany: State University of New York Press.

———. 1998b. "Reactor Control and Environmental Management: A Cultural Account of Agency in the U.S. Nuclear Weapons Complex." Ph.D. diss., Johns Hopkins University.

———. 2004. "Bioterrorism: U.S. Public Health and a Secular Apocalypse." *Anthropology Today* 20 (5): 8–13.

———. 2006a. "Post-Katrina, Pre-Pandemic America." *Anthropology News* 47 (1): 32, 36.

———. 2006b. "Welcome *and* the People Talk Back: Anthrax 2001 Public Communication Lessons." Paper presented at the meeting "The Public as an Asset, Not a Problem: A Summit on Leadership during Bioterrorism." University of Pittsburgh Medical Center, Center for Biosecurity, Washington, DC, February 3–4.

Schoch-Spana, Monica, Allison Chamberlain, Crystal Franco, Jonathan Gross, Clarence Lam, Andrew Mulcahy, Jennifer B. Nuzzo, Eric Toner, and Christiana Usenza. 2006. "Conference Report, Disease, Disaster, and Democracy: The Public's Stake in Health Emergency Planning." *Biosecurity and Bioterrorism: BioDefense, Strategy, Practice, and Science* 4 (3): 313–319.

Schultz, Majken. 1995. "Comparison between Cultural Perspectives." In *On Studying Organizational Cultures: Diagnosis and Understanding,* 149–65. Berlin: Walter de Gruyter.

Schwartzman, Helen B. 1993. *Ethnography in Organizations.* Newbury Park, CA: Sage Publications.

Selmeski, Brian R. 2006. "Navigating the Slippery Slope: Balancing the Practical Benefits, Ethical Challenges, and Moral Imperative of Security Anthropology." Unpublished ms, Kingston, ON.

Shore, Cris, and Susan Wright. 1997. "Policy: A New Field of Anthropology." In *Anthropology of Policy: Critical Perspectives on Governance and Power,* ed. C. Shore and S. Wright, 3–39. London: Routledge.

Sidel, Victor W., et al. 1962. "The Physician's Role in the Postattack Period."
    New England Journal of Medicine 266 (22): 1137–45.
Simons, Anna. 1997. *The Company They Keep: Life Inside the U.S. Special Forces.*
    New York: Free Press.
———. 1999. "War: Back to the Future." *Annual Review of Anthropology*
    28:73–108.
Simpson, Brian W. 2002. "Far from a Madding Crowd." *Johns Hopkins Public
    Health Magazine.* http://www.jhsph.edu.
Smithson, Amy E., and Leslie-Anne Levy. 2000. "Ataxia: The Chemical and
    Biological Terrorism Threat and the U.S. Response." Report No. 35. Stimson
    Center, Washington, DC.
Strauss, Claudia. 1992. "Models and Motives." In *Human Motives and Cultural
    Models,* ed. R. G. D'Andrade and C. Strauss, 1–20. New York: Cambridge
    University Press.
Transactional Records Access Clearinghouse. 2003. "Department of Homeland
    Security—the First Months: A TRAC Special Report." Syracuse University,
    Syracuse, NY.
Trebilcock, Craig T. 2000. "The Myth of Posse Comitatus." *Journal of Home-
    land Defense,* October. http://www.homelandsecurity.org.
Trotter, Robert T., II, and Jean J. Schensul. 1998. "Methods in Applied
    Anthropology." In *Handbook of Methods in Cultural Anthropology,*
    ed. H. R. Bernard, 691–735. Walnut Creek, CA: AltaMira Press.
Tucker, David. 1997. *Skirmishes at the Edge of Empire: The United States and
    International Terrorism.* Westport, CT: Praeger.
U.S. Department of Justice. Office for State and Local Domestic Prepared-
    ness Support, Office of Justice Programs. 1998. "State and Local Domestic
    Preparedness Stakeholders Forum, Proceedings." Draft. Office for State
    and Local Domestic Preparedness Support, Office of Justice Programs,
    U.S. Department of Justice. Washington, DC.
U.S. Commission on National Security/21st Century: Hart-Rudman Commis-
    sion. 2000. "Seeking a National Strategy: A Concert for Preserving Security
    and Promoting Freedom—the Phase II Report on a U.S. National Security
    Strategy for the 21st Century." Washington, DC: The Commission. http://
    govinfo.library.unt.edu/.
———. 2001. "Road Map for National Security: Imperative for Change—
    the Phase III Report on a U.S. National Security Strategy for the 21st Cen-
    tury." Washington, DC: The Commission. http://govinfo.library.unt.edu/.
U.S. Federal Civil Defense Administration. 1950. *Survival under Atomic Attack:
    The Official U.S. Government Booklet.* Washington, DC: Government Print-
    ing Office.
U.S. Northern Command. 2004. "Homeland Security vs Homeland Defense."
    U.S. Northern Command, Peterson Air Force Base, CO.
Vandercook, William F. 1986. "Making the Very Best of the Very Worst: The

'Human Effects of Nuclear Weapons' Report of 1956." *International Security* 11 (1): 184–95.

Vise, David A. 2000. "Drill Shows Cincinnati Unready for Terror D.C., Prince George's County to Participate in Tests of How Other Areas Respond." *Washington Post*, April 28.

Warren, Shields. 1966. "Civil Defense—Fact or Fraud?" *Proceedings of the American Philosophical Society* 110 (3): 153–55.

Waskow, Arthur I. 1965. "Social Science as Systematic Anxiety: A Case Study in the Civil Defense Dialog." *Journal of Conflict Resolution* 9 (2): 264–87.

Waugh, William L., Jr. 1990. *Terrorism and Emergency Management.* New York: Marcel Dekker, Inc.

———. 2000. *Living with Hazards, Dealing with Disasters: An Introduction to Emergency Management.* New York: M. E. Sharpe.

Weart, Spencer R. 1987. "History of American Attitudes to Civil Defense." In *Civil Defense: A Choice of Disasters*, ed. J. Dowling and E. M. Harrell, 11–32. New York: American Institute of Physics.

White, Geoffrey M. 2004. "National Subjects: September 11 and Pearl Harbor." *American Ethnologist* 31 (3): 293–310.

Wicks, David. 1998. Organizational Structures as Recursively Constructed Systems of Agency and Constraint: Compliance and Resistance in the Context of Structural Conditions." *Canadian Review of Sociology and Anthropology* 35 (3): 369–90.

Wilmsen, Steven. 1998. "The Money Pit." *Boston Globe*, June 7.

Winkler, Allan M. 1984. "A Forty-Year History of Civil Defense." *Bulletin of the Atomic Scientists* 40 (6): 16–22.

Wolfe, Alvin A. 1978. "The Rise of Network Thinking in Anthropology." *Social Networks* 1:53–64.

Working Group on Governance Dilemmas in Bioterrorism Response. 2004. "Leading during Bioattacks and Epidemics with the Public's Trust and Help." *Biosecurity and Bioterrorism: BioDefense, Strategy, Practice, and Science* 2 (1): 25–40.

Wright, Susan. 1994. *Anthropology of Organizations.* London: Routledge.

Zabusky, Stacia E. 1995. *Launching Europe: An Ethnography of European Cooperation in Space Science.* Princeton, NJ: Princeton University Press.

———. 2000. "Boundaries at Work: Discourses and Practices of Belonging in the European Space Agency." In *An Anthropology of the European Union: Building, Imagining, and Experiencing the New Europe*, ed. T. M. W. Irene Bellier, 179–99. Oxford: Berg.

Zarlengo, Kristina. 1999. "Civilian Threat, the Suburban Citadel, and Atomic Age American Women." *Signs: Journal of Women in Culture and Society* 24 (4): 925–58.

Zilinskas, Raymond A. 1999. *Biological Warfare: Modern Offense and Defense.* Boulder: Lynne Rienner Publishers.

INDEX

nuclear attack: civil defense in
nuclear age, 24–32; preparedness
for, 140–41
Nunn-Lugar-Domenici Domestic
Preparedness Program, 34

Office of Civil and Defense Mobiliza-
tion (OCDM), 28
Office of Civil Defense Planning, 25
Office of Civilian Defense, 25
Office of Homeland Security, 35. *See
also* U.S. Department of Home-
land Security (DHS)
Oklahoma City bombing, 32, 134
On the Beach (novel and film), 28
Ortner, Sherry B., 17–18, 20, 172
outsourcing, 162–63

participant observation, 21, 55–62,
104–5
pathfinders, 176–81
PATRIOT Act, 35–36, 109
patrolling, 110–11
personal protective equipment
(PPE), 124–25
police officers. *See* law enforcement
policy community: and agency,
19–21; and cooperation, 171–72;
defining first responders, 81–82;
definition of, 79; and experts,
162–63; flexibility of, 80–81, 91,
171–76, 185, 189, 212; formation of,
79–80; and generative practice,
89–91; issues facing, 99–102; and
jurisdiction, 82–83; nature of,
19–21, 22–23; pathfinders, 176–81;
and private sector, 82; private/
small group communication
in, 86–89; role of meetings, 86,
87–88; secrecy in, 98–99; sense of
community in, 160–70; size and
complexity of, 46–47; tempo-

rary task-based organizations,
197–206; usefulness of anthropologists to, 220–22; visibility
of, 84–89. *See also* homeland
security; interagency relations
policy opportunities, 220–22
Port Security Initiative, 198–99
Posse Comitatus Act, 154
postal workers, 82
Powdermaker, Hortense, 59
practice: codification of, 173–75;
impact of, 229–33; and narratives,
167; and networks, 47–51; and
the policy community, 89–91;
practice theory, 15–21. *See also*
flexibility
Presidential Decision Directives
(PDDs), 33, 155; Homeland
Security Presidential Directives
(HSPD), 36, 37–38
Privacy Act, 55
private sector, 82
profiling, 113
public discussion, 147, 225–27
public fear, 28
public health: and bioterrorism
funding, 155–57; and counterterrorism, 34; Emergency Medical
Services (EMS), 185–86; and incident management, 191, 192; and
interagency relations, 162; mass
care clinics, 151–52; watching role
of, 111–12
public trust, 149, 169–70, 225

Radiation Control Program, 78
Reagan, Ronald, 30
red teaming, 134–35
Reid, Richard, 117, 168, 187
Reilly, Thomas F., 203
relationships, 186–88; institutionalization of, 173–75, 174–75;

personal, 164–65; with research subjects, 7–11, 52, 57–60, 73–74. *See also* affiliations; interagency relations; networks

research community. *See* policy community

response. *See* incident response

responsibilities. *See* roles, responsibilities, and leadership

Ridge, Tom, 203, 204

risk-analysis model, 140

rivalry issues, 70, 161

roles, responsibilities, and leadership, 36–39, 69–74, 143–53, 176–81

Rubinstein, Robert A., 20, 49, 58

Rudman, Warren, 31

Safire, William, xx

Sahlins, Marshall, 12–13

Salvation Army, 67

sampling, 49–51

Sassen, Saskia, 89, 90

SATURN. *See* Massachusetts Statewide Anti-Terrorism Unified Response Network (SATURN)

Schoch-Spana, Monica, 223

Schwartzman, Helen B., 164

screening, 112–16, 160

secrecy, 23, 52–55, 98–99, 119–20. *See also* informant confidentiality

secure, definition of, 139–43

security cameras, 109–10

security metaphors, 223–24

Selmeski, Brian, 9

September 11, 2001. *See* 9/11

shelter programs, 26, 28–29, 30

Shore, Cris, 46, 79

situated knowledge, 206

social context, 32, 102, 139–40

Soldier Biological and Chemical Command, 45

sovereignty, 89–90

space and place, 121, 121n8

special operations units, 68–69, 69n4

state sovereignty, 89–90

Strategic Defense Initiative, 30

"study up," 14–15, 62

subjectivity, 18–19

surveillance. *See* guarding; watching

Swift, Jane, 71, 179, 203

systematic observation, 57

tacit knowledge, 59, 124, 206–14, 222

targets: guarding of, 116–21; hard and soft, 136–37; identification of, 133–39, 141–42; *vs.* vulnerabilities, 134

temporary task-based organizations, 197–206

terminology, xviii–xxi, 165–66

terrorism: bioterrorism, 156–57; as a growing threat in 1990s, 32–35; and hazard assessment, 131; and the military, 154; preparedness, 133–34; and sovereignty, 89–90; as a term, xviii–xix. *See also* counterterrorism

Terror Tip Line, 108

threat assessment. *See* hazards, assessment of

Tokyo, sarin attacks in, 134

TOPOFF exercise series, 27–28, 134

transnationalism. *See* globalization

Transportation Security Administration, 113, 160

Truman, Harry S., 26

trust: within policy community, 186–88; public, 149, 169–70, 225

United Freedom Front, 45n1

U.S. Border Patrol, 67

U.S. Coast Guard (USCG), 67, 83, 137, 145–46, 188, 198–99